To/ June & Ken,
what a joy to meet fellow
Brits a long way from home.
Shine your light & love

Linda

Marmalade
and
Machine Guns

Marmalade
and
Machine Guns

16 COUNTRIES, THREE CONTINENTS, 12 YEARS AND
ONE SUITCASE: ONE WOMAN'S QUEST TO HELP DISASTER-
STRICKEN COMMUNITIES BACK ON THEIR FEET

LINDA CRUSE

JOHN BLAKE

Published by John Blake Publishing Ltd,
3 Bramber Court, 2 Bramber Road,
London W14 9PB, England

www.johnblakepublishing.co.uk

www.facebook.com/Johnblakepub `facebook`
twitter.com/johnblakepub `twitter`

First published in hardback in 2012

ISBN: 978-1-85782-876-4

British Library Cataloguing-in-Publication Data:

A catalogue record for this book is available from the British Library.

Design by www.envydesign.co.uk

Printed in Great Britain by CPI Group (UK) Ltd

1 3 5 7 9 10 8 6 4 2

Papers used by John Blake Publishing are natural,
recyclable products made from wood grown in sustainable forests.
The manufacturing processes conform to the environmental
regulations of the country of origin.

Every attempt has been made to contact the relevant
copyright-holders, but some were unobtainable. We would be
grateful if the appropriate people could contact us.

This book is dedicated to my two wonderful children,
Gail and Graham, who inspire me every single day.

'Two roads diverged in a wood, and I –
I took the one less travelled by,
And that has made all the difference.'

Robert Frost

CONTENTS

CONTENTS

ACKNOWLEDGEMENTS

My chief collaborator in the writing of this book has been Wanda Whiteley. Her enthusiasm, expertise and encouragement have always been boundless. She calls herself 'the manuscript doctor' but she really does have the power to turn base metal into gold.

Huge thanks to Stuart Higgins for producing the rabbit out of the hat – what a friend!

And for those men and women with vision, too many to mention individually, who have supported and encouraged me on along the way, who include: Sir Richard Branson, HRH The Prince of Wales, Peter Hopkirk, Tessa Brewer, Gwendolyn and David Fall, Greg Barton, Jean Olewang, Peter Avis, Sue Hale, Andrea Baron, Ivor Wood, James Kidner, Isabella Ward, Evelyn Webb-Carter, Clive Alderton, Andy Cope, Gowri Motha, Rajendra Bajgain, Emily and Spencer Klein, Angie Miranda, Cathy Heinecke, Kutira Decostérd, Simon Matthews, Elizabeth English, Avril Price, Paul Choong, Steve Buckley, Brian Solomon, Nelofar Currimbhoy, Tweedie Brown, Richard Morrison, Janice Lee, Doreen Virtue, Molly Harvey, Marie Diamond, Julia Hausermann, Christiane Pedros, Mylene Soriano, David Arkless, Sarah Summers, Jane Keightley, Mujeeb Khan, Geoffrey Bush, Mary Mills-Brown,

Randy Langendorfer, Carlos Rojas, Alan Hassenfeld, Harold Goodwin, Shahnaz Husain, Sheila Crowley, Richard Street, Eric Taylor, Karen Jones and Michaela and Alfie.

The generosity of friends who gave me temporary residence in their gloriously beautiful hotels so that I could take some time out to write; Chris and Mike McHugo of Kasbah du Toubkal, Morocco, Andrea Bonilla and Hans Pfister of Harmony Hotel, Cayuga Group, Randy and Carlos of Monte Azul both in Costa Rica and Karen Emanuel of Jicaro Lodge in Nicaragua.

Appreciation and admiration goes to the numerous companies who I have worked alongside over the years, who have sponsored projects and volunteered including Manpower, SAGA, Cadbury's, Virgin, Hasbro, Nestlé, KPMG, PSG, Thai Beverage, Deloitte, Accenture, Standard Chartered, Shahnaz Herbals.

A special thank you must go to my darling friend Jan Slater, present and steadfast through thick and thin, ready with a hanky to dry my tears, a glass of wine to celebrate and kindness and love beyond measure.

Lastly huge thanks go to my wonderful family: my Mum and Dad who instilled my sense of wonder and adventure and who gave me the confidence to follow my heart and passion. And through all my craziness have cheered me on along the way. My Dad handed me a TS Eliot quote one day: 'Only those who risk going too far can possibly know how far they can go'.

So many names and places in this book have had to be changed to respect the individuals' privacy and guard their personal safety. I wish, in so many cases, that I had been able to name them and honour the sterling work they are doing in such difficult circumstances. To these unsung heroes: thank you.

My Mission

A NOTE FROM THE AUTHOR

For as long as I remember I have always felt that I was on a 'mission'. From a very young age I was driven by an unquenchable thirst to serve something greater than myself, but for a long time I didn't know what, where or how.

Marmalade and Machine Guns looks back on an incredible journey – humbling, exhausting, stressful, challenging but rewarding beyond measure.

I drifted into nursing and loved it – but it was not enough. At the age of 39 I leapt into the frontline to help those in dire need living in some of the poorest and most challenging areas of the world.

For over 12 years I have moved from project to project with just one suitcase. It's taken me all over the world – to every continent, way off the beaten track. I have assisted in catastrophic natural disasters such as the Asian tsunami, the Pakistan earthquake, in conflict zones, with tribes deep in the Amazon rainforest, nomads in the deserts of Uzbekistan and in high mountain areas such as the Himalayas and Atlas Mountains, and refugee camps – Burmese, Afghan and Tibetan.

Born and raised in the United Kingdom I realise that my journey has been somewhat unusual. Some people admire me, others think I am crazy.

With great regularity I have little or no access to clean running water, reliable electricity, dependable food supplies, a comfy bed, a hot shower or a safe shelter. All of these things I used to take for granted. I don't now.

The journey has not been short of adventures and misadventures. I have lost a few lives – escaped from a rebel army, evaded rape, been wrongfully arrested, been held at gunpoint, survived severe altitude sickness and hypothermia and had my face slashed open, having to stitch myself up in the absence of medical help.

These experiences of life, near death and suffering have given me an insight into life and its meaning, real and practical, gained first hand through living life on the edge. I have learnt the meaning of unconditional love, strength, forgiveness, courage and compassion from unconventional teachers – an 11-year-old tsunami survivor who lost not only her parents and siblings, but also her teacher, her home and most of her friends, a 16-year-old Burmese refugee blown up by a landmine, left blind with no legs, surviving in a no-man's-land camp, not welcome in his host country yet never able to return to his own – my list of teachers is endless.

And along the way I have imbued the wisdom of indigenous visionaries – Amazonian shamans, Tibetan lamas and Indian gurus. Much of my work carried out with the backdrop of parental anxiety – my son is also regularly on the frontline with the Rifles in Afghanistan.

So why did I write this book? To remind us all to get passionate about living; to tune in to our own intuition, compassion and courage; to learn from the extraordinary ways people confront fear, face death and find joy and happiness in the most dire circumstances.

So there it is! See you on the frontline! Don't forget to pack your head torch and most importantly your sense of humour.

With love, onwards and ever upwards...

Linda x

'In the end, it's not going to matter how many breaths you took, but how many moments took your breath away'

shing xiong

PREFACE

HOW IT ALL BEGAN

At the age of 36 I decided to change my life. And not just in a small way.

The realisation that I needed to do so came to me quite suddenly – and terrifyingly – one night as I was driving along a motorway. Worn out after a sales conference and desperate to get home, I wanted to pull the duvet over my head and sleep forever. The road was almost empty, fortunately for me. One second I was driving along, trying to stay awake; the next I was blind. A moment of stabbing pain behind my eyes, then everything went black. I don't know how I managed to pull into the hard shoulder; instinct, I suppose. Anyway, there I sat, whimpering in fear. Praying to a God to whom I hadn't given a thought in decades.

My sight returned a few hours later. But in that time something in me had changed. It wasn't a nice feeling. It was disturbing, frightening. What I saw in those hours of blindness was that the life I had been living was stifling me. I was an adventurous child of adventurous parents. We weren't the sort of family to holiday to the nearest seaside resort each summer, like everybody else. We took the car and zigzagged across Europe. My parents were both committed Cub Scout leaders and I worked hard for every badge; out in all weathers. Taking the mottos very seriously: 'Do a good turn daily' and 'Be prepared'. On our family camping holidays we would sit out under the stars, while my dad taught us their names. He would say to us, 'Vive la difference! The world is just waiting to be explored.'

I became a single mother in my early twenties and that, understandably, reduced my scope for adventure. I adored raising my two children but the free-spirited life with wide horizons that I later found so exhilarating simply wasn't open to me. I did what mothers in my situation do: got on with the job, my own needs well and truly buried. I watched my two wonderful children grow and I got in the groceries, paid the bills, raced to pick them up from school. Rushed headlong through each day. Much of what I had was good. But I was in a meaningless job, selling something I didn't believe in, eating the wrong foods, drinking too much and crying under my duvet at night.

When a friend asked me what I wanted for my birthday, I asked for a blue suitcase. For three years it sat in the corner of my bedroom, where I could see it. I tacked photos from travel magazines on a cork board on my wall, and marked out my route with pins on a big map of the world. I dreamed and I planned. I put a little money away each month. And although I had to carry on working for another three years, I was much happier. I had something to aim for. I didn't know anyone in the field of international aid work but that wasn't going to stop me.

Then the right time came – the year my son left home to join the army and his older sister went to university. They were happily following their dreams. My job was done. We sat down for supper one summer's evening in July. I looked at my darling children, all grown up, and said, 'Is it OK if I leave home?'

We laughed together, nestled up close on the sofa.

'Go Mum! We are right behind you.'

PART 1: HEADING FOR DISASTER

Working in Disaster Zones

'If you are going through hell, keep going.'
Winston Churchill

CHAPTER ONE

BRING IN THE CLOWNS

Khao Lak, Thailand, 2005

When a single event is so traumatic that our hearts are wrung by the sheer horror of it, we discover that for the rest of our lives we remember exactly where we were and what we were doing when we heard the news. It was like that when Princess Diana died or when the twin towers fell.

So it was that on Boxing Day, 2004, at a time when millions were getting ready to eat turkey leftovers with their families, the whole world heard the news that the Asian Tsunami had delivered its deadly blow. The facts were almost incomprehensible: waves up to 100 feet high had killed over 230,000 people in fourteen countries, devastating their coastal communities. It was simply one of the deadliest natural disasters in recorded history.

At the time, I was in Uzbekistan. It was the end of a tough year; and an unforgiving winter. I was sitting in my room, late in the evening, and I switched on my laptop. When I scanned the news headlines I was brought bolt upright with shock. It was the first time I had ever come across the word 'tsunami' and I flicked quickly from site to site, feeling a sense of mounting horror as I did so. It was clear that, with millions left without food or shelter, the race was on to save lives.

I grabbed my coat and dashed out into the thick snow to look for my closest friend, Habib. On the streets of Tashkent it seemed that no one had heard the news. Life was continuing as normal. A stocky streetseller, proudly displaying her knee-length beige popsocks, shouted to me, 'Come and eat. It's delicious!' Normally I would have been tempted to buy a bowl of *plov*, the national dish of lamb, onions and carrots, but I couldn't stop. A group of old men, drinking industrial-strength vodka in their woven *tubeteika* caps, called out their greeting, '*Na sdarovie!*', blithely unaware of the news that was rocking the world.

Habib was at his normal spot, entertaining businessmen in the local restaurant. He was always a generous host and the table was laden with food, pots of black tea and a mind-numbing variety of empty vodka bottles.

'Have you seen the news, Habib?' I screeched over the top of the high-pitched Uzbek lute music. 'I have to go there!'

'What did you say?' Habib cupped his ear, then held up a hand. 'Hold on a minute.'

I had to wait while the waiter performed the usual lengthy tea ritual, pouring tea into a cup from the teapot, then pouring it back again, three times. I usually enjoyed these ancient traditions – the repetitions that symbolise *loy* (clay) which seals thirst; *moy* (grease) which isolates from the cold and danger; and *tchai* (tea or water) which extinguishes the fire. Tonight, though, I was breathless with impatience.

'There's been a terrible disaster. I need to talk.'

'Give me 30 minutes and I will get rid of these guys. Meet you at your apartment.'

The men looked quite drunk so I guessed that it wouldn't be long before the meeting was brought to an inevitable close.

I dashed back to my room. Where to start? Remembering that a great friend of mine was in Colombo working for the Red Cross I quickly shot her an email offering my help.

She replied by return. 'Linda, it's a mess here. Aid has started to arrive but much of it is being impounded by the Sri Lankan government. It's just sitting on the tarmac. I wouldn't advise you to come. You'd likely get impounded too'.

I sat back in my chair and paused to think. I was feeling in the grip of an utterly unstoppable drive to help. I decided against making contact with family or friends – I could hear their comments: 'You can't just pitch up. It's a full-blown disaster area. It'll be chaotic. You don't know anyone there. I doubt you will even be allowed in.'

I called Thai Airways. 'I need a one way ticket, Tashkent–Bangkok, please. Is there any availability for tomorrow?'

The woman on the phone gave a disbelieving laugh. 'The planes are flying empty. Only three seats sold. Who would want to holiday there now?'

When I told Habib I had bought the ticket he was furious. 'You are one crazy woman! Let the army sort out the chaos. If you really must go, wait at least until they've cleaned up a little.'

He looked at me, then sighed, realising he was wasting his words.

'OK. I will book the taxi. And then we'll crack open some bottles. We can't let you go without a bloody good send-off.'

Then he wrapped me in his arms in a great big bear hug.

That evening, full of merriment and tears, glasses raised in endless toasts, marked the end of my project in Uzbekistan. It was as if a new door had suddenly opened and I needed to walk through it. I was compelled to enter the unknown room, even though I knew it would be full of horrors. The only way I could do it was to keep my eyes closed. *Don't think too much. Just go.*

The next day I staggered onto the plane, feeling completely numb. The combination of champagne and vodka had done a good job at anaesthetizing my brain. Chilled and hungover, I pulled my thick winter coat tightly around me. With that and my fur-lined boots I knew that I would look a strange sight on arrival in Bangkok. I hadn't been to Thailand for over twenty years but the thing I remember most strongly was the intense heat and humidity.

In my hurry to leave, I hadn't had time to research the facts. I had no idea of the geography of the tsunami-hit areas. I flicked through the headlines of the Bangkok Post to find out which were the worst hit areas, then turned to the map page of the inflight magazine. It seemed the tsunami had caused the most damage at Phi Phi Island and Khao Lak. I worked out that I would have to take a domestic flight to Phuket from Bangkok. 'How bad can it be?' I thought to myself as I stretched out across four empty seats. 'I will be fine.' Then the alcohol took over and I was dead to the world.

I opened my eyes but couldn't see a thing in the thick, black churning water. My body was being pummelled by what felt like blocks of cement. And then I thought, "this is what it's like to drown".

Survivors of the tsunami know what it's like to be drowning – to hear and feel the indescribable noise of the sea. After going through that, I've become aware of my own mortality. The experience brought home to me the importance of family and the brevity of life. If there's something you've not said to a loved one, make sure you do, because you don't want to be left with regret. Your whole life can change in one second.

Flashbacks don't just disappear. There are people who,

although not physically affected by the tsunami, were affected mentally. For me, it serves as a constant reminder to enjoy life to the fullest.

Tsunami survivor

My aid work career has never been a conventional one. I prefer to work as an independent consultant, contracted to, but not employed directly by any organisation. This gives me lots of freedom to find projects, write my own script, fulfill a task, and deliver with the aim of making myself redundant. It also means that I could take my own initiative, research issues, assess situations and propose effective and sustainable solutions. Most importantly for me, it enables me to take my own risks.

In the case of Thailand, my mission was entirely unplanned – very much a case of 'leap and the net will appear'. I didn't know what I was getting myself into, nor did I have any idea how long I would be involved with this particular project. All I knew is that I had to go.

Unlike the eerily empty plane I had boarded in Tashkent, the domestic flight from Bangkok to Phuket was full. Every nationality was on that plane: distraught relatives, diplomats, and rescue service men and women in fluorescent jackets bearing the name of their organisation.

My 'doubt gremlins' were having a field day: 'They won't even allow you off the plane. Do you have an official badge? Look at you – in winter coat and boots. It's 30 degrees in the shade out there!'

I was sweating when I got off the plane. I knew that I didn't look anything like an aid worker: more like an ignorant tourist from Outer Siberia. I decided to flash my UK driving license at officials if they questioned me. I collected my case and strode purposefully past the chaotic groups of police and army personnel, focused on finding the taxi rank. As I exited the air-conditioned building, I gasped for breath. It was like walking into a wall of heat, stifling and fierce.

'*Sawadee ka*. Welcome to Thailand. Where do you want to go, Miss?' The taxi driver brought his hands together in a *wai*, a Thai greeting to show respect, lowering his head as he did so.

He opened the door and I jumped in. 'Khao Lak, please,' I said quietly. My driver turned around in his seat and stared at me.

'You do not want to go there. Not good place to visit. Not now.' His face was concerned, presuming I was an ignorant tourist.

'Please just take me there,' I repeated, not meeting his eyes.

'I can't, Miss. The police tell us only army or rescue workers.'

I quickly grasped at a lie. 'I am with the forensic team,' I said. 'My colleagues are already there. I would be so grateful if you can help me to find them. Please.'

A second's pause, then the driver drew out of the airport, heading north in silence. I looked for signs of the disaster but saw none. Tall palm trees lined the streets, and with the clear blue sky and strong sunshine it felt like just another day in a tourist resort. Then we came to a halt behind a long line of traffic.

'What is happening?'

'Army checkpoint.'

'What are they looking for?' I asked.

'Journalists, disaster tourists,' he said. 'Thieves. Men steal children from the camp. Bad things happening.'

'I really must get through. Is there a side road we can use?'

My pleading voice must have moved him to help. He drew out of the long line of cars and edged past them slowly one by one. They held a mixed bunch and I could see that many had cameras. When we reached the front of the line, armed police were waiting next to high rolls of barbed wire. My driver got out of the car and strolled up to them. They spoke for a moment and although I understood none of the words, their body language was obvious. It was a 'no'. I was sure of it.

Damn, I thought, closing my eyes.

On hearing laughter, my eyes opened. Two army personnel and my driver were peering at me through the window, grinning. My comically overdressed appearance must have reassured them that I was not a disaster tourist.

The barbed wire was rolled back and we continued our journey on the deserted road in silence. Feeling my driver relax a little, I finally plucked up the courage to ask him some questions.

'Is your family OK?'

'Yes, thanks to Buddha. They were on the hill in Phuket town.'

'Where were you?'

'Working. That day always busy. I was lucky. I take Japanese man to his hotel at Patong beach. We heard screams. People running. Cars... bikes... everywhere.'

He paused and I waited for him to go on. 'Japanese man shout at me, "Turn car around. Drive to hills. Fast".'

'How did he know what it was?' I asked.

'I don't know. "Just do it," he shouts. "It's a tsunami. Get to high ground. Quick!"'

The driver told me how people were scrabbling at the doors of his car, climbing on to it. He was scared he would run someone over. His passenger asked him to let in as many people as he could then they were away, driving fast for the higher ground, away from the wave and the horrors of the seafront.

I sensed my driver would relive the scene every day for the rest of his life. His first thought was that terrorists had struck. The noise of the wave slapping onto the concrete buildings was like a bomb going off. His eyes looked haunted when he told me of how he looked into his rearview mirror and saw a huge rolling black mass of water.

9

'But you managed to drive clear.'

'Yes. My passenger, he saved many lives.'

After that we slipped back into silence. Later, he pulled the car over to the side of the road.

'Missing Persons Identification Post,' he told me. 'Your friends might be here.'

I got out of the car. What I saw was overwhelming. Boards of photos, messages, and pleas to find loved ones – sons, daughters, babies. And then in a horrible juxtaposition, alongside the happy holiday snapshots were pinned photographs of the dead, their bodies bloated, bruised and battered. Any distinguishing marks were ringed in pen – tattoos, scars, anything to help identify the badly disfigured bodies.

I read the messages, one by one, tears falling.

'I have lost my child, she is only two. We got separated. She only speaks Swedish. Please help. She will be so scared.'

A few people stood beside me in silence, hungrily scanning the board for clues. For a sign of hope.

Standing there, by those boards of photographs and that desperate group of survivors, was the first time that the enormity of the situation really sank in. The number of dead, injured, missing or lost was still just an estimation: Confirmed Dead 5,395; Estimated Dead 8,212; Injured 8,457; Missing 2,817; Displaced 7,000.

We continued on, my driver slowing every now and again to point something out. At times it felt like a macabre parody of a tourist outing. We passed a spectacular Thai temple whose golden roof tiles sparkled in the sun, little bells tinkling in the breeze.

'Miss, they put the bodies here.'

I couldn't help wondering at that. All those bodies decaying in the heat and humidity.

'It's the best place for them. A holy place,' he said.

My driver went on to say that it was getting to the stage now where the temples were unable to cope with the constantly rising number of corpses. Volunteers were trying to slow the decomposition process, using dry ice, and the bodies were each photographed and tagged with identification codes. However, many of the relatives were confused because the black and swollen faces of the victims had mostly become unidentifiable.

As we drove on the scenery changed dramatically. It now looked like a nuclear bomb had exploded, destroying everything in its path. The land was scarred, flattened, wiped clean.

We reached the top of the hill and he parked. We both got out of the car and stood in silence, looking down on the sweeping bay of Khao Lak. I couldn't seem to focus on anything. The sight was so ghastly my brain simply could not process it. A surreal concoction of floating trees, household equipment, upturned cars, suitcases, pillows, bits of houses. The driver slipped a pair of binoculars into my hands. Close up it was even more horrifying. I could see bodies caught up in the debris, washed up on the beach, limbs tangled and trapped in the branches of uprooted trees. The ocean was coated with debris and oil. Several boats and a passenger barge were drifting without a crew. A few boats were moving about under power, searching for survivors or bodies.

I walked away from the driver and sat down abruptly on the cliff edge. My heart was racing. I could feel the sweat trickling down my back and my mouth was so dry my tongue felt enormous. It wasn't just the sight of all that destruction that shocked me. It was the smell. The putrid smell of decomposing bodies was all-pervasive. So bad that it made me heave.

My senses were on overload and I felt I was going to faint. Sticking my head between my knees, I pinched myself hard. *I don't think I can do this ... it's too much.*

As a nurse I had encountered death fairly regularly, tending to

11

the victims of horrific road traffic accidents and attempted suicides. But this was different. Here, it was the scale of death, the sheer enormity of it that made me want to turn tail and run. I vomited.

I fished blindly in my bag for my mobile phone hoping that I had a signal. I dialed one of the few numbers I knew by heart. My friend picked up on the second ring.

'Jan, it's Linda. I'm in Thailand.'

I heard her catch her breath. She could hear I had been crying. 'Are you on your own?'

'Yes…no…With a taxi driver.' My chest was heaving and the words were coming out in sobs. 'It's awful…I'm at Khao Lak…You can't imagine…I don't think I can stay. I thought I could help but I can't…I feel so stupid.'

Ever practical and calm, Jan said, 'Do you have some water with you? It must be very hot. Have a big gulp. Splash some on your wrists and the back of your neck. Do it now.' She paused while I scrabbled for my bottle. 'Sit quietly for a bit. There's no rush. You've travelled a long way. Have you got your lavender? Put some under your nose. Call me back in an hour or so. Don't think, just rest.'

Jan's calmly rhythmic list of instructions managed to soothe me. I did exactly as she instructed then closed my eyes and drifted off into a half sleep.

The next thing I knew someone was massaging my shoulders, the touch gentle and reassuring. I turned to see that it was a Buddhist nun, dressed in grey cotton. I remained motionless and accepting, my body grateful to be receiving such healing.

Another nun appeared in front of me. 'We are from the north,' she said. 'We have come to help. In any way we can.'

It was then I saw that a few small pick-up trucks had stopped near our car. Dozens of men and women, all dressed in the same loose grey cotton trousers and tunics, were setting up camp. They moved about silently, hardly speaking. Seeing them in action was like watching angels on earth. Every movement they made seemed to speak of unconditional love and compassion.

I got up and brushed down my clothes, my strength restored. I was here to work. I asked the driver to turn the air conditioning up as high as possible. I had a lot to do.

We drove slowly down the hill towards the beach. The scene was like one from a disaster movie. The water had left a terrible trail of destruction: cars had been thrown on top of buildings, some overturned and resting on their roofs, as if a giant had picked up and thrown a child's dinky toys.

We drove past resorts crumpled like boxes of matches. Boats had been hurled into the sky and parking meters bent to the ground. A tangled mess of debris. Miles and miles of it. Buses and boats obstructing the streets. Cars slammed into buildings. Electrical poles down. Broken glass everywhere. On the streets, work crews were cleaning wreckage and pumping water out of buildings, presumably looking for bodies.

I could not take it all in. 'It's like a war zone'.

A pick up truck drove past us. As it passed the tarpaulin flapped up in the wind and I caught a glimpse of a pile of bodies, legs hanging out of the back.

Inland, lakes had formed, their floodwater full of chairs, palm fronds and other debris.

'I brought a Japanese news crew here yesterday.' I turned my attention to my driver with some relief. 'They asked me to take them to see the police boat that had been guarding the Prince.'

He told me that the boat had been out at sea when the wave hit. The Prince on his jet ski. The wave had lifted their twenty-metre, 50-tonne vessel and thrown it like a golf ball two miles inland. They all had died, the Prince included.

It was impossible to imagine the power of the tsunami. I supposed that with stuff flying around at such force and with the wires in the water, if you weren't crushed or sliced to death you might be electrocuted. It was a living nightmare.

It was beginning to get dark. 'Where are you sleeping tonight Miss?' the driver asked.

'I don't know.'

'Miss, no hotels…all washed away,' my driver said. He looked uncomfortable, on edge. 'I have to go home now. Too many ghosts.'

'You can feel them?'

'They fill my car. I stop at the temple and put them out before I go home. But my mother unhappy. She says she smells them on me.'

Listening to him, I felt goosebumps all over, thinking of the lost souls, clamouring for attention.

'Where have the survivors settled?' I asked, changing the subject.

'The camp is at Ban Nam Khem, 35 kilometres north of Khoa Lak,' he said. 'The town is gone. Three waves. Nothing left.'

'How many people are in the camp?' I asked.

'About five thousand,' he said. 'Maybe … four hundred children. Many orphans.'

I lapsed back into silence. My driver turned to look at me, suddenly protective.

'Come back with me, Miss. You can't stay there. No water. No electricity. Too many ghosts.'

His words didn't change my mind which was quite made up. The camp was exactly where I needed to be…ghosts and all.

'Don't worry, I'll be fine,' I said, rather briskly. 'You need to get going. Please can you drop me at the camp. Thanks, but I can manage perfectly now.'

A little later, he slowed and pointed out two enormous fishing trawlers. They must have been thrown like pebbles, only stopping because they had hit a concrete building.

'Here we are, Miss,' he said. 'Easy to find the entrance. Just look for the boats.'

Ahead of us, as far as the eye could see, was a vast sea of canvas. Thousands upon thousands of tents, all colours, pitched without an inch between them. We drove past mountains of old clothes and piles of blankets. I spotted one young woman with blonde hair, holding an infant in her arms and asked my driver to stop. I leapt out of the car and went up to her. She looked exhausted.

'I'm looking for the camp manager,' I said.

With a limp arm, she pointed vaguely in the direction of a large army tent.

I didn't want to let the driver go until I had found someone who might be able to help me so I left him in the car and made my way cautiously into the tent. Inside, a saffron-clad monk sat cross-legged on a platform in the centre, leaning forward, deep in discussion. His skin was wrinkled and covered in tattoos. I had read how the ink is hand-tapped into the monks' skin while prayers are said. The patterns all have different meanings, symbols connected to their spiritual faith, nothing meaningless or crass as we often we see in the West.

The monk was talking to a Thai police officer who was kneeling in front of him, hands tightly clasped. I guessed he was important as his uniform was covered in stripes.

I turned to my driver, who had crept in to stand beside me.

'What's happening?' I whispered. 'Why is he on his knees?'

'Asking for advice. Shh! Let me listen.

'He wants to know where he send his team.'

I wasn't used to a country where the army generals and heads of police defer to the holy men.

15

'He looks very old,' I whispered.

'Maybe, over 100 years old. Very special monk. Thai people buy his spit. Keep it for protection.'

The driver looked at his watch, anxious to leave. 'I'll find someone who can help you.'

He walked over to a Thai volunteer and spoke quickly to him, then turned to bid me farewell.

'He will show you where to sleep tonight. I must go now.'

The driver wished me luck and got back in his taxi. Seeing it drive off made me feel suddenly alone and very tired. I needed somewhere to rest, as well as food and water, although I didn't hold out much hope of getting any sustenance that night. I was led by the volunteer past rows of tents. Inside some of them I could hear the sound of quiet sobbing. Outside, children were lying listlessly, with dazed eyes wide open. We passed the first aid tent where queues of injured survivors were waiting patiently to have their dressings changed.

The volunteer led me to a communal tent. 'I'm afraid you'll have to sleep here tonight,' he said, with a light touch of his hand on my arm. 'It's all we have.'

Before I could thank him he had slipped away into the night. I stepped into the fug of the tent. A few people stirred but no one said anything. There were more than twenty of them, lying in haphazard rows, trying to sleep. I saw bandaged limbs, stitched faces, ripped and dirt-stained clothes. At first I couldn't see how I could possibly find a space but then I spotted a slither of a gap between a sleeping toddler and an elderly lady. She had a patch over one eye and was moaning quietly which didn't bode well for my sleep. I put down my rucksack. It was suffocating inside the tent, absolutely boiling. I decided to go back outside to find the bathrooms.

Scared I would get lost in the maze of tents, I carefully counted

16

them as I walked until I reached the end of the row. I smelt the portaloos before I saw them. No running water but at least there was some privacy. I reached for my hip flask of industrial-strength Mekhong whisky and my toothbrush. I was used to improvising and I reckoned this was better than risking water anywhere near my stomach. I swallowed the last mouthful, after brushing my teeth, and it burned as it slid slowly down my oesophagus. Definitely medicinal: hopefully I might get a few hours' sleep.

Without electricity, there was complete darkness. My trusty head torch, my lifesaver in many a situation, helped me safely back to the tent as I picked my way over a mass of guy ropes.

In spite of the whisky, I was awake the whole night. Overhead, helicopters patrolled the night skies with an ominous drone. In the adjoining tent, I could hear Australian voices. I couldn't help listening in to their conversation. It was like being read the strangest bedtime story.

'You know, on the day before it hit, an old woman visited Ban Nam Khem, just up the road from here,' one of them was saying. 'The old lady asked for water. Apparently she warned them that a disaster was coming. Now they think she was Buddha in disguise. Think they've been punished for not heeding the warning.'

All night my mind buzzed with images of old women and lost souls and what I might find when daylight came. I may have dozed for an hour. At sunrise, the camp was up and buzzing and I sat up wearily, relieved that the long night was over. I could smell fried rice being cooked. How I longed for a strong black coffee!

I stood up and picked up my sleeping bag, rolling it tightly and slipping it into its cover. My neck and back were stiff but I knew they would feel better once I was up and about. By now the tent had emptied out so there was space for me to make my ablutions. I achieved what little I could and, not for the first time, thanked God for wet wipes. I didn't have to dress as I had slept in my clothes.

'Thank goodness for perfume,' I thought, rummaging in my bag for a mirror. I wish I hadn't. God, I looked rough.

'Let's see if lipstick will help,' I said to myself. Then I dragged the brush through my hair. 'There. That's as good as it is going to get today!'

I didn't hang around – the tent was quickly becoming an oven. To orientate myself, I decided to take the short walk to the seafront to see how the beach clear-up was coming along. I was joined by an volunteer called Judd, a junior school teacher from Manchester. When he heard I had just arrived he happily filled in a lot of the gaps for me, keen to talk.

'You know, the wave was over 11 metres high when it hit this part of the coast,' he said.

'Why was it so bad here?'

'Because of the shallowness near the shoreline. It hit twice and in between the two waves, the sea just disappeared. Got sucked out, like the plug being pulled in the bath. Fish left stranded.'

'How far did it go out?' I asked.

'They say over a mile of beach was left exposed. Can you believe it?'

I asked him what would happen now. He said that he had heard that it would be a long time before the locals would be able to grow crops again. The salt water from the ocean had poisoned the freshwater and the soil and it could be years before they would be clear of contamination.

We had reached the beach now. I looked along the debris-strewn sand and paused, placing a hand on Judd's arm.

'Look. Over there, Elephants'.

We moved closer, curious to know what they were doing on the beach. We saw then that some were clearing rubble or transporting heavy cutting equipment while others were carrying sheet-wrapped corpses, tied to their tusks. It brought tears to my eyes seeing these gentle giants, going about their work with such grace and care.

'Did you know, not one animal bone was found post-tsunami,' Judd said. 'They knew the wave was going to hit hours before it did.'

I told him that I had always heard that animals have a sixth sense, some sort of vibrational awareness that humans have long lost.

'Makes sense,' Judd said. 'I was talking to a local tourism guy who told me his elephants broke loose from their chains two hours before the wave hit. Just walked up the mountainside, cool as cucumbers.'

Talking to Judd made me feel a little more grounded. I was glad to have company on my walk. Afterwards, I made for the mess tent, picking my way carefully over broken glass. There I found the same Buddhist community I had met on the road. A quiet grey army, working in rows: cleaning and chopping vegetables; cooking huge vats of food; and brewing urns of tea. They had hundreds of survivors to feed and already a long queue for breakfast was forming. The line was silent, heads drooping, the only movement coming from a few children running in and out of it.

At times like this, I felt myself drowning in the sea of grief. 'Do something practical,' I thought, squaring my shoulders.

I walked in the direction of the first aid tent. A little girl with a dirty face and tattered clothes toddled up to me with outstretched arms. She buried her face in my chest.
What's your name?' I asked. 'Have you lost your Mum?'

'She has lost everyone, 21 people in total, all the pillars of her life. Her mother, father, siblings, friends and teachers', a deep voice spoke from behind me.

I turned to see a man, standing next to one of the stretchers. He smiled at me.

'Hello, I'm Tim. Volunteer doctor. Arrived yesterday.' He looked down at the little girl with gentle eyes. 'She's called Shine – or that's the name we've given her. The morning before the wave hit, her Mum and Dad had dropped her off at Grandma's house on the way to work. Mum was a chambermaid and Dad a porter at the holiday resort on the beach just over there,' Tim pointed towards the sea.

'Hotel took a direct hit from the wave. They're still missing. The Grandma lived in a house across the road from the beach. Amazingly, she survived along with Shine. The Grandad is paralysed from the waist down though.'

I looked at the tiny girl holding on to my legs, then knelt down on the grass, holding her tight.

'Are you here to help?' asked Tim.

'I'm a nurse,' I offered.

Tim's eyes lit up. 'Well, roll up your sleeves. There's lots to do!'

Tim carried on with his work, suturing a head wound. 'Let's hope it's a calmer day than yesterday. With the constant rumours of more tsunamis on the way there was a continual stampede to higher ground.'

'I can see why they would.'

'Yeah, well, many people are staying in the mountains without food or water because they fear another hit. I have a theory that the looters stoke the panic by spreading gossip that more waves are coming.'

'That's awful.'

'Well, I for one am staying put. What will be will be.'

'What do you want me to do?'

'Well, there are a few things I should warn you about,' he said. 'Look out for signs of malaria. Mosquitoes are a real problem.

They're breeding in the stagnant water and there aren't enough nets in the camps.'

He told me that the army fogged the camp twice a day so to be careful not to breathe in the pesticides when they did. Tim smiled as he spoke but his face was drawn.

'Dengue fever is another one to look for. Particularly in the young,' he said, breaking from his work for a moment to look at me. 'Hope I'm not putting you off. Don't want you to do a runner.'

I shook my head and smiled at him. Reassured that I was made of sterner stuff he bent his head over his work again and continued with his list.

'They're getting little fresh drinking water so look out for cholera, diphtheria, dysentery, typhoid and hep A and B.'

'Can we get them to hospital?'

'Not really. Both Takuapa and Thai Muang are overflowing,' he said. 'No, we have to do what we can here first.'

Tim looked as if he hadn't slept for days. His eyes were sunken and ringed with shadows. I reckoned he must be in his early thirties but he looked so exhausted he seemed older. His white coat wasn't going to be white much longer: already it was streaked with dirt and bloodstains.

'When did you arrive, Tim?'

'I was working close by in a hospital in Singapore,' he said. 'I came straight away. Took unpaid leave. It's the least I could do.'

'How long will you stay?'

'As long as I am needed – no timetable.'

The power of one. I took strength from the thought. Unsung heroes working miracles, helping to heal the land and the people.

I set to work. There was no running water in the first aid tent so I took out my wet wipes and tried to clean up. A couple of broken sun-loungers were covered in sheets and what dressings we had were piled up in a laundry basket someone had fished out of the debris. There was a big queue for my services so I set to work briskly. I was mainly treating deep, swollen lacerations. The wounds had become infected after being immersed in dirty water and left exposed in the heat and humidity.

'*Sawadeeka*. What is your name?' I asked the 12-year-old girl at the front of the queue. She limped up to me and stood there, saying nothing. Her face was expressionless. She lifted up her sarong to reveal multiple deep gouges in her legs.

'What happened to you, then?' I asked gently.

The young Thai man who was with her replied, 'We are not sure. She says she was trapped under some trees. Then a car scraped over her. Now she doesn't speak.'

'Are you her brother?' I asked.

'No. We cannot find her family. I found her.'

Once I had dressed the girl's wounds, she leaned over and put her arms around my waist. We both found comfort in the hug. During the course of the morning I tended to other children. Like the girl, many of them were mute with grief and the shock of their ordeal. I had heard that there was a children's tent somewhere in the camp where volunteers were working with the children who had been orphaned or whose families needed support. I decided to set out at lunchtime to find it.

'Tim, I'm going to take a break if that's OK,' I said, wiping my hands. 'I thought I'd go and see what they're doing in the children's tent.'

'Yeah. Good idea,' he said. 'I've heard they're doing wonderful work there. It's hard to know how to comfort the kids.'

He told me that he had treated a little boy who had been found clinging to a piece of wood that had lodged in the top of a coconut palm. He had watched his four-year-old sister being swept away.

'What's happened to him now?'

'Well, the real problem is that even if the poor things have survived the wave, the sand and seawater getting into their paranasal sinuses means infection sets in,' he said. 'He's got it in his lungs and heart. There's not a lot we can do about it. Even with blood transfusions many of them don't survive.'

I could hear the children's tent long before I found it. The wonderfully joyous sound of guitars, and the clapping and singing of the volunteers was a welcome relief from the heavy weight of tension and grief that hung over everything in the camp. A jolly, middle-aged woman greeted me with a hug.

'Welcome to children's world.'

'You sound like you come from the mid-west,' I said to her.

'Yup, from Winsconsin. Dairy country,' she said. 'A sheet of ice at this time of year. My children are all grown up – so here I am!'

She introduced herself as Anne and led me into the large canopied area they had set up.

'My group ranges from the youngest survivor here, baby Dee, who's just 25 days old, to this great bunch of teenagers.' She pointed to a group of girls and boys sitting at the knee of a volunteer who was playing guitar.

'Are most of them orphans?' I asked.

'Yes. But not all. Some of them have parents who are so traumatised, they're not up to caring for them at present,' she explained. 'They're consumed with worrying about how they're going to survive. They haven't just lost their families. It's their livelihoods too.'

She took my arm and led me to the next tent. 'Come and see what we're doing.'

A large blue plastic sheet was spread out on the floor. Every inch of it was covered with large pieces of paper, on which children were working with paintbrushes, completely absorbed.

'We have set up an art therapy programme here. Take a look.'

I walked slowly along the rows of children. Their little heads were bent over their work so that most of them didn't notice me. I was impressed but also deeply shocked by what I saw, never having encountered traumatised feelings expressed in this way, and on such a scale. It was a huge outpouring of images and, sometimes, words. One child had drawn a big wave carrying stick men high into the air, the sea full of smashed boats and floating coconut trees. She had painted a man standing on a rock, arms outstretched, shouting 'Help!' I am used to seeing bright children's pictures, cheerful with yellow suns and colourful scenes. Here, it was a different vision. The colours the children had chosen were predominantly dark.

I moved closer to see what one teenage girl was writing. She was clutching a pink teddy bear in her left hand, while she wrote in big black letters: 'I hate Tsunami – it took my father, my sister and my uncle. I hate Tsunami.'

'It's extraordinary,' I said to Anne. 'Until now the children I've seen have been barely able to communicate. Here you've got such an outpouring. It's mind-blowing.'

Anne took me to the side of the tent to explain. 'Their psychological recovery will be a very long process. You see there are multiple layers of loss and grief. Every child has lost many pieces from their everyday framework: loved ones, a teacher, school friends, as well as their homes, their toys, their playgrounds.'

'Presumably the things they experienced will never leave them. The images will remain with them for life?' I said.

'Yes, of course, for most of them. But the healing power of the art therapy process really does make a difference, particularly as many of them are still unable to talk about what happened, as you've seen.'

'The colours they're using are so dark.'

'I know. It's to be expected. They're expressing their night-mares. But, you know, the rewarding thing about this work is that you get to see lighter colours starting to come in. But it does take time.'

I looked over at the teenagers. 'How is it working with the various age groups? Do they express their hurts differently?'

'They do,' Anne said. 'We've noticed that the one-to-fives don't eat or sleep well. Most of them are so scared of water that they're refusing to shower. The most demonstrative group seem to be the six to tens who want to be held a lot of the time.'

'And the older ones?' I asked.

'That's different too. As you might imagine, we're finding the older teens quick to fire up, hot-tempered, moments of aggre-ssion,' she said. 'It isn't helped that they're not sleeping much.'

'What about the younger teens?' I asked.

'They're different again. Tend to internalise their stress. We're getting a lot of complaints about headaches and stomach aches.'

Anne sighed. 'The thing is that they're not sure if they feel loved any more. They've lost their parents after all. Some of them clearly don't feel they've got the strength to fight on. It's heartbreaking.

'And what isn't helping is that the adults are living in constant fear of another tsunami and they're passing the fear on to the children.'

For a moment, the jolly, upbeat Anne had vanished and she just looked tired and sad. 'Linda, it's hard for everyone. We don't see many smiles around here.'

Just then a group of nuns, or 'earth angels' as I liked to think of them, appeared quite suddenly like some glorious annunciation. One of them called out, 'Ice cream! Who would like some ice cream!' and, in a second, they were swallowed up by excited paint-covered children. Each one came away with a dollop of ice cream in a bread roll.

Something about the fevered creativity in the tent was catching. My brain was buzzing with ideas, coming so thick and fast that I felt almost giddy with the desire to do something. With every hour I spent in the camp I was getting a clearer picture of how to help. I had been pondering on how I would involve individuals from multi-national companies: those with the funds and know-how to help rebuild livelihoods and the general infrastructure of the country. But my experience in this tent, with these troubled children, had my thoughts spinning down entirely different tracks. What could I offer them?

Anne had said that it had been vital to move quickly. The longer the children had to wait to get help the longer they would take to heal. As I walked away from the children's tent I looked back at their paintings fluttering in the warm breeze, hung up to dry on makeshift washing lines. My mind was spinning. What could I do for them, right now?

In the food tent I sat alone playing with my bowl of noodles, the sweat dripping from the end of my nose. I longed for a large glass of water and a shower. I vowed never to take water for granted again. My phone bleeped. It was a text message from my parents, checking up on me. Something in that connection suddenly triggered an idea.

'Magic!' I shouted, only realising that I'd said the thought out loud when the small boy sitting next to me nearly fell off his chair.

I come from a family of magicians. My grandfather, although an amateur, was awe-inspiring. My father carried on the tradition. Now in his seventies, he still wows crowds at friends' parties, sawing my mother in half. As a child I was riveted by dad and granddad's tricks. They taught me some of the simpler ones and they've come in handy over the years.

'What does magic do?' I asked myself. The answer was simple. *It brings joy to people.* But it wasn't just that. You see, there's no need of language with magic. And, with hundreds of children up and down this battered coast sinking under layers of grief...

I picked up the phone. 'Dad, I need your help. Can you get me the phone number of the President of The International Brotherhood of Magicians?'

I barely had to explain. My Dad got it in a millisecond.

'Look, I'll ring you straight back,' he said. 'D'you know, I think this might just work. Good luck, darling.'

In a few minutes I was on the phone to Dan, the president.

'Well, Linda, this one is new to me,' he said cautiously. 'I can see how you'd need doctors and builders...but magicians? It seems a strange idea.'

I could almost hear the cogs in his brain clicking as they turned the thought over. We were silent a moment. *I know it will work. Please see it too.* I was willing him to say yes.

'I'll tell you what I'll do,' he said at last. 'We'll let the members decide. Why don't I announce the idea then we'll wait and see if anyone responds.'

I thanked Dan and put the phone down. *Please, lord, let all those wonderful children's magicians be inspired to come!* I willed them not to think too hard about it, but just to hop on a plane.

My prayer was answered. Not quite as instantaneous as that but it happened nonetheless. Within a few weeks, my first volunteer magician had left London for Phuket. Attired in the uniform of his profession – brightly-coloured waistcoat and dickie bow – Michael the Magician took the camps by storm. Dripping with sweat, melting daily in the unforgiving swelter, he performed at least three shows a day for three weeks. He performed to crowds of children and adults – on the beach, in schools or in the survivor's camps. And no matter who his audience were – sea gypsies, widowed old people, orphans, or traumatised hotel staff – they delighted in the show.

In no time, Michael was being followed about everywhere he went, greeted with shouts of 'Abracadabra', like a pied piper weaving his spell. The show needed no words, he made his own magical stories with his actions: producing rabbits, making silk scarves disappear, twisting balloons into animals. He was like a bright butterfly flying around the blackened stumps of a devastated forest.

When he performed his magic show to the children of Ban Nam Khem School, the parents came early and squeezed in the back of the room. The magic seemed to take the tension out of their shoulders, smoothing away the lines of worry...for a while at least. The school had taken a particularly severe blow: out of a total of 450 students, 150 had been washed away by the wave. Michael's audience was blindsided with grief, having lost so many friends and siblings.

'Michael, please come back soon,' I heard the head teacher say. 'Your magic is helping the children to find joy in life again. It is the first time I have seen them smile in months. Your magic wand is really working.'

News of the magician's success must have travelled. One morning, I found an email in my inbox:

Dear Linda,

Would a circus be of any use to you and your recovery work? We have a small children's travelling circus, based in UK, and would love to help? We can entertain almost anywhere – we're very mobile. And for small groups we can teach skills. Altogether very therapeutic.

Hope to hear from you soon.
Arabella

Yes! I knew it! Out of one little seed…It is like magic how ideas spread and grow, almost without effort. All you need is creative thinking and the will to make it happen. It was an inspired idea.

'Bring in the clowns!'

In no time at all we had jugglers, stilt walkers, fire-eaters and Giggles the Clown roaming up and down the survivor camps, spreading a bit of happiness as they went. The circus stayed for six weeks and in that time they brought a ray of magical sunshine everywhere they set up. They also gave circus skills workshops and trained camp volunteers to perform tricks so that their legacy could be continued after they had left.

One group I had heard about but hadn't worked with were the Morgan people, a tribe of sea gypsies who had been devastated, like the other coastal communities, in the Tsunami. They kept themselves to themselves and few Thais dared go near them. Over the years dark myths had grown up around the sea gypsies and mothers would hurry their children away when confronted with a group of Morgans. Unsurprisingly, given the fact that they were feared and reviled by other Thais, they hadn't chosen to join the survivor camps. Instead they had formed their own compound, constructing makeshift shelters from brown hessian strung between bamboo poles and draping them with fishing nets.

I felt particularly determined that no group should miss out on the mobile circus experience so I sought out the sea gypsies' community elders to ask their advice. They accepted our offer with alacrity, giving us the permission we needed to enter their compound.

'Why not?' said one of the old men. 'The children will love it.' He gave a wheezy laugh. 'If the adults don't like it, they will let you know when it is time to leave.'

We bribed three reluctant taxi drivers to take us to the sea gypsies' camp. The cars, loaded down with colourful props which had been crammed into every available space, weaved their way through a complex maze of side streets. The place was thick with a viscous slurry of mud, sand and debris. We made slow progress. Everything and everyone was covered in dirt and the place smelt of rotting fish.

The village elder greeted us and led us to a small raised area in the middle of the camp which was to be our stage. I loved how enthusiastic and cheerfully adaptable the circus troupe was, thinking nothing of setting up in such squalid and pitiful surroundings. Immediately, Giggles the Clown, Jill the Juggler and Freddie the Fire-eater set to work, whistling happily, hanging their blue silk backdrop and setting up the sound system. They refused to be spooked by the handful of locals who passed by the stage, every one of them unsmiling and suspicious. We knew that the circus group must look a surreal bunch to the sea gypsies, as strange as men from Mars, so it was no surprise that they weren't welcomed with easy familiarity.

'Let's play some music,' said John, once he had donned his Giggles the Clown outfit. 'That might draw them out.'

Soon, the Pink Panther theme tune was blaring out and Jill the Juggler, dressed in orange afro wig, with yellow oversized sunglasses and a twirling bow tie, got out her juggling balls. She marched to the music, up and down the platform, tapping her big red clown shoes in an exaggerated fashion with each step.

All was still quiet on the street.

Jill then threw three red balls high in the air – then four – then five – then six. Higher and higher they went. She passed them under her legs and behind her back.

Aha! I saw out of the corner of my eye a few children approaching, dragging their mothers by the hand. Then an old woman carrying a chair plonked herself down in front of the stage. We were on a roll.

The circus troupe, wearing floor-length wizard coats and silly hats, took a bow. The gathering audience was greeted by Freddie who squirted water from a flower in his lapel. Giggles had them captivated when he brought out his magic colouring book. Miming dramatically, he flicked the pages and, on realizing they were blank, stared at them then looked at the audience with the saddest expression, wiping away pretend tears. Suddenly, scratching his head, he had an idea. His eyes lit up, and he ran into the crowd. With his wand he tapped the children's coloured shirts and did the same on the blank book.

By now the children were jumping up and down and screaming with excitement, desperate to take part. Giggles jumped back on stage and dramatically flicked his book again. 'Ta-daa!'

'Woweee!' the audience squealed as each page was revealed, full of brightly-coloured pictures. The adults broke into applause and the children cried out for more. The ice was well and truly broken.

There was only one moment when the circus nearly came a cropper. It was when Jill the Juggler brought out a magic change bag. She began by walking around the stage and into the audience, proudly showing her big plush red velvet bag. She turned it inside out, showing everyone the sparkly blue lining so they could see it was empty.

Jill had spotted a crowd of teenage fishermen who had gathered at the side of the stage. She went up to them and pointed at a heavy chain one of the lads was wearing around his neck, inviting him to put it into the empty bag. Then, raising her arms like a conductor, she yelled, 'Hocus Pocus!'

So far so good. 'Hocus Pocus!' the crowd replied. With a flourish of her magic wand and another raucous, 'Hocus Pocus!' she turned the bag inside-out again. The chain had completely vanished. The small group of teenagers looked decidedly uneasy.

The crowd was still laughing and cheering but I was feeling anxious, watching the teenagers become increasingly agitated. A moment later, the biggest of them jumped onto the stage and stood in front of Jill, glaring at her. At this, the crowd was suddenly quiet. Jill may have been alarmed but she didn't show it. With a showman's flourish, she grabbed the magic change bag and trilled, 'Hocus Pocus! Ta-daa!' Out came the chain, glittering in the sunshine, and the crowd, who had been holding their breath, relaxed. Then they clapped even louder than before.

Fred the fire-eater concluded the show as the sun set over the sea.

'If only my wonderful Grandad could see this,' I thought to myself.

When I had flown to Thailand from Uzbekistan I had no idea how long I would stay. It turned out to be nearly two years. Once I had seen what effect the entertainment was having on all the tsunami survivors, not just the children, I approached Cadbury Schweppes who liked the project and offered the funding to expand it. Together we devised a psychological recovery programme called 'Laughter: The Best Medicine' which we rolled out to a much wider territory.

Cadbury wasn't by any means the only company to get involved. A host of others came forward in the months following the tsunami, offering all kinds of help. Individuals too kept on arriving…builders, teachers…even a seamstress who taught the girls a new and useful money-making trade.

Magicians and circus performers weren't the only ones to offer entertainment to boost morale: sport turned out to be another winner. The CEO of Everton Football Club, Robert Elstone, came out to get involved in the setting up of a football league at

Ban Bang Muang school in Khao Lak, led and sponsored by Paul Choong senior vice president of Thai Beverage. His players coached groups of kids, who were to be seen in the schools and camps wearing their strips with pride.

One evening I was sitting in the camp manager's office with a group of the remaining foreigners. He had called a meeting as he felt we had reached a new crisis. We listened to this elderly Thai man with respect. He was clearly feeling under pressure. He told us that most charity workers who had sprung to the aid of the Thai people initially were now leaving in droves.

'There were 70 straight after the tsunami,' the camp manager said. 'Now that number is down to 20 and falling all the time. The hard fact is that the larger charities have already left.'

He didn't need to explain: we spoke often about it in the camps. The Thais who were constantly looking over their shoulders in grief and despair, reliving the trauma of the waves, were not aware that a whole new crisis lay ahead of them.

'There's no work for these people. What are they going to do? They can't live on handouts forever.' The man put his head in his hands. Usually reserved and not one to show emotion, now he couldn't help himself and his voice wobbled as he spoke:

'What is going to happen to these homeless people three months, six months, a year from now?'

I left, needing some quiet time to mull over his words. We had experienced the sheer force of the collective response to help immediately following the crisis. Now we just needed to impress upon businesses and individuals the importance of the recovery phase. They needed to be inspired to continue.

I for one wasn't giving up.

CHAPTER TWO

TEACH A MAN TO FISH

The devastation caused by the wave was only the beginning of the problems for the Thais. Not only had their families, friends and homes been taken, but for most of the people living on the southern coasts and islands, their livelihoods had also been washed away.

Working in tourism had been a pre-destined path for many years. The local school children knew their career options from a very young age: hotel gardener, cleaner, laundry worker, bellboy, assistant in a dive shop, or a tour guide if they had a flair for English. The big wave had changed all that.

Ninety per cent of the local population had been employed in the tourist industry. Now, nine thousand hotel rooms were down to nine hundred. Over half of the airport taxi drivers had lost their jobs, as had hundreds of bar staff, waitresses and diving instructors. Every week, with the decline in tourist spending, merchants were losing millions of dollars and thousands of jobs were at risk in the local communities. Most survivors did not have the money to repay their debts and resume their lives. Many had lost their homes and land and were forced to stay in relief centres. The few hotels that were going to be rebuilt would not be ready for a couple of years.

I have always been a firm believer that the only sustainable way out of poverty is through business. I had witnessed enough fruitless handouts in the past that had vanished as quickly as if dollars had been flushed down a toilet. It was a no-brainer – we simply had to find alternative business ideas for these workers. Tourism had always been an easy cash cow for the locals but there had to be other income-generating activities we could identify. We had to find other profitable business opportunities in the area other than tourism. Otherwise, it would be like beating one's head against a brick wall.

But how? I knew that I needed an ally. I called Miss Soonpon.

Miss Soonpon had been a teacher for over twenty years and was loved and respected by every family in the community. Schoolteachers are the most trusted figures in Thai society, after the King and the Buddhist monks, obeyed without question. Miss Soonpon, by far the most experienced teacher in her school, had taken on the role of social worker as well. Families with any type of social problem would wait patiently to see her after school, knowing that from her they would receive practical, calming and wise words.

Her school was in a deprived area in the outskirts of Khao Lak, its 300 children from poor families. The teachers had painted cartoons on the crumbling concrete walls but this couldn't hide the general dilapidation of the place. As the school building hadn't actually been damaged by the tsunami, the school itself wasn't being supported by any local charities, although many of the children's lives had been affected by the disaster. Miss Soonpon was determined to help the struggling families, coming in early in the morning and staying late after class to give them advice. She was unfailingly jolly, calm and practical and I too came to rely on her heavily, barely making a move without consulting her first.

She was short and stocky, with large brown glasses that perched on the end of her nose seemingly doing nothing as she always looked over them. Her short, spiky grey-speckled hair gave her a jaunty look and she went everywhere with a broad smile, always followed by five or six children clinging to her skirt. They circled around her as if she were the Pied Piper, holding her hand, skipping along beside her, gaining comfort from her presence. We met often. I knew I could rely on Miss Soonpon to come up with a list of those most in need as she knew every family in the community. We decided that first she would announce our plan to everyone and then invite all those interested in getting involved to an interview at the school.

'They'll feel more comfortable there,' said Miss Soonpon. 'The staff room, after class has finished, will be perfect. They will be able to open their hearts.'

What she didn't say was that honesty and truth were expected in this almost sacred place. With so many people fighting for survival, the situation had understandably created opportunists. Not that we really had to worry about that: Miss Soonpon knew the families inside out and would ensure that those who really needed help would get it. Without her wisdom and inside knowledge, we probably would not have got a fair, workable and respected project off the ground.

We were flooded with requests for help. By the end of the week Miss Soonpon's desk was heaped with papers. People had poured their hearts out on the page, sharing their crises. The stories were heartbreaking.

'Where do we start?' I asked. 'Each one of them needs help right now.'

Miss Soonpon said, 'You have your vision, you know your goal. Break it down into manageable, bite-sized chunks. Day by day. Five new families at a time. Don't fret, Linda. I will take the letters home this weekend and select the first five families.' She beamed at me over her specs. 'They will all get their turn'.

As much as I trusted Miss Soonpon to fulfil her end of the bargain, I had another worry: me. I wasn't qualified to provide all the business advice these people were going to need. Moreover, there was no one in the local area I could call in.

One morning, as I doodled on my pad of paper, hoping for inspiration, an idea came to me: 'There is an abundance of creative business brains sitting in Bangkok. Company executives who spend their days putting together solutions to challenging situations!'

I started to make notes, fired up now, writing quickly. The first thing everyone would have to acknowledge was that the survivors of the Asian tsunami would need to become entrepreneurs. Otherwise, the future staring them in the face was bleak. Although the majority had no previous commercial experience, no opportunity to acquire business skills and no access to loans they did have a few key entrepreneurial qualities. Courage and determination, and the overriding hunger to pick themselves back up.

I now needed to prepare a compelling business case for the business community in Bangkok and my possible backer – The Prince of Wales International Business Leaders Forum. I would then work with the companies in Bangkok to identify opportunities for new income-generating ventures. Then, once we had selected those with the most potential we would develop a simple business strategy for each new entrepreneur.

I knew something was still missing. An idea was hovering at

the edge of my mind, niggling at me. There was still one thing I hadn't addressed. Once armed with a new business idea, how would the survivors be able to develop it on their own? They wouldn't have the necessary level of skills or knowledge.

Then the idea came to me. I bit my biro so hard that ink spilled out the end of it: 'Mentorship!' That was the answer; we needed to build in ongoing support. Partner each entrepreneurial survivor with a business friend who was prepared to share their business skills. They'd need to support them, be there for them when they felt confused or frustrated, when they met an obstacle they didn't know how to overcome. Hold their hand, guiding them in whichever area they needed support – market expansion, accounting, advertising, customer service. This could be weekly at the beginning, face to face or by phone, moving to monthly once the entrepreneur became more confident.

'These businesses are always being asked to write a cheque,' I thought, knowing that this would grab their attention. 'They're being offered a project they can really sink their teeth into, one that isn't all about money.'

Later, as I pushed the send button on the ancient faded computer keyboard of my laptop, I closed my eyes and visualised the request winging its way to The Prince of Wales International Business Leaders Forum in London. I had my fingers crossed. All I could do now was wait.

I had a reply by return. The email was from the boss himself, Robert Davies, who thought the idea was excellent. He wanted to bring eight of IBLF's business leaders to visit, so that they could see for themselves how they could kickstart the whole initiative. I was overjoyed.

Not for the first or last time I sat and cried with thankfulness. It reminded me that all we have to do sometimes is ask.

The first five families arrived at the school the following Wednesday afternoon. I arrived at 4.30 to prepare for the interviews. To my surprise they were all there waiting, sitting on the grass, talking and eating.

Thai people have a love of food which borders on obsession. It has been said that if a Thai person isn't actually eating, they will almost certainly be thinking about food. When I approached the group on the grass, I was offered a plastic bag of tea which I accepted with thanks. I knew the street-seller. He had a stall outside the school gates. A painfully thin, elderly gentlemen with a heavily lined, sunburnt face, he made the takeaway tea by first scooping crushed ice into a plastic bag, then pouring hot tea on top which melted the ice. Last, with a few skilful twists and a flick of the wrist, he sealed the bag around a straw. Ingenious.

As I drank my tea I wondered how many ideas like this, simple yet clever, these families would be able to dream up with our help.

That afternoon the interviewees filed in, family by family, fighting their shyness. Asking for help was their last resort – with every penny of their savings gone, they came because their backs were against the wall. They had nothing left. The first family – parents and daughter – sat in a huddle on the sofa facing us, looking cowed. Miss Bani was dressed traditionally in a light batik sarong tied firmly in a knot around her waist. The colours in the fabric had faded to an amorphous blob of grey, the whole piece held together by heavy darns. Her oversized white T-shirt was frayed at the neck. On the front and back was printed a slogan: 'DTAC Happy' with the local phone company's logo, and underneath it was a smiley face which looked horribly out of place next to the mother's anxious expression.

'Thank you for coming today,' Miss Soonpon said cheerily. 'You are amongst friends, so let us see how we can help you.'

Her voice broke the tension in the room. Miss Bani took the lead.

'We are so sorry to bother you, teacher,' she said, her eyes filling with tears.

'Never mind that,' replied Miss Soonpon, the school teacher in her taking control of the escalating emotion in a matter-of-fact way. 'Take a deep breath. Now, tell us your story.'

The words came rushing out like a dam bursting its banks. 'I was a cook in a beachside hotel in Khao Lak. I love my job. I earn enough money to feed all of us. My husband had a car accident.' She pointed at his missing foot. 'This is our daughter Puk. She's eight'.

Puk was motionless, like a rag doll. Her eyes were wide open, staring into space, head resting on her mother's lap.

'She hardly ever talks,' Bani stroked her daughter's head. 'She lost so many friends'.

Miss Soonpon nodded sympathetically, encouraging her to continue with the story.

'It was my day off. I was at the village pump doing the laundry. Thanks to Buddha we live at the foot of the mountain.' She glanced at her husband. 'We heard it coming. He can't run – but somehow we got him up the hill. The wave took all our possessions: our clothes, my daughter's school books, our food. Everything smashed, washed away, gone.

'The hotel is gone. There is nothing left.' Her shoulders slumped but then she remembered what she had to say and sat upright, clearing her throat. 'Miss Soonpon, it's been six weeks now since I've worked and we can no longer feed our little girl.'

It was a difficult thing for a mother to say and a difficult thing for us to hear.

'I cannot take care of her anymore. There are no hotels for me to work in. It's all finished. Can you feed her?'

Tears were streaming down her face now. 'I try to be strong, but I have to accept it that there is nothing I can do. I feel so ashamed.'

I wanted to scream, 'Yes!', to throw my arms around her and give her money for food. Sensing this, Miss Soonpon indicated for me to remain seated.

I took a breath. This wasn't the way. Giving money would be a sticking plaster at best. After two months the family would need money once again.

Miss Soonpon took the lead, realizing I couldn't speak. 'We understand your situation and we are going to help you. But not as you have requested.'

An agonised sigh came from the silent husband, as if a guillotine had just come down. Khun Soopon continued quickly, with a confident smile. 'Listen, it is good news. We are going to help you to set up a new business.'

At this, Bani looked even more upset. 'I am not a business-woman! I am a cook.'

On seeing the beads of sweat on his wife's face, her husband took her hand and squeezed it lovingly. I spoke then, hoping to reassure them. 'I appreciate that but now is the time to look at a different future, a new career.'

'I only know how to cook,' Bani repeated.

'Trust us. All we ask is for you and your husband to spend a few days reflecting on your skills and your resources. How you would like to make a living if you could. Then look at your local community needs and see whether your idea fits. This is how you will come to realise a new business idea. A way you can earn money. A way you can be independent again. This way, you'll be able to feed your family.'

It was obvious that Bani thought we had gone mad. She rolled her eyes in disbelief.

'You may not believe it possible right now to become a successful businesswoman. But surely it's worth a go. What do you think?'

Bani sat back and nodded. I could see she wasn't convinced but we had said enough for one day.

'Don't worry, we have a team of experts to help you think about what will work. They'll guide you. It's a new beginning.'

Miss Soonpon spoke quickly to the family in Thai. Her words were obviously reassuring as the expression on their faces relaxed a little. Then they rose and with the customary gesture, a *Wai*, we all said farewell with heads bowed and hands clasped in front of our chests.

'See you in a few days', I called after them as they walked away. The little girl turned and waved, with the tiniest hint of a smile.

Miss Soonpon called for the next family to come in. I took a steadying breath – this was going to be one hell of an afternoon. I was relieved that we only had five families to interview.

Miss Wati entered alone. She was a tiny woman. Her fragile, bony frame looked utterly swamped in her oversized clothes. A dirty gauze dressing, stained yellow with pus, was hanging loosely under her chin. Above it, her face was strained, with hollow cheeks and dark rings around her eyes. Miss Soonpon indicated gently where she should sit.

'I don't know where to start,' Wati mumbled quietly, head bowed. Her hands fiddled nervously with her bag. 'It's all such a mess.'

'We know. Just start when you are ready. Here, have a sip of water. We are here to help you,' the schoolteacher said.

'I worked in the laundry at a beachside hotel in Khao Lak. I have worked there for years. It's in the basement. I had come up for my normal break, to take some fresh air. It gets really hot down there with all the driers. I was sitting on the grass deciding what to cook for supper when I heard a low rumbling noise, an odd sound like I had never heard before.'

Wati's voice trembled and she paused for a sip of water.

'I saw a wall of water – it must have been eight metres high – rushing straight towards me. It was like something from the movies. All I could hear was screaming, crashing, crunching.

'I remember thinking, I don't want to die. Not now. It's not my time! And I ran as fast as I could. But in my panic I ran back downstairs into the laundry. The wave followed me. I was like a doll in a washing machine. Round and round, up and down, over and over again. The pain in my ears and eyes was terrible. I heard my bones crack as they smashed against the walls. Something sharp ripped my skin. I could not breathe.'

Wati paused and lifted her arm, an action that took some effort, and touched the shaved concave area at the back of her skull.

'I was left lying in a pool of rubbish, coughing out the muck. The smell of sewage made me vomit. I knew I had to get out if I was to see my son again. One arm was useless. I don't know how I managed to get up the steps. Dragged myself on my stomach. Then luck smiled on me. A foreign man ran past me and I threw myself in his way. Grabbed his hand. The next thing I knew I was lying on the mountainside. I suppose the *farang* must have carried me there. I never saw him again but I thank Buddha every day for his kindness and pray for his soul.'

Wati fell silent and looked out of the window at her son playing football on the grass. Miss Soonpon leaned in close to me, speaking quietly. 'Wati has been in hospital since the tsunami. She was only released yesterday. She's had a lot of internal bleeding and she's still in a great deal of pain. She is also troubled with nightmares, depression, and panic attacks. She tried to commit suicide, Linda. Her husband is still in hospital unconscious. They believe he was hit by a car.'

'Is that their only son?' I looked at the little boy playing outside. 'Yes, just the one child. He's five.'

We explained to Wati about our plan for her. She didn't flinch. 'Only one thing I know. I will never work close to that sea again.'

It was the beginning of a rollercoaster eighteen months. At the start, I visited all the families at least once every two weeks, and called them every week to check they had not hit any unseen obstacles. Very often they were bursting to share a new success with me. I had no idea at the beginning how long I would have to stay on this bruised and battered coastline but one thing was clear: if anything was to be achieved then my physical presence was needed. My job was to broker the right partnerships, trouble-shoot problems, give encouragement when obstacles got in the way and a sympathetic shoulder to cry on when it all became too much. Above all I was there to help provide the daily inspiration these new entrepreneurs needed to keep going forward and not give up. After all, these were a people not only embracing the challenge of starting a new business but also bowed down in grief and haunted by their experience, many of them with debilitating physical injuries. In despair, some were being driven to suicide, which was an entirely new phenomenon in their community and one which was confounding local leaders and the Thai government.

My daily field work took me back to my days of district nursing when I had to try and juggle my patients, figuring out my timetable according to their geographic location and busy lives. In Thailand, I quickly got to know who got up early, ate late or had to pick up children from school. There were always unexpected events and emergencies I had to help with. Equipment would break; someone would have a last-minute hospital appointment; a mother would ask me to accompany her

45

to the monastery to pray for her lost son. When such things happened I would take out my red pen and rearrange my day. 'Mai pen rai' I would mumble, trying to remain calm. *The best laid plans...*

As the number of families we were helping increased, my days became longer. Soon, it became impossible to stay long. Leisurely visits were out of the question. I found myself constantly looking at my watch and always had to refuse a second cup of tea. My day always ended with a careful review of my notes. How were the families progressing? Was I missing anything? What else could we be doing? I would then email a concise report to my team of businessmen and women in Bangkok. They studied the figures and came back to me with any comments. I had to ensure that the business team was kept abreast of any social, psychological and environmental factors that were having an effect on a family's livelihood recovery. It was my job as field worker to be the team's eyes and ears.

My day would always start super-early. Rarely by choice. A raucous combination of screaming roosters and barking dogs would wake me. Even earplugs were useless against the din. The stray dog situation has become almost uncontrollable in Thailand. In Bangkok alone, as many as 300,000 stray dogs wander the streets, largely thanks to the Buddhist religious practice of selfless acts.

Buddhists are taught to revere living creatures and 'make merit' with acts of kindness which supposedly reduces a person's suffering in the next life. Few merit-making acts are as public or entrenched as feeding strays. Each evening at dusk, merit-makers across Thailand dump leftovers in the street, often laid on a banana leaf or a scrap of cardboard to dignify the meal.

'Giving food is among the simplest and truest forms of merit making,' says Phra Mahajatuphom Thummopalo, a monk and radio disk jockey at Bangkok's Thammongkol temple. 'Knowing that the monks are devoted to sustaining all life, Thais often drop their unwanted dogs at temple gates after dark. When food is scarce, monks will actually forego dinner to feed the strays. We have a lot, we give. We have a little, we also give.'

There were good days and bad days. Mostly I managed to keep upbeat. Sometimes, though, it all got too much. When that happened, homesickness would roll in and I'd miss my family and friends in the West. Then, all too soon, I received word that the West was coming to visit us.

The IBLF had promised to visit and the first group of international and national businessmen and women arrived in the April of 2005. They visited Phuket, Phang Nga and Krabi. Dubbed 'the Tsunami Business Task Force', their job was to assess the local needs not only in Thailand but also in India and Sri Lanka. The task force was made up of fifteen representatives of some of the world's leading businesses, including Accenture, Alcan Inc., Thai Bev, Cadbury Schweppes, Deloitte, ERM Group, Manpower, Nestle, and Standard Chartered.

They decided to visit Thailand first. When I was told that the business leaders would be with me for only two days I felt stumped. The distances were vast: most of our time would be wasted driving from one place to another. I pondered the problem for days, finally deciding that using helicopters was the only way it would work. But how on earth was I going to swing that one? I took a deep breath and picked up the phone. I decided to call the Admiral in charge of tsunami relief at the Navy Base at Cape Panwa, at the foot of Phuket Island.

Maybe it was crazy to think that the Navy would spare two helicopters at the request of a foreign woman. But at the time that did not even enter my head. I had no doubt that it was a good idea.

The next day I was received at the Navy Base with all the pomp and ceremony that only the military can pull off. Luckily, I always have one nice frock with me and on this occasion I pulled out the stops with lipstick, perfume and blow-dried hair. The Admiral, who must have been in his fifties, had a formidable presence. He stood straight-backed in his immaculate uniform to greet me, shoes and buttons gleaming. I glanced down at my pumps, relieved that I had remembered to give them a wipe. He asked me to sit. I started nervously but he was a good listener. Soon I was pouring out my plans and goals and all the while his gaze never left my own. He asked all the right questions and was very decisive once he had all the facts.

'Of course they've got to see what's going on first hand. I think it's a splendid idea.' He scratched his chin. 'Tell you what. I will give you two eight-man helicopters for two days.'

I nearly fell off my chair.

'Let us know where your business leaders are staying and we can pick them up from there – it will save time. And why don't we conclude their visit with a trip to our Navy base for a presentation of our military strategy for recovery?'

'Thank you so much, Sir,' I stuttered, feeling overwhelmed.

'You are very welcome, young lady. Your passion to help the Thai people at the grassroots – at the very heart of our problems – has moved me deeply.'

Later that evening at the café, I sat with some of my fellow volunteers who had huddled round to find out how I had got on. I grinned at them and raised my beer glass in a salute.

'I needed helicopters. They had them!' was my response. 'There's never any harm in trying.'

The two days flew by. The business leaders, who were accompanied by the British Ambassador, were tireless. Snatched from their comfortable lives, they visited the worst-hit areas, never once flinching at the dirt, the heat, the grief or despair. They talked to disabled survivors, orphaned children, and fisherman, all the while listening to their needs.

On the second day, I had planned an unusual dinner for the group. It had occurred to me that the main stakeholders in the recovery process after any catastrophic disaster, which always include the government, the military, the media, the charitable sector and the business sector, don't always talk to each other. Each is heavily engaged in vital work, always frantically trying to meet deadlines and achieve their goals, and in Thailand I had witnessed some overlap. It was clear that these groups needed to communicate. I was hoping that my dinner could kick-start that process.

My dinner guests needed to be from the top of the tree, no middle-management or lieutenants. I needed CEOs and Admirals. The group that was later billed as the 'Disaster Rapid Response Team' was made up of leaders of the following groups:

- *The government of Phuket* (responsible for the population and recovery strategy)
- *Private sector* (business skills and resources for emergency and livelihood recovery)
- *NGOs* ('strengthen the buffalo to plough the field': generally they are the ones with the strong local contacts and experience)
- *Military* (strategy, manpower and equipment)
- *Media* (often first on the scene – the Thai public donated more aid money to the leading TV channel in Thailand than the they did via the government because the camera crews were reporting the developing situation, minute by minute, and communicating the immediate need.)

The Governor of Phuket, Udomsak Uswarangkura, thought the dinner was a marvelous idea. As did the head of the main national TV channel, a senior representative of the Red Cross, and two admirals. Their presence around the dinner table at the Sheraton Hotel in Phuket that second night sparked a real plan of how best to work together. The information was later used as part of a powerful publication, 'Best Intentions, Complex Realities'. Now that we had agreed channels of communication I knew that the relief and recovery work would be as effective and sustainable as it was possible to be. There would be no more overlaps and time wasting.

Watching the large group around the table engaged so energetically in their subject was heaven. I sat back in my chair enjoying the scene, while the conversation sparked back and forth, taking on a whole dramatic life force of its own. There was no need for small talk that night. The Ambassador, who was sitting opposite me, caught my eye at one point and winked, leaning across the table to say, 'You did good Linda. What an evening!'

I appreciated the praise, but nothing came close to the joy Miss Soonpon and I felt when we visited individuals and families that we had helped and found their lives had been changed for the better.

One time we ventured deep into the jungle to visit Lek. Lek was a five year old girl with HIV contracted from her mother. Lek's mother had died of AIDS only a month before the tsunami killed her father. Now she was being cared for by her aunt Miss Piu. They had relocated deep in the jungle after the tsunami and were finding it impossible to make ends meet. Initially, Khun Soonpon had asked if we might be able to pay for Lek's HIV drugs to help the family. I hoped we could find a better solution.

Piu was a single mother, not only having to care for five year old Lek but her own two little girls as well. She couldn't go out to work. When we first met it was clear that she was a bright and energetic young woman, open to starting her own business. It had only taken her a day to work out a viable plan. She told me that where she lived it was a considerable distance to the nearest garage to buy petrol. She reckoned that she had spotted a gap in the market. My mind boggled as she spoke: was she suggesting that she erect petrol pumps in her front garden?

As our truck made its way through the rolling green mountains, lush and jungle-covered, ethereal mists swirled in the slowly warming morning air. I had taken extreme measures to ward off mosquitoes as I knew we'd be working in their playground. As well as wearing long trousers tucked into socks, boots and a long-sleeved, high-neck shirt, I engulfed myself in clouds of mosquito spray and put an even more potent and toxic chemical repellent on my clothes and shoes.

As we approached their house, I jumped out of the truck, excited. I could sense that everything was going well. Lek came running up, giggling and clutching my leg. I picked up the little girl and gave her a big hug. Then we went into the house to find her aunt.

Piu's idea had been to create a shed at the front of the garden in which she would place petrol drums and recycled coke bottles. Each would contain either petrol, diesel or engine oil for motorbikes and farm vehicles.

The business brains in Bangkok had confirmed that it was certainly a viable business and one where she could earn money from home and care for her family at the same time. For less than $100 she purchased plastic drums, glass pumps and the wood to build the small outhouse. The news of Piu's new enterprise spread fast and her brother came from Surat Thani to see if he could help. Soon he was busy building the shed.

Piu was bursting to tell me how she was getting on. She held out her hands to greet me, standing tall.

'How is business?' I asked, although the question hardly needed asking.

'*Khop Khun Ka* [Thank you] Linda we did it! People love it. My customers are steady and regular. I even have enough to pay back the money I borrowed for Lek's drugs'.

We sat together on the step of her little house in the jungle and had tea. The atmosphere was magical. It was at times like these I knew that everything we were doing was worthwhile.

Not every case was such a straight-forward success story. Some of the people we were helping were much more fragile. Miss Son was one of them.

She had been working as a chambermaid at a beachside hotel on the morning the wave hit. Normally, the guests would have vacated their rooms, leaving them free for her to clean and tidy, but they'd been partying hard the night before. Miss Son was still finishing the first floor rooms when she heard a deafening crash. She turned towards the noise. The last thing she recalls was seeing a poolside chair flying straight at her through the bedroom window.

Miss Son woke up days later in hospital. She had ingested so much dirty water her lungs had developed multiple abscesses. The doctors had feared this would kill her before she regained consciousness. They had been pumping her with IV antibiotics while friends kept a vigil at her bedside. When she did come to, she was in agony. She had a dislocated left shoulder and a broken right arm, wrist and fingers. A pin was put in her arm and her wrist and fingers were put in plaster. But no matter what combination of painkillers the doctors put her on, they could not seem to control her pain.

We had to find a way to help her as she was the breadwinner of the family. Her husband had died two years before in a bike accident and she was caring for her elderly parents and her five year old son. Thankfully the three of them had been away visiting relatives, far from the beach, on the day of the tsunami.

Miss Soonpon asked me to visit Miss Son at home. 'Linda, this is a difficult situation. She is very sick but she is a proud lady. She wants to work.' She paused, looking worried. 'To be frank, I don't think it is possible, but if we don't give it a go I am afraid she will only get more depressed.'

Collecting some fruit on the way, Miss Soonpon and I took a local *tuk tuk* to Miss Son's house. Her elderly parents were sitting outside on the wooden porch playing with Ralee, their little grandson.

'Have you come to see Mum?' Ralee said, grabbing Miss Soonpon's hand. 'She is in bed.'

We followed the boy into the house. In a darkened bedroom, we found his mother.

'I am so happy you came. I am just getting up. I am fine.' Her voice sounded weak.

'I have a great business idea. Just need your help with it.' It was humbling to hear her words, so full of spirit. 'It's just the pain … if only I could control the pain I would be fine.'

We helped her get up. She winced with pain every time she moved. When we asked her how she was, she brushed our words aside. 'Let's have some tea and I can tell you what I would like to do.'

We sat and listened carefully to her idea.

'I would like to set up a laundry business from my home. I have the space. It can be plumbed in here,' she said, pointing to a space in her outhouse. 'The garden is very sunny so the clothes will dry in no time. I love ironing.'

For a moment I was silent, unable to imagine her having the strength to lift an iron, let alone wet sheets and towels.

'The market is great,' she continued. 'Once I have the equipment – a washing machine, iron and ironing board – I will have customers. What do you think? Can you help me?'

Neither of us had the heart to dishearten this brave woman. But both of us were having the same thought. How on earth would she have the strength to lift the sheets from the machine onto the line?

Our silence alarmed Miss Son. 'I have no other choice. Please. I have no one else to help us.'

'I am concerned about your health,' Miss Soonpon said gently. 'What did the doctor say?'

'He said there is nothing more they can do. He hopes my body will adjust to cope with the pain. I'm sure he is right. I'll be fine. Soon.'

Honestly, I doubted it. 'Is there any other lighter business we can help you with?' I cast around wildly, hoping for inspiration.

'Linda, I don't feel strong enough to leave my house to sell things at the market or at school. If I work from home I know I have the option to lie down if the pain gets too much. My parents can always help.'

I very much doubted that, having seen how elderly and physically handicapped they were.

'We will work something out for you. Don't worry,' I said with a confidence I didn't feel. 'Now, you go and get some rest.'

My business advisors were moved by Miss Son's plight but, like us, thought it likely that her business would fail. The next week, however, we decided that we should give it a shot. This was against our better business judgement but we agreed to build in extra support somehow. The equipment was bought and installed. When Miss Son saw her gleaming washing machine, iron and ironing board she smiled. For a fleeting moment her face looked softer, no longer tense from holding the pain.

'Start slowly, pace yourself,' I advised her. 'Just work a few days a week and see how you feel.'

Every other day I popped by to see how she was. At first, seeing the washing blowing on the line, I was encouraged. Maybe we were wrong and she'd be fine.

At the end of the second week, Miss Son called me in tears. 'I am so sorry. I cannot work this week. I know I am letting you down.'

'Of course you aren't,' I tried to reassure her. 'You've done brilliantly. Of course you'll have bad weeks. It's only to be expected.'

'You trusted me. And I am letting my family down. But the pain is too much. I give in. What is the point of living?'

I rushed straight to her home.

'You have been so brave,' I said, holding her gently in my arms. 'We tried too much too soon, that's all. Forget feeling guilty. We have to sort out this pain. I am going to Phuket International Hospital to get you an appointment and a second opinion. You are not alone, Miss Son.'

She put her head back on the pillow and slept.

The doctors and physiotherapists of Phuket International Hospital advised us that an intensive course of ultrasound treatment and daily physiotherapy might help. It was a gamble as her muscle damage was extensive. It took six months of therapy and daily visits to get Miss Son back on track. Her business remained small. She agreed to work only two days a week, to take on light laundry only, and to call one of her friends to help her if the pain became too great. She earns enough now to keep the family afloat and a young niece is slowly taking over most of the workload.

These more difficult cases, those men and women like Miss Son who had chronic physical or mental problems, we formed into cooperatives. With a tight community support network they could call each other for help at times when they could not manage.

They also needed some lightness in their lives to help ease their depression. We organised a schedule of activities that regularly brought them together. I asked my fishermen friends if they could take them out on the boats; we organised picnics in the forest; and we took trips to temples on auspicious days and received blessings from the monks. They shared their problems and found comfort in that.

It wasn't only the locals who needed light relief. The volunteers, immersed every day in the reality of people's physical and mental pain, needed beers, laughter and dancing to ease the tension. Bone-weary, at the end of a long, hot, dusty day, many of us would gather at the Marley café. It was a small place with a large picture of Bob Marley hanging jauntily above the bar, a pair of gigantic black speakers on either side. It never failed to make us feel at home. The chef, knowing how little home comforts put a spring in our step, did his utmost to provide them. One day peanut butter appeared on the menu to a shout of applause, and his mashed potato would have made any trucker's café in Bolton proud to call their own. At ten o'clock the dancing started. No one waited to be asked. We threw ourselves into it, bopping about, young and old, losing ourselves in the moment.

Of all the people we met and helped, the ones that illustrated best for me how utter hopelessness can be turned into overwhelming joy was the fishermen. It was a close friend of Miss Soonpon, Mr Ya, who first introduced me to them. One beautiful Sunday morning we set off on his bike to meet his friends. We got to the waterfront at ten and I was shocked to see so many fishermen sitting idle, in small groups dotted along the beach. We approached a huddle of men who were taking refuge from the sun under a tarpaulin held up by four sturdy bamboo posts. They were sitting on blue plastic beer crates, the younger ones playing dice, others reading newspapers. On a wooden platform in the middle was a golden Buddha, five foot high, adorned with garlands of flowers. A wooden sign was propped against a post. 'Boat Trips. 100 baht' painted on it.

'How long are these men going to sit here?' I thought to myself. 'Waiting for tourists who never come.'

When the fishermen saw Ya they gave him a hug. I received a slightly suspicious handshake. They pulled up a couple of crates and we sat down. I knew better than to push myself forward. Thai fishermen are a traditional bunch, proud and macho. A woman poking her nose into their business and issuing instructions would go down particularly badly with them. The whole thing had to be handled sensitively. Ya took the lead, immediately explaining why I was with him, speaking in rapid Thai, arms gesticulating vigorously.

One of the fishermen came forward, a wiry slip of a man dressed in a Cristiano Ronaldo football strip and sporting a huge number of amulets around his neck. He introduced himself as Sadee. The others hung back from the conversation at first, letting the smaller man be their spokesman. Ya had warned me that the fisherman worked in gangs and each had their own patch. They had a strong hierarchy. Knowing that, I was alert to their body language and the group dynamic, knowing that I could easily put my foot in it.

Luckily Sadee spoke a little English and with my *nik noi* [smattering] of Thai, plenty of body language and the odd drawing, we managed okay.

I was full of questions. How many fishing boats and long-tailed tourist boats needed replacing? Which boats could be salvaged?

What equipment had the fishermen lost? Did they have lifejackets? (Health and safety would be high priority now for tourists.) How many boats would they need now that there were fewer tourists and less fish needed as a result? I knew that my business people in Bangkok would need me to give them specifics.

Sadee explained that the fishermen had tried to form themselves into co-operatives. That way, they could take turns to fish in the boats they had. This had helped maintain morale and prevent their families from starving. But it wasn't enough.

'Surely, you should be building new boats. And you could sell them. You'd have a business.'

'The Andaman Sea is very deep. The boats need to be fast and strong. We don't know how to build them.'

'What if you learn how to build them?'

'We haven't got master shipbuilders or boatyard space.'

'Then we must find a master shipbuilder to teach you how to build them. Everything's possible.'

My business team agreed that the fishermen needed support. If we could help them set up as boat-builders then they would have an additional means of earning a living and a reason to get up in the mornings. We knew that corruption was a possibility, as it always was once funds started to pump in. In order to make sure that the money reached the right hands we decided to use the group scrutiny process: fishermen must identify each other as real fishermen.

Now that a plan had been established, the work could begin. I started to get things sorted, sourcing wood up and down the coast and finding a retired shipbuilder from the Phang Nga province who was prepared to teach the fishermen how to build boats. As the fishermen threw themselves into the project I sensed a breath of new life energising the small fishing community.

'No better time to learn a new trade,' I said to Ya.

Over the next year the fishermen became my close friends. I loved to sit with them on the beach at sunset sharing a bottle of the local Mekhong whisky. As well as the whippet-like Sadee who, as spokesman, was always given a nudge by one of the others whenever I approached, I got to know many of the others. One of them, Arak, was a legend. An expert at spear-fishing, he would dive without oxygen to great depths, returning to the surface many minutes later with a prize barracuda. He looked like Neptune with his long flowing hair and bulging calf muscles. He had a jagged, angry-looking scar on his right cheek which looked like an old knife wound but I never asked how he'd got it.

Evenings at the beach were magical. Once the handful of holidaymakers had returned to their hotels, the fishermen's families would gather. They'd toss fish onto a barbeque and one of the young lads would get out his guitar. We feasted on a catch so fresh it tasted better than anything you could hope to find in a Michelin-starred restaurant, grilled to perfection and served with a dash of chilli sauce.

The boatbuilding project was a wonderful success. Every time a new boat was lovingly and painstakingly completed I would get a call:

'Come on Linda, we need to launch the boat. We know you are busy but you need to come. You are our lucky charm.'

It seemed that for it to be a success, not only did the fishermen need to consult a monk on the most propitious time to launch and build an altar of offerings on the beach, but they needed me on board for luck. What they didn't know was that I couldn't swim. When I was five, a severe ear infection had caused both my eardrums to perforate. After many operations I resigned myself to the fact that I would never be able to get water anywhere near my ears again. Now, I was put in the bizarre position of having to ride choppy seas in a long-tailed boat.

'Feel the fear and do it anyway.' I heard the whispered words of my Tibetan master driving me on.

I wasn't the only one to feel fear. When the sea was at all rough, I would crouch with the others, wrapped in a waterproof, and I would sense that these hardy survivors were thinking about the tsunami.

As Christmas approached, a year since the tsunami had struck, I felt torn. I badly wanted to see my family but I knew I would find it hard being back in England. Being so close to misery and deprivation every day had made the thought of Christmas difficult to stomach. I didn't want to be a humbug but I felt too raw after what I had seen and shared with the tsunami survivors to head into a crazy world where commercialism was running riot. I could imagine what it would be like: streets heaving and people racing in and out of shops, stressed if the latest toys had sold out. I couldn't do it.

I asked Ya if he and his gang of fishermen and their families might join me for a Christmas party on the beach.

'I've never heard of Christmas, Linda, but you know we're always up for a party!'

I threw my arms around him.

Christmas Day 2005 on Rawai beach brought home the real joy of Christmas to me, something I realised I hadn't truly felt in years. We decorated a pot plant with red and green streamers and hung coloured wool balls on its branches, kindly crocheted by Miss Soonpon. I had even managed to find a box of crackers at Tesco Lotus.

'Go on, tug! Tug hard! Don't be scared!' I shouted at these fearless men of the sea.

By the time the crackers were pulled and their contents had spilled out on the sand we were all in hysterics.

We feasted on jasmine rice, Tom Yam Kung (spicy shrimp soup), Phat Thai (fried noodles), stir-fried vegetables, chicken curry soup and plate after plate of scrumptious fish.

'We have a gift for you, Linda.'

I was embarrassed. 'Really, you shouldn't have!'

Arak, the gentle giant, stepped forward. 'I carved it and Sadee varnished it.'

He held out an exact replica of a wooden longtailed boat, resplendent with coloured swags – exactly the same as the ones we had launched, but in miniature. I was lost for words.

'We love you, Linda!' they cried, standing and raising their glasses. 'Happy Christmas!'

Seeing I was about to blub, Arak said, 'Everyone in the sea! It's a beautiful night for a swim!'

Later, as I watched the families leave on their motorbikes, still wearing their paper hats with pride, I felt my heart brimming over.

I came back three years after that first visit to Thailand to see how the fledgling businesses were getting on. Virtually every single one had taken off. Many had expanded, others had diversified. It was so heartening to see that entrepreneurial flame still burning so strong.

I visited the home of Miss Bani, the first person we had interviewed in the schoolroom four and a half years before. I was delighted to find that the small business we had helped her set up was now running very successfully. I was greeted by a very different person from the despairing woman in the smiley-face T-shirt that I had met with Miss Soonpon. She looked taller, calmer, more confident.

'Come, I want to show you something,' she said, taking my hand. She caught me looking at my flip-flops and understood my concern. Her house was on the edge of overgrown jungle and I was terrified of meeting a king cobra.

'You can borrow my husband's rubber boots. They should fit you.'

Bani led me through an avenue of tall trees. We walked in silence. The forest was dense, with lines and lines of trees, the sun barely managing to break through the canopy of leaves. We finally reached a small clearing in which stood a sizeable wooden shed. As we walked up, her husband emerged from it and shook my hand.

'These rubber trees have been in our family for generations. We have five hundred. They produce at least eight sheets of rubber per day,' Bani told me.

'How much does that fetch,' I asked.

'A sheet sells for fifty baht. We earn about four hundred baht a day.'

My business mentors had pointed out that rubber was an excellent way forward for those lucky enough to own land. It used to be a thriving local industry on the coast until tourism took over. The trees were there to be farmed and they were happy to invest in the pressing machines, tin trays and knives to make it happen. Thailand, they told me, is on track to become the world's biggest rubber exporter.

Beaming with pride, Bani told me that their weekly income was now four times greater than it was when they had been working in the tourist industry. And the business was growing all the time.

'My husband collects the sap each morning,' she told me proudly. 'Watch, he'll show you.'

Bani's husband took out a heavy curved metal knife that he had tucked in his leather belt. He held the point to the bark of the tree and, pressing hard, he carved a deep diagonal channel about a foot long around the trunk. Immediately a thick white gluey sap oozed out. Then, taking a half coconut shell which was hanging from a nail in the tree, he began to harvest the rubber.

'He has to work through the night with his team as the sap needs to be collected at the coolest time of day, before sunrise.'

I was then taken into the shed where we stood under rows of honey-coloured sheets the size of a bathmat. Bani showed me how the rubber is processed and then told me to take off my boots. She emptied some of the coagulated rubber onto the concrete floor.

'Now, walk on it. Be careful not to slip.'

I felt like I had been transported to a French vineyard, pounding the juice out of the grapes. The rubber was cool and slimy and squelched up between my toes.

Bani was like the captain of the ship, in full sail now. 'We then cut the rubber into sheets and put them through this old washing mangle to flatten and squeeze them even more. That's hard work.'

'How do you get them to market?' I asked, drying my feet on a towel.

'It's easy. An agent from a Bangkok rubber company comes to our door every two days.'

'You really have got things well sorted,' I said with admiration.

'Not just that,' she said proudly. 'We're now looking to get a machine to process glue. We're expanding the business all the time.'

As we walked back to the house I asked her how her daughter was getting along. I remembered the lifeless little girl burrowing into her mother's lap on the sofa at the school.

'She is so much happier. Her teacher says that she is much more lively at school. Joining in with the others. Everyone says she is blossoming!'

When it was time for me to leave, Bani gave me a hug. 'We still

MARMALADE AND MACHINE GUNS

talk to our business mentor every week who gives us good advice,' she said. 'But we miss you, Linda.'

Another day I went to visit Miss Wati, who we had also interviewed at the school. For her, depression had been the most disabling thing after the tsunami. Yes, her body still bore the scars, but from the moment she had started her own business she came to life again. Wati liked to cook, and the more people appreciated her food, the more it inspired her.

'Your business people gave me seven thousand baht to set up my mobile shop.'

'And how has it been going?' I asked her.

'It's very busy down at the construction sites. I've been worked off my feet. I can hardly produce enough to keep the men happy,' she said, smiling.

In the eighteen months I had been working with the families I had kept up with her success. At first, she would call me every day, bursting with excitement, telling me that she had sold all of her chicken in only a few hours.

'And have you managed to expand at all?' I asked.

'I've started to experiment with other foods. Cakes and salads. I cook the food that I know they'll want to eat.'

'How is your son?'

'He's great. Got new shoes. And I've signed him up for the school trip,' she said proudly.

'I have been hearing such wonderful things about you,' I said, taking her hands in mine. 'You've been such an inspiration to everyone. You're a great business mentor, I hear. A real natural.'

'Who would have thought it?'

I knew that she too was remembering the broken person we had met that day at the school, full of the hopelessness of her situation.

People always talk about the power of networking or 'word-of-mouth'. It is vital in work like mine. Otherwise we'd be forever planting small seeds without the projects ever taking root. It's hard to be out there spreading the word when you've got your sleeves rolled up and you're doing the work on the ground. You need friends with influence on your side.

Some people are especially gifted networkers; nothing gives them more pleasure than bringing the right people together to make the best things happen. The British Ambassador, my friend David Fall, is one of these very special people. He believed in what we were trying to achieve and was one of our most powerful evangelists. He rang me one day, towards the end of my time in Thailand, and suggested that I meet Mr Tirawat, Chairman of the Thai Red Cross and one of HRH Princess Sirindhorn's advisors. It was a meeting that was to spark a wonderful new initiative, one which still continues today.

Mr Tirawat met me in the Four Seasons Hotel in Bangkok. Although dressed immaculately in dark grey suit and gunmetal silk tie, there was nothing staid about him. He bubbled with energy and smiled all the time. He was fond of Britain, having been educated there. Speaking perfect BBC English, Mr Tirawat explained that HRH Sirindhorn's charity hadn't thought of working with the business world before. They were keen to preserve the traditions in the villages in which they worked and would question whether the business sector could possibly offer the same level of sensitivity. Surely any business people involved in charitable work would ultimately always ask, 'What's in it for us?'

He had heard a little about Prince Charles's desire to involve businesses in the issues that affect their local community. I told him that the IBLF were breaking new ground in Thailand. The generosity of the business men and women in Bangkok coupled with the extraordinary entrepreneurial spirit of the locals was a wonderfully powerful partnership. And it wasn't entirely selfless: businesses had reported that their employees were feeling happier and more engaged in their work and productivity was up. It was working for everyone.

Mr Tirawat spoke fast. 'I think this is very exciting. As long as the Princess's charitable advisors are assured that your business people won't be imposing their big city ideas on the small rural communities I'm sure they might want to get involved.'

'I can see why they'd be cautious,' I said. 'A Royal charity needs to be. To be honest, it wouldn't be the first time a partnership between the charitable and business sectors has raised a few eyebrows. They do make odd bedfellows.'

'Look, I want you to meet the Princess. Can you come to Phuket next week?'

I had heard a little about the detailed protocol involved when meeting a member of the Royal Family. Mr Tirawat proceeded to brief me further. It was a little intimidating.

'You cannot greet her with bare arms. And no open-toed sandals.' He glanced at my clothes. 'I'm afraid trousers aren't allowed. And no black.'

It is lucky he warned me. Everything I possessed was a no-no.

'You must never turn your back on Her Royal Highness. When you need to leave, you should walk backwards.' He looked at me, up and down, assessing my height. 'Your head must never be above hers so bend your knees and keep low.'

I had a vision of myself bent double, like some crabbed old crone. No high heels then.

'Only speak when you are spoken to and do not offer your hand. Her Royal Highness must make the approach. She will shake your hand if she wishes.'

The Thai royal family is adored by their people. Each day, on the streets, the national anthem blares out from speakers at 8am and 6pm. Everybody stops what they're doing and stands still in reverence. On the day HRH Princess Sirinhorn came to visit the Red Cross projects in Phuket a huge crowd had gathered. On the street there was a holiday atmosphere, excited heads craning to see, flags waving. I had no idea if the Princess would talk to me. I had heard that there was a specific royal language that Thais had to speak if they were addressing a member of the Royal Family. As a result, any room they entered was usually silent, commoners not daring to open their mouths in case they made a mistake.

I stood in line, melting in my long-sleeved dress, worrying that my mascara would be making its way down my cheeks in runnels of sweat. The princess walked along beside her army officials, stopping now and then to talk to children and old people. She wore a pale blue safari-style trouser suit. Occasionally she paused to write something in her notebook. Then she stopped in front of me. I made a low curtsy, keeping my head bowed.

'I have heard about your great work. You are a real action woman.'

The Princess took my hand and looked into my eyes. There was something in her unwavering stare that impressed me. She was clearly deeply involved with her work, tenderly concerned about the plight of her people.

The next day I received a phone call from the palace.

Things moved quickly. Once I had described to HRH Princess Sirindhorn's senior charitable advisor, Mr Kitti, how the partnership would work and how the private sector could be a positive force for good she wanted to give it a try.

They picked a tough case.

Huay Loi village, on the Thai-Laos border in north-east Thailand, is a forgotten place, in part of what was known as a 'red area'. During the war against communism, over twenty years ago, many government ministries were stationed here. After the war it became a ghost-town. Many of the villagers who stayed on were ex-soldiers. None of these former communists would give up their guns, although they weren't supposed to have them. They'd had a tough life, many of them hiding out in the hills during the worst of the troubles. Things weren't much easier two decades later. The land was forbidding, crops never flourished, and the hillsides were scarred with increasing levels of deforestation.

Taking a group of senior business executives to Huay Loi village would be a tall order. I sensed that this would be one 'Seeing is Believing' trip they would never forget. I had to trust that the experience we provided would be one that engaged their minds and hearts. Talking to the locals, getting a taste of what their daily lives are like – this is what sparks creative thinking. I'd seen it happen before. I trusted it would again.

Sitting at a table in Bangkok with Anat, CEO of Cadbury; Simon, Country Manager of Manpower; Paul, Senior Vice President of Thai Beverage; and David Fall, the British Ambassador, I outlined the plan for our trip. I couldn't help wondering if the lack of amenities would put them off. I shouldn't have worried – these were men who let nothing stop them once they'd committed to an idea. They were bright, buoyant and flexible people. The cut-and-thrust world they inhabited had made them fit to meet just about any challenge.

'A bit like being back in the scouts,' Anat said, eyes sparkling with fun.

When we all met again at the airport they seemed different. There was no sign of the frazzled business executives in expensive suits I'd met a few weeks before. Instead, in their polo shirts and chinos, they really did look like a group of boy scouts, eager to be off on an adventure.

It was pitch black and misty when we arrived at our hostel close to Huay Loy village. There we had cold showers by torchlight and ate a simple supper of stir-fried rice. Next morning we set off for the village, winding along rough, dusty tracks in our minibus. A Thai song was playing on the radio and the men burst spontaneously into song.

We were met by the village leader, a wiry, muscular man in a threadbare brown vest and red bandana. His face and arms were etched with old scars. He took us to the schoolroom where we sat down with a group of male villagers. He opened the discussion, speaking bitterly of the hardship the village had endured during the communist fighting. He described how many of them had hid in the hills for years living off the almost barren land, like animals. After the war, they were abandoned, forgotten.

The only time his voice softened was when he spoke about HRH Princess Sirindhorn. I looked up at the picture of her hanging on the schoolroom wall, festooned with yellow ribbons, in pride of place. He told us that the Princess had given them hope for the future.

We were taken on a tour of the village, along overgrown, muddy tracks, breathless and sweating. As we passed a cluster of bamboo huts with banana leaf roofs I sensed, from the little flickering movements inside, that eyes were following our every step.

Miss Pongpan, one of the Princess's charity advisors and our host, described the worst of the problems the villagers faced.

'The villagers have no access to clean tap water. They have to bring water up from the river here, in eleven tank stages, using gas.'

We peered over the river's edge, barely able to glimpse the water it was so far down.

'They've all got intestinal parasites from drinking the water.'

She pointed at the hillsides. They looked as if they had been scored by a large knife. 'The only way they survive is by clearing the forests. The land gives so little back that they need more and more of it. We need to find them a different living.'

We met the women of the village. They were sitting in the shade with their babies. They giggled nervously at first, a little alarmed at having the men sit with them. Many of them were pregnant. When we asked them what they did with their day, there was a collective shrug.

'Not much. Do what is needed round the house. Look after the children.'

'Are you happy?' asked Anat.

'It's our life.'

When we asked if they might like to learn a new trade, one with a guaranteed market, the question was met with listlessness.

'We have the children to care for. That's what we do.' Another shrug.

I wondered how we were going to spark the necessary entrepreneurial spirit in Huay Loy. It was going to be an uphill struggle motivating such a malnourished, under-confident group of people. They were used to getting nothing, so expected nothing.

Our group of business people weren't deterred by any of this. They'd been dealt a difficult case but that wasn't putting them off. There were obvious problems that needed to be sorted:

- *A lack of clean water.* To that end Cadbury organised for water tanks to be installed, properly sealed so that the rainwater didn't get contaminated.
- *The village's remote location, making it impossible to get produce to market.* Here, Thai Bev trucks returning to Bangkok after having made their deliveries were put to use.
- *The villagers' lack of skills and self-confidence.* Manpower

70

offered training and in a short time they were making bamboo furniture and handicrafts which were sold from the Princess's charity outlets.

- *The lack of nutrients in the soil making it unsuitable for standard crop growing.* It was decided that mushroom-growing might become the perfect income-generator for the villagers. With the right transport, they could sell this high-end crop to the city hotels.

In no time, the schoolchildren and their mothers were learning how to grow mushrooms and the general air of lethargy pervading the village was transformed into one of industry. With a bit of help the village was able to turn itself around.

HRH Princess Sirindhorn was delighted with the success of the new partnership and it is one that is still flourishing today.

By February 2006 the time had come to say goodbye to those brave-hearted, generous Thais with whom I had spent such happy times. Part of me didn't want to go, couldn't bear to be parted from my friends, but I felt that my work was almost done here. There was a great team in place who could keep the projects moving forward and I knew that it was time for me to get my teeth into something new. I was hoping, with the IBLF's help, that I might be able to use the model we had worked with in Thailand in some other place, equally in need of our help.

I was dreading saying goodbye to my fisherman friends. Along with Miss Soonpon, they would forever hold a place in my heart. I was dry-mouthed and tense on my last morning as I walked down to the beach. The first thing I saw was a crowd of people on the shoreline. Then I spotted Mr Sadee. He was wearing his Manchester United football strip, a sure sign that something out of the ordinary was happening. He gave me his usual bone-crushing handshake.

'What's happening?' I asked, indicating the crowd who were standing with their backs towards us.

'Come and see Linda', he said, hopping from foot to foot with excitement.

On our approach the crowd parted. It was then that I saw what they had been looking at. At the water's edge lay a gleaming long-tailed boat, its bow loaded with offerings and garlands. On its side was painted in twelve-inch white letters: LINDA CRUSE.

'Look! Look inside!'

I grabbed the warm wood, lifting myself up to see over the side. I read the words inscribed there: LOVE YOU.

I couldn't speak.

'We'll never forget you, Linda,' Mr Sadee said.

'*Kop, khan, ka*, my dear friends,' I stammered through my tears. 'I will never forget you either.'

Mr Ya stepped forward and lit the firecrackers. Then, as the air exploded all around us, the fishermen inched the boat forward on its rollers.

'Come on, Linda. Get in!' they shouted. 'Time to go!'

CHAPTER THREE

A MAN'S WORLD

Pakistan, 2006–8

I was sitting with my team of business leaders in Bangkok when I first heard about the earthquake in Pakistan. The news was just coming through and we listened to it together.

'Right, you'll be off then, Linda,' Simon said.

How well he knew me!

I was naïve to think that Pakistan would be anything like Thailand. Did I think I could dive in, do the job, and leave with a chorus of friendly cheers? Perhaps. But I would soon know better. That energetic community spirit which extended itself to foreigners – so obvious in Thailand – seemed barely present in Pakistan. There, as it turned out, supplies sent to the disaster area were being looted, often as not, before they reached the desperate families in need. And foreign journalists and aid workers were being sent home in droves, their employers unable to vouch for their safety. Kidnappings, suicide bombs, mob killings. It wasn't a good place to be. Westerners felt unwelcome in Pakistan. And if you were white and female you were the guest nobody wanted at their table.

My first mistake was arriving at the airport on my own. I hadn't organised any official transport. It wasn't an oversight – I like to see a situation for myself without having to be under any umbrella of protection. For that reason, too, I had chosen a local guesthouse rather than a large hotel. What I didn't realise was that by doing so I was putting myself and others in danger.

I walked out onto the airport concourse. There was a large crowd. I felt hundreds of eyes staring at me with such intensity it was as if they were burning a hole in my chest. I understood how Beckham must feel walking out onto the pitch at Wembley Stadium. For a moment I wondered if my skirt was tucked into my knickers. Then I remembered that I looked different – pale skin, blonde hair. I hadn't an inch of flesh in sight below my high-necked top but it was enough to cause a stir. I began to feel a bit panicky, unable to see the exit, or a way through the crowd. Then, hearing the magic cry of 'Taxi!' I walked briskly in the direction of the voice.

Like a miracle, the sea of white *shalwar kameeze* parted, allowing me to walk right through the middle. I felt a little dazed. Then a man approached me.

'Where are you going, Miss?'

'I need to reach my guesthouse.' I handed him a crumpled piece of paper on which was scribbled the address.

He took it and, without stopping to glance at the address, ushered me quickly to his car. Inside it there were no door or window handles. I looked at the dashboard. No meter.

'What's your rate? How much will...?'

The driver, a tall man who had managed to fold himself into his tiny Suzuki with great agility, cut me off mid-sentence:

'Listen, Miss. I will take you to your guesthouse.' He looked at me, unsmiling. 'You are lucky to have me as your taxi driver. A woman travelling alone. It's dangerous.'

He told me to sit in the middle, keeping away from the window. I had the feeling that this was as much for his safety as for mine. We wove our way through brightly-painted jingly trucks, belching out thick black smoke. Ordinarily, I would have delighted in the chaotic scene – carts laden with melons, local buses crammed with passengers, bodies hanging by their finger tips from every conceivable ledge. But with the taxi-driver's dark warnings my spirits had been damped down. And it wasn't just that – I had found the atmosphere oppressive from the moment I got off the plane. Why? What was it? I'd been all over the world and never had quite this feeling – as if I was in a truly alien place.

As the cab continued its journey, braking often to avoid children selling cigarettes to the drivers, the answer dawned on me: there were no women. No grandmas, wives, little girls. And I couldn't recall having seen any from the moment I walked onto the airport concourse. The taxi driver dropped me off at the guesthouse and drove away quickly. My welcome wasn't much warmer inside. The manager seemed equally perturbed that I was a woman, travelling alone. I was shown upstairs to a dingy room with peeling walls. I closed the door and sat down on the bed. I couldn't relax. The taxi driver and guesthouse manager's jumpiness had rubbed off on me. I got up and pushed a chair under the door handle.

'I'd give anything for a nightcap,' I thought to myself. No such luck.

Next morning the manager could hardly hide his delight when I told him I was leaving. As he said goodbye, I almost heard the words hanging in the air: 'And don't come back.'

During those first days and weeks in Pakistan there were many times I wanted to cut and run. There aren't many places, desperately in need of aid, where charity workers are at risk. Pakistan is one. I was repeatedly advised to leave the country but stubbornly I stayed on, even when my main sponsor, the IBLF, pulled out of the project, unwilling to take further responsibility for my safety. By that time, I had fifty businesses interested in setting up sustainable projects. There was no way I was going to leave.

The Pakistan earthquake was a disaster on an enormous scale. Thousands were dying of thirst and starvation, families huddled without shelter in the blistering sun. Aid wasn't reaching them fast enough and it was pitifully inadequate. Unlike Thailand, the country wasn't a popular holiday destination so it wasn't a story so close to home. The global media covered it only briefly. Tsunami aid money kept on flowing. Pakistan was left to cope almost alone. Thirty thousand square kilometres at the foot of the Himalayas were devastated, towns and villages razed to the ground. Before the earthquake the population was already living at subsistence level. No one had anything put by for a rainy day. Any hiatus and they starved.

I needed to get to the main refugee camp at Balakot. At the bus station at Islamabad, I joined the crowd queuing for the bus. It was my first day in Islamabad and my nerves were still jittery. I found myself singing a Monty Python song in my head, *I'm a lumberjack and I'm OK*, horribly aware that every bit of me was being scrutinised by a hundred pairs of eyes. As planned, I was setting off on a recce to the earthquake area. I had no escort and was starting to realise that this wasn't a good idea.

Then a stroke of luck. A white-haired man came up to me, greeting me with a nod.

'*Asalam allikum*,' he said. 'Are you off to the earthquake area? Please may I introduce myself. I am Dr Ghas.'

I realised this was the first time anyone had spoken to me with any warmth since I'd arrived in Pakistan. I explained to him that I was heading to Balakot. He said that he too would be going that way, although he was waiting for some medical supplies and wouldn't be there until later.

'Are you waiting for someone?' He glanced around the bus station.

'No, I'm alone.'

At this he looked serious. He said he hoped I didn't mind his giving me advice. There was something in his tone that made my stomach churn all over again.

'Your bus will make many stops. Sit at the back. When it stops, hide yourself. Bend down below the window so you cannot be seen.'

He paused, understanding my distress. I didn't want to hear it. I didn't want it to be this way. The constant watchfulness. Doom-laden advice. It made me bristle although I knew the man only wanted to help.

He spoke gently. 'These areas on the north-west frontier are sensitive. The people are very poor, very...' he searched for the right word, '...emotional. It's best they don't see you're a foreigner.'

'What would they do to me? Throw stones?'

'No. They will kill you.'

I tugged at the scarf around my head, feeling stifled.

'It's okay. I'll speak to the bus driver. I know him. I will say you are my friend.'

Dr Ghas told me to get on the bus. Standing outside any longer would only attract more attention.

'When you get to the camp, go straight to the army base. Ask for the Major in charge. Tell him I sent you. Don't talk to anyone else.'

I thanked him and got on the bus, moving to the back. My legs were shaking. I sat down and pulled the grubby curtain across the window, shielding myself from view. I sat for the whole journey huddled, face down, barely moving. Feeling afraid every time the bus stopped.

I was met at the bus stop in Balakot by one of Dr Ghas's friends, a man called Gullam. Dr Ghas had called him while I was on the bus, suggesting that he took me on a tour of the worst-hit areas. We would wait for him at an agreed spot on the way to a place called Mitakot.

Gullam drove slowly, skirting landslide rubble and wide cracks in the road. As far as I could see, in every direction, were piles of grey rocks and huge gaping craters. It looked like the surface of the moon. There was hardly a building standing.

'Balakot was where the two plates collided. They tell me the mountains moved sideways. The earth moved upwards with a jolt. Then crashed down.'

'There's nothing left,' I said, half to myself.

'It was a beautiful city.'

We waited in silence for Dr Ghas on the mountain road. He arrived in an ancient green army jeep, tooting the horn with a flourish.

'I finally managed to get us a ride. Almost impossible to find a driver.'

The one he had managed to find had a very nasty limp. He'd had a metal rod put in his leg and only used one foot on the pedals. He never once used his brakes, only the clutch, even on the tightest of bends. I wondered if we would make it to Mitakot.

We drove for over an hour, climbing constantly. I couldn't see a single house left standing. When we got out it was freezing cold and raining. I was thankful for my walking boots as the ground was covered with rubble. Finally we reached some makeshift shelters, a few tents and tarpaulins, some drapes woven together.

Dr Ghas called out, '*Salam Alikum,*'

A tall thin man with a speckled beard appeared from a shelter.

Behind him a handful of male villagers. He was wrapped in thick white blankets. On his head an Afghan turban. He didn't say anything, just stood there for an age, staring.

Dr Ghas broke the silence. 'We are here to help. I am a doctor.'

The man moved forward to greet us. He led us through what remained of their homestead. They had lost everything – families, homes and livestock. He told us that the buffalo had been crushed in their stalls. Every last chicken had been killed when the henhouse collapsed.

'We haven't had people up here. The weather has been too bad.'

They knew they wouldn't get housed before winter set in and were resigned to having to live in the tents. They didn't know if they would survive. I had heard that truckloads of blankets, sleeping bags and warm clothes, earmarked for the earthquake survivors, were being sold in the local markets.

We walked silently behind the villagers. There was nothing to say. We were led to the one remaining shelter and there Dr Ghas patiently listened to each man as he voiced his needs. I watched their faces as they spoke, gaunt with worry. I could hear but not see the women, whispering in the shadows at the back of the tent.

Eventually Dr Ghas said we had to go. 'It's getting late. We need to get back before dark.'

He told the men that he would return each week to check how they were doing physically. In the meantime he would make sure that dry food rations, tents and blankets were sent up to them.

It took us a half-hour to get through the army checkpoints and into the camp. We were body searched and our documents checked several times over. By now it was getting late. We were shown into an army tent and told to wait for the Major.

When he arrived he wasn't pleased. 'What is she doing here?' virtually spitting the words.

Dr Ghas spoke quickly to him in Urdu.

The Major turned to me, red-faced with anger. 'Didn't you know there was a curfew? It's for your own safety. You shouldn't be here.'

I stammered that I didn't know.

'I am sorry. I didn't know either,' Dr Ghas said. 'Look, where can she stay? It's too late to set out now.'

The Major wasn't angry any more – he had more pressing concerns. 'Bridges and roads are collapsing. We've got no hospitals. And on top of that, there's looting and fighting breaking out everywhere. He wiped his face with his sleeve, exhausted. 'I'm sorry. Both army and refugee camps are off limits. No foreigners.'

Dr Ghas looked worried. There was nothing to say so we took our leave.

'Linda, it's too dangerous to drive now. Too many thieves and bandits on the roads.'

'I am so sorry to be such a problem. What choices do we have?'

With no hotels left standing in a fifty mile radius we had only one option. Dr Ghas led me to a concrete house, which belonged to one of his friends. The top floor had collapsed, its roof resting on the earth. It was a tangled mess of broken glass, metal beams and rubble.

'Wait here,' he said. 'I'll see if any part of it is safe.'

I'd been told about the frequency of aftershocks. It wasn't surprising that the refugees weren't using the place for shelter. The building was on its last legs. The slightest tremor and it wouldn't stand a chance.

Dr Ghas reappeared, covered in dirt and dust. 'I've found one room that should be okay. Take my arm and watch your step.'

I didn't think I would sleep a wink that night. Dr Ghas had warned me about ghosts. The whole area was full of them, he told me. Next door had been a girls' school. All four hundred students died, buried alive in the rubble.

'We heard their murmurs for nearly an hour. We dug for days but not one was rescued.'

I lay down on a broken, damp sofa, covered in fragments of rubble. Shafts of moonlight shone through the gashes in the wall. Dr Ghas, having shared his fears about ghosts, was soon snoring. exhausted. I blessed him silently. Without his help I wouldn't have got by that day.

I lay awake for a long while, saying prayers of protection and peace for all those who had suffered. In my hand I gripped a powerful talisman of a revered monk, given to me by my fisherman friends.

It was the end of my second day in Pakistan. I knew I had to wise up if I was to be able to stand many more.

And wise up I did.

In the two years I lived and worked in Pakistan we saw numerous suicide bombers wreak havoc in the cities. Some, like Karachi, were almost completely out of bounds. I was based in Islamabad which was slightly safer, but worry of attacks still peppered our conversation. Even charity workers were at risk. Rumour had it that many of them were CIA operatives. Some undoubtedly were – they stood out a mile in their perfectly pressed *salwar kameeze*. In some people's minds, we were all potential spies in disguise so every aid worker's life was in danger.

Embassies pared down their staff and sent the families of their employees home. They had set up a useful warning system. Whenever there was a gunman or bomber on the loose, or even word of a protest, we were alerted immediately by text message. Every day we were sent messages to be vigilant, with reminders to avoid shopping centres, mosques, restaurants, hotels or the diplomatic enclave where the embassies were situated. Living in a state of high alert was new to me but I swiftly learnt to sense the mood, feel an atmosphere, tune my radar, detect potential danger. We went everywhere clutching our cell phones, anticipating the worst.

The only way to calm my fraying nerves was to keep my head down and work. Over the following weeks, I came up with a plan of action. We'd leave the disaster relief to those aid agencies which were best primed to deliver the necessary emergency supplies. My job was to focus on livelihood recovery, and the start-up of new business ventures. There were many Islamabad-based businesses and multinationals wanting to get involved. We researched several possibilities then settled upon one area where we reckoned we'd be able to deliver.

In the northern region of Sindh, dairy farmers were barely scraping a living. With only a small number of cattle – nothing as large as a herd – most of them were easy prey for middlemen. In their hands they were blackmailed and squeezed so that they made almost no profit. Often their families would go hungry. There was a need in the cities for milk. Pakistan, it had been estimated, was the sixth largest producer of milk in the world but from the amount that reached the market you would never have known it. The dairy companies were desperate to access this 'white gold' but had so far failed to change the system. Our task was to help these poverty-stricken smallholders bring their milk to market.

It was the classic fair trade model. We just needed to implement it. Clearly, these small dairy farmers needed to form a cooperative, cutting out the need for middlemen. I enlisted the support of large dairy companies to provide the necessary locally-situated tanks and distribution. With a team in place to train the farmers, giving them advice on milk quality, antibiotics and animal care, milk yields would rise and farmers would start to see a real change in their income.

I had the most unlikely of allies during my time in Pakistan, one who was to become my staunchest friend. My driver, Faisal, was a Pashtun from Swat valley, near the Afghan border. Taliban country. Faisal belonged to a community where women would be chastised for showing their face in public, let alone travelling around unaccompanied, bossing farmers about. Initially, Faisal had a professional regard for me as his passenger (and meal ticket) but over the months this grew into real affection and respect. He often offered me advice, increasingly engaged in the work I was doing. A wiry man in his late twenties with thick black beard and moustache, he had a wife and three small boys back home, a hundred miles from Islamabad. He only got to visit them every few months.

I learned many rules to protect my safety but I disregarded the one which stipulated that you should change your driver frequently. Keeping the same driver was a known hazard. Any employee who knew too much about your daily habits and schedule could be used by terrorists. Keeping Faisal, though, was a risk I was prepared to take. From the first, I liked his air of calm and attention to detail. The moment I exited a building he was by the car door, ready for me to slip away. His initiative saved me on numerous occasions and he was the one that dried my tears whenever things became too much. Faisal was the one person in Pakistan who kept me smiling.

It was to Faisal I went for help when I needed to buy a burkha. I was getting ready for my first trip to the dairy country of northern Sindh province. I would be going alone. My assignment was to assess the most practical ways we might organise scattered dairy farmers into cooperatives. I needed to do my best to fit in with local custom if I were to have any chance of them listening to me. That meant wearing a burkha. I asked for Faisal's help.

In the shop, we both scanned the rails.

'What about this?' I held up a pale blue cotton burkha.

He gave it a quick glance. 'No madam. That is an Afghan chadri.' He told me that Westerners call it a shuttlecock burkha. 'You'll need that when you go to the north-west frontier province. Or in Peshawar or the refugee camps. Not Sindh'.

I could see why it was called a shuttlecock burkha. The top was shaped to grip the head and looked just like the top of a shuttlecock. There was just a small area left open for the eyes, which was covered by latticework.

'How on earth do you get around? My eyesight's bad enough as it is.'

'It's an art, Madam,' he said, then adding as a cosy afterthought: 'My grandmother was knocked down by a car. She didn't see it coming.'

I smiled to myself as I watched Faisal handling the burkhas. He was becoming increasingly engrossed in his task. As fastidious as a Saville Row tailor.

'Look at the trim,' he held out one with a small diamante YSL logo. 'Hmm, perhaps not suitable for Sindh farmers.'

He handed me one with a mandarin collar. 'I think this will be long enough. We can't have your walking boots showing.'

I gave a twirl as I exited the changing room. 'What do you think?'

I had thought the burkha looked like a shapeless dressing gown but Faisal's eyes lit up with delight.

'Oh, madam! You look beautiful.'

How funny! I thought, Faisal had seen me in a variety of clothes – trousers and shirt or tunic – all, in my mind, perfectly attractive. But the burkha! I could tell that it blew him away. You could see it in his eyes.

'Now try on the *hijab*. You must cover your blonde hairs.'

I could never get Faisal to use 'hair' instead of 'hairs'. He would always argue his case vehemently.

A few minutes later my hair, ears, neck and chest were covered with the *hijab*. Faisal's work was done. He stood back to admire his work of art.

'Beautiful, Madam!'

Faisal was upset that he couldn't accompany me to Sindh.

'You can't come, Faisal. It's too far to drive. I must fly. I will be okay – especially now I have my burkha!'

I missed him dreadfully. I had got so used to having him with me. We were unlikely friends, in many ways, but it was odd how little things managed to bridge the cultural divide. We ended up agreeing to alternate his Islamic religious music (which was driving me mad) with my Abba tape. Faisal grew to love *Mamma Mia*, especially *Supertrooper*. Whenever I walked out of a building after a meeting, I would often hear it blaring out of the car. If he'd known what the film was about – a hippy free-thinking woman, presented with several men, any one of whom could be father of her child – he would have been horrified. Strange world.

I travelled light, packing only the essentials, which included a small can of hairspray, scissors and a whistle – my emergency kit to repel unwanted attention. I hoped it would not be needed. My embassy colleagues were none too pleased that I was travelling to Sukkur, the main town in Northern Sindh, via Karachi. The whole area was a no-go zone. There was little they could do about it, though, as I was being funded by a Pakistani industrialist and a local Pakistani NGO. They could forbid their diplomats from going to Karachi but they couldn't prevent my doing so.

I boarded the plane which would take me from Islamabad to Karachi. A new private airline, carrying businessmen mainly. I had just settled into my seat, my nose already deep in a magazine, when a stewardess hurried over.

'I wonder if you wouldn't mind moving?' she asked. 'I'm very sorry but we need to rearrange the seating.'

She looked flustered. The plane was waiting to take off. A woman was standing in the aisle. I wasn't able to see her face but I could hear a note of hysteria in her voice. She was stubbornly refusing to move.

'Why can't she sit there?' I asked crossly. 'There's an empty seat.'

The stewardess explained that the passenger was refusing to sit next to a man. I knew that custom dictated that a woman shouldn't sit next to a man who was not her husband or a member of her family, but I was surprised that someone as well off as she would make such a scene. Particularly as she had chosen to board a plane she must have known would be full of men.

I sat down in the empty seat, next to a grey-suited man, wondering what I might find. He smiled at me. 'Sorry about that,' he said, holding out his hand. 'May I introduce myself. I'm Tariq. I work for Pfizer in Karachi.'

I felt like laughing. Hardly a big, bad wolf!

I was looking forward to my evening in Karachi. A friend from the IBLF who worked for Unilever in Bangkok had arranged for me to meet a Pakistani colleague of his, a woman working in Karachi named Ayesha. This was the first time I had been invited to have a meal with a Pakistani woman, one on one, and I was excited. So far I had failed to find a single Pakistani woman willing to befriend me. I wanted to understand how life was for them in this country, get stuck in with the local people, but I was no nearer getting to know any of them than I was when I arrived. Women were kept sequestered. It was very much a closed society, one which I was not allowed to penetrate.

Ayesha's driver met me at the airport. He handed me a letter.

Linda,

Welcome to Karachi. Don't be alarmed but there was something I forgot to tell you. It's very important that you don't use your mobile phone whilst being driven in Karachi. There's been a spate of hold-ups. See you at the Fujiyama restaurant, on 17th floor of the Avari Towers. Can't wait!

Ayesha

Ayesha was waiting at our table. She stood to greet me and held both my hands with great warmth. We sat near the window and looked out at the lights of city twinkling below us. She apologised for her message. She hadn't wanted to alarm me but with over eleven thousand murders recorded the previous year and ten times that number of mobile phone thefts you had to be extra careful. She explained that Karachi is the economic hub of the country and it attracts mafia gangs as well as the very desperate poor, looking to survive.

'The police are pretty ineffective. The underworld actually keeps things in fairly reasonable order,'

She told me that it was common for gangs of four or five men to enter an office building, ask for the valuables to be handed over, then stay for a cup of tea.

I very much enjoyed my dinner with Ayesha. We spoke about Unilever's latest campaign, 'Dirt is Good'. Apparently, with so many anxious parents keeping their children off the streets, safely inside their apartment blocks, kids weren't building up healthy immune systems. They were playing in environments that were too clean.

'They should have the right to play outside, ride bikes, jump in muddy puddles. Climb trees.' Ayesha spoke passionately. I could suddenly see her as a child, how she must have railed against the restrictions that kept women back.

'Otherwise, how can they possibly learn about the world around them?'

I could see why parents did keep their children indoors though. They were at constant risk of being snatched and held for ransom. Who would want to risk that?

I was longing to find out what it was like being an independent businesswoman living in Pakistan. Ayesha was a rare species. She spoke with pride about her work. The company rewarded her well. She told me that there was an increasing number of career women, particularly in fashion or event management, but you had to be tough. Many ended up relocating overseas. She'd fought hard for her freedom, something I took for granted. Occasionally, I detected a wistfulness. She'd taken a lonely road.

'I'm in my mid-thirties. My marrying age has passed,' she told me. 'It was my choice. My parents received many marriage proposals for me. But if I'd taken that path I couldn't have worked.'

'Has that been hard for you?' I asked.

'It wasn't a hard choice for me. But it was hard for my parents.'

That night I stayed in the Sheraton, one of the two foreigner-friendly hotels in Karachi. I slept fitfully. The hotel's idea of security was a bit of a joke. They had installed a metal archway, as you find in airports, but if you were a woman passing through and the alarm beeped, the security guards didn't dare frisk you.

The next morning I was the only woman on the plane. When we arrived at Sukkur, the centre of dairy farming in Sindh province, I was instantly surrounded by four armed police.

Here we go, I thought to myself.

My host NGO had decided against having guards on this visit, having explored the pros and cons with me.

I continued to walk on, wondering what I should do next. Then a very thin boy, no more than fourteen years old, came up to us. His feet were so encrusted with dirt that I had the urge to get out my nailbrush and give them a good scrub. He greeted me then spoke quickly to the police. He pointed to a small rusty car.

'I've been sent to take you to your hotel.'

I got in gratefully. Two of the police climbed in too. I had no idea what was going on and no one to ask. I suddenly missed Faisal. I looked out of the window, breathing steadily to calm my nerves. The landscape was surprisingly green. I had read that the city controls one of the largest irrigation systems in the world and waters ten million acres of farmland by means of its seven huge canals. Without the Indus, the whole area would be desert. A beautiful place, but a hotbed of political unrest.

We reached my hotel safely. I asked for a room on the first floor. Once inside, I checked the windows were locked and drew the curtains. Then I moved the bed as far away from the window as possible. I had seen the damage bomb blasts could wreak. It was the shards of glass from windows that usually maimed or killed.

Another lonely night, feeling scared.

I took out the one book I had brought with me. A volume of Rumi poetry. I loved the smell and feel of its brown leather cover; the Persian art on each page. I opened one at random.

> *Forget safety. Live where you fear to live.*
> *Destroy your reputation. Be notorious.*

I could hear voices and the scraping of chairs outside my room. I didn't dare open the door. Then a boy came upstairs bearing a tray. He knocked at my door, calling, 'Room service'. I opened it and took the tray. As I did so, I caught a glimpse of the two police guards, sitting on either side of my door, rifles propped against the wall. I closed the door quickly. Seeing them there gave me no comfort. I guessed they were there not so much to check that no one got into my room but to make sure I didn't get out. I was their prize goose.

Later that night the men's raucous laughter turned into a drunken scuffle. Some person or thing was thrown against my door. I lay in bed terrified, imagining that they would break it down and rape me. I put my fingers in my ears and tried to imagine a few of my favourite things – like one of the Von Trapps.

Mahdi came to pick me up the next morning. He worked for a local Sindhi NGO, and had elected to be my guide. I had heard about Mahdi on the charity grapevine. He was well-liked, having worked unstintingly for twenty hard years. Although his faith in what he was doing had been battered over time, and he had little belief that whatever his charity managed to achieve would ever be sustainable, he slogged on diligently, never giving up. Over the months I got to know Madhi I never failed to marvel at how hard he worked – long hours, every day of the week, without rest. A man with a big heart.

He was waiting by his battered old car, wearing a crumpled white shirt and black trousers. His face was creased with tiredness but he broke into a warm smile when he saw me. He asked me how my night had been. I cast a glance at the two policemen watching us from their truck and told Mahdi how they hadn't left me alone, and that it was making me nervous.

'Don't worry, I'll talk to them. Trouble is, they see a foreigner and think there's money to be made.'

Mahdi went over and spoke to them. When he came back he shrugged.

'They're coming along. I drove the price down but they could get nasty later. It's better we lose them.'

This was all new to me but I trusted that Mahdi knew the ropes and that everything would work out. I looked at the two policemen in the back of their open truck, rifles on their knees. Their clothes were pulled tight across their pot bellies, buttons almost popping. They looked poor and it made me feel suddenly sorry for them.

Mahdi had arranged for me to meet the farmers later, in the afternoon. First, as a gentle warm-up, he was taking me to visit a women's compound. I was very curious to see it and hoped the women wouldn't be too shy to talk to me. We pulled up outside and waited for Leena, Mahdi's colleague. He wasn't allowed inside the compound. A fifteen foot stone wall circled it and the door was made of thick metal.

As Leena and I entered there was a sudden flurry of activity, almost as if people were escaping a sandstorm. The children ran to hide and many of the women put blankets over their heads, as if hoping this might make them invisible. They were sitting in groups in a big sandy courtyard which reminded me of a prison yard. It was empty except for an old broken bed frame pushed up against the wall and a tree, under which three baby goats were sleeping. On one side was a mud hut, in pretty bad shape.

We went over to a group of women who were sewing. We were greeted by the oldest in the group, who must have been eighty or so. She had a large gold nose-ring. Leena spoke quietly to her in the local Sindhi dialect. By now, I was beginning to feel faint with the heat and I scrabbled inside my rucksack to find my fan. It was a Spanish one, black and lacy, with a flamenco dancer painted front and back. I flapped it back and forth frantically.

Instantly there was a ripple of tittering amongst the women. I offered the fan to the old woman who didn't take it. After a second's pause one of the younger women grabbed it out of my hand and fanned herself. It was then passed from hand to hand with much giggling, until finally it reached a young girl who ran across the yard to try it out on a goat.

Now that the ice was broken, the women began to talk to Leena. A little later, when they went to make the tea, she filled me in on their conversation.

'The lack of schooling is a problem in the village,' she said. 'Everywhere it's the same. The government teachers hardly ever show up.'

I asked her why.

'They don't usually get paid so why bother.'

She pointed at a group of children, sitting on the bed frame. A teenage girl was reading to them.

'The mullah comes by regularly to check how they're getting on with the Qu'aran. That's the only book most of them ever get to see.'

We were led to the mud hut, inside of which were the living and sleeping quarters. The room housed twenty women and ten children. It was sparsely furnished but immaculate, the sand floor raked neatly. We sat down on blue plastic mats and were given small glasses of chai. Leena was longing to find out if the women had decided to accept her charity's offer of micro-finance loans. It had worked well with some of the other women's compounds.

She spoke with energy: 'You're already doing well selling eggs. This way you'll be able to buy goats to breed in time for Eid.'

Eid marks the end of Ramadan. I had witnessed the mass slaughter of goats, camels and buffalo in Peshawar, the streets running with blood, and I never wanted to again. But with even the poorest families believing they had to sacrifice an animal, although many have to borrow money to do so, it presented a sound business opportunity.

The women were silent, sipping their tea. Not exactly a picture of enthusiasm.

Then one of the women spoke. 'We have to work in the fields. I don't think that...'

Another woman interrupted her. 'The men take our money for their tea bill. They sit around at the cafe. When we walk past, after work, we have to stop and give them everything.'

None of them wanted a loan. What was the point in working harder when they would never see a penny of their earnings.

A young woman sighed. 'We are just breathing, not living.'

Apart from ten minutes at the end, when I taught the children 'Heads, shoulders, knees and toes,' it had been a dispiriting visit. As the women waved goodbye I felt a sudden pang. I had the freedom to leave; they did not. And for the millionth time in Pakistan, I found myself counting my lucky stars.

It was time to meet the dairy farmers themselves. We needed to head out to a smaller town called Jacobabad. It was reputedly one of the hottest places in South Asia. In June the temperature can reach 55 degrees centigrade. I was boiling already and it was a mere 35 degrees. I couldn't imagine what 55 would feel like.

As I got into Mahdi's car I could see the police hurriedly dismantling their sheesha pipes and throwing them in the back of their truck. If I was feeling a bit flat after my visit, Mahdi soon changed that. He decided now was the time to shake off the police.

'This may look like a heap but let's see what it can do,' he said.

Mahdi kept an eye on the rearview mirror as he wove nimbly in and out of camels, horse carts and trucks. The way he used his gears almost had me wondering if he had been a racing driver in another life. Once we could no longer see the truck, he turned sharply into a side street and stopped.

'We've lost them. It wasn't that hard, was it?'

I was laughing.

'How about a Kulfi to celebrate?' Mahdi was still glowing from the adrenalin rush.

After we'd finished our ice creams we got back in the car. Later, on the road to Jacobabad, our jubilation at having lost our armed guard waned when we found our way blocked by a political protest. Who knows what had sparked it. The Bhutto family seat is in Sindh province and there was always political ferment. Mahdi stopped the car and turned off the engine. We were gridlocked. He looked worried.

'I'm going to take a look. Don't move.'

He jumped out of the car, returning a moment later red-faced from running in the midday sun. 'We'd better sit tight. There are no shops or restaurants where I can hide you.'

He asked me to crouch down in the footwell and covered me with a shawl. 'You okay?'

'No point in being anything else,' I said, feeling anything but okay.

I could hear shouts. Glass shattering. Mahdi sat smoking, pulling at his beard.

'Keep still. They're close. I can see the banners.'

The car shook from side to side. The mob was banging on the glass with fists and sticks. A man jumped on the bonnet. I sensed someone peering into the car. They flipped the door handle just above my head.

A moment later, the crowd had passed by.

'You can come out now,' said Mahdi. 'You must be suffocating down there.'

I felt surprisingly calm. I got back in my seat and soon we were moving again, to a chorus of cheers and hoots, the drivers relieved to be about their business once more. Mahdi suggested we stop at a restaurant to freshen up. He emerged from the bathroom drenched and grinning, shaking his wet hair playfully like a dog.

We met the farmers in the grounds of their landlord's house. Mahdi explained that it was very tribal in rural Sindh. Each landlord had their own set of rules that even the local government had to obey. He advised me to watch my step and address the landlord with deference. It was he, the master, who had given his permission for me to come. Mahdi was as nervous as a cat, although he tried not to show it in case he rattled me. He wasn't fluent in the local dialect so had arranged for one of the educated villagers to be my translator.

'I don't know how they'll react to a woman,' he fretted.

'Well you soon will,' I said, feeling no fear at all. I must have been getting used to it.

We were met by a man in a bright white suit. He looked as if he was going to a costume party as John Travolta. Mahdi saw my look of incredulity and explained that the man had probably never seen a Westerner in the flesh. All he had to go on was what he would have watched on TV. Like me wearing a burkha, he had dressed to blend in with my world to make me feel at home.

I followed the man, leaving Mahdi in the car. As I walked through the gate my heart almost fell through my boots. Close to a hundred men, all wearing white salwar kameeze and brightly-coloured Sindhi hats, were sitting on benches in a circle, three or four deep. Each had a gun resting on his knees, AK47s or big rifles.

At times like this, I always thank god for my school drama classes. My stage was a large wooden bed frame covered with a tapestry blanket. At each end, tribal police sat like a couple of bookends, nursing impressive-looking firearms.

I took a breath, then walked up to the stage with as much dignity as I could muster. I inclined my head at the assembled crowd who were staring at me with eyes like saucers. I realised in that moment that I had forgotten to cover my head and this had inadvertently added to their shock. I wasn't sure how to start. The men looked so confused that I was certain that whatever I said wouldn't be heard. I dithered for a second, not wanting to choose an icebreaker which might make them reach for their guns.

'Salam Alikum.' I spoke very slowly. The white-suited man translated every word.

'My name is Linda. I am from England,'

There was a shuffling among the men when they first heard my voice. I made sure that my body language was as relaxed as possible, hands resting loosely on my knees.

'I am a social worker. We want to help you earn more money.' I paused to let this sink in.

'With more money you can take care of your families, pay for teachers or doctors, build a well. Maybe even buy more livestock.'

I laid out the facts simply. If their yield was one litre a day per farmer, I suggested they could multiply that by four. I spoke of the middlemen, the Paccha Dhobis, and how the farmers would no longer need to sell to them under the new scheme. I didn't speak for long. I just wanted to engage them at this stage. I told them I would be back once they'd had time to talk about the project with their community.

As I finished, the landlord came forward from the back of the crowd. He was a tall, handsome man in his thirties with an air of authority and ownership. He spoke perfectly enunciated English with flawless grammar.

'You're a very unusual lady,' he said, shaking my hand.

I asked him where he had learned to speak such impeccable English.

'I'm an Oxford graduate,' he replied.

I wasn't sure if I had managed to impress him. There was a hint of mockery in his tone but I didn't detect any hostility or derision. I sincerely hoped he would support our project. We couldn't do it without him.

I flew back to Islamabad, both hopeful and doubtful, a feeling I had experienced many times before.

Dairy companies in Pakistan were crying out for more milk to feed the urban population but seventy per cent of the milk produced was consumed in the rural areas. Meat was too expensive for the rural smallholders, so milk provided the main source of protein in their diet. The dairy companies and farmers had tried to work together in the past but the partnership had quickly broken down. The smallest cogs in the wheel – the scattered farmers in the least accessible rural areas – were those I proposed to visit first. Getting them organised had proved to be the main sticking point before so I knew I had better to iron out the creases before we launched the project. Otherwise it might prove unsustainable.

I waited in Islamabad until Mahdi contacted me, saying we had been given the green light. I drove back to Sukkur and he drove me deep into the Sindh countryside. At one point, he overtook a man wobbling dangerously on a motorbike weighed down by four large metal urns, two strapped each side.

'That's a Kaccha Dhobi,' he said. 'They collect milk from the villages. Sell most of it to the Paccha Dhobis. Their partners in crime.'

'Doesn't sound very hygienic. Passing through all those hands.'

'Not only that, but a lot of tampering goes on,'

Mahdi explained that the middlemen add ice to the milk to keep it fresh which dilutes the milk solids by thirty per cent. The water contaminates the milk. Then, in order to mask the fact that the milk had been diluted they add vegetable oil and whey powder to boost the fat content. Antibiotics and peroxide are commonly used as preservatives.

'And none of this is regulated.'

The Paccha Dhobis had the farmers in a stranglehold, Mahdi told me. Whenever the latter had an urgent need for money, a sick child or a wedding perhaps, the Paccha Dhobis would offer to lend them the sum, with a great show of benevolence. The cow would then be mortgaged and in return for this magnificent favour, the middlemen insisted on a reduced rate per litre for a year.

'The farmer ends up getting a third of what the Paccha Dhobi receives from the distributor.'

'So they're screwed.'

'The system has been entrenched over generations. Hard to change,' Mahdi said.

By the time we reached the compound, which belonged to an open-minded farmer named Adil, my blood was up. I was determined to help change things.

We walked through a gate in the wall into a dry and dusty yard. Mahdi went to find Adil, telling me to wait. I looked around for a shady place to hide from the sun but there wasn't any to be found. A pair of buffalo were tethered in the corner and a dog was asleep on a pile of dry mud. Nothing else, save a few chickens pecking at the dust.

'Salam Alikum,' Adil walked up to me, smiling. 'Mahdi tells me you are interested to learn about our lives.'

He took me over to meet the buffalo and patted one fondly on its bony back. 'They are how our family survives.'

Mahdi told him we had passed his Kaccha Dhobi on the way.

'We sell him about forty per cent of our milk. The rest we drink ourselves.'

'Isn't that quite a lot for one family?' I asked.

'We've no way of keeping it cold so we drink what we can in the morning – the first milk of the day – then sell some to the Kaccha Dhobi. The second milking we drink or throw away.'

We walked with Adil as he led the buffalo across the compound to a water trough. I asked him why he kept them tethered.

'That's what we've always done. They're safe and that way, they don't do any damage to the land.'

The buffalo sucked in the water in great noisy slugs. It was clear that they would be much better off if they were able to stand in the shade and have constant access to their water trough. I guessed that their milk yield would rise if that were the case. I made a note to find out by how much. Sometimes the simplest changes have the greatest effect.

Adil's eyes lit up when I explained that we were looking at how the farmers might never again need to deal with middlemen. I asked him if he might also be interested in hearing about new ways of raising his milk yield.

'We are just simple farmers. All we do is what we've always done. Learned from our fathers and grandfathers.'

He straightened his back, looking me in the eye. 'I would like to hear what you have to say.'

Following the 'rule of three' we distilled the information into three key messages for the farmers, which would give quick and powerful results.

- Give the animal shade and keep it cool.
- Do not tether the animal and allow it adequate food and drink on demand.
- Wash the cow one hour before milking.

The latter alone would increase milk production by one litre. An animal, on average, was currently producing four litres a day. If a farmer implemented these three key changes, plus some additional care such as vaccinations, the amount would rise to as much as twelve litres.

Once all the parties were on board, keen to embrace the partnership, my role as broker began. We hoped that the initiative would spread from village to village, as word of its success spread.

One of our main objectives was to bring everything the farmers needed to their door. Mentors from the milk company and charity advisors visited the farms regularly to train and advise. Farmers were given access to cost price feed, vaccinations and medicine. A vet called at the farms regularly. Most importantly, in a move that eliminated the need for middlemen, the milk companies supplied chillers and tankers for the daily collection of milk. A few months down the line, the farmers were seeing a real change in their weekly income.

It is amazing how, when things begin to change for the better (or worse, for that matter), you see a domino effect. The villagers in this project experienced a real and exhilarating change in their fortunes. But it wasn't just that. As each new micro-entrepreneur's income rose, so did his dignity. The women, whose job it was to look after the animals, also felt their self-confidence growing. With this newfound financial security and confidence the village took on a new life. Soon there was a new school building, water pump, laundry and children's play area, and other villages asked to join the scheme as word spread.

It wasn't only the farmers who benefitted from the project. Through it, the milk company increased its market share and consumers witnessed laudable company ethics at work. When a company is seen to be helping marginalised and vulnerable communities, it is valuable, not only in terms of PR, but also because of the boost in company morale. Bosses invariably witness their own employees becoming happier and more motivated.

I had almost become used to sitting in the middle of a group of men, talking milk quotas, whilst they stared at me googly-eyed, rifles on their knees.

But not quite.

I also hadn't given up hope of meeting a Pakistani woman who had managed to make a go of her own business. But so far it had proved elusive.

All I had met was a group of women in Gilgit, in Northern Pakistan, who had been given the money to make cushion covers by a well-meaning charity worker. Now the covers were collecting dust in a corner, and the women were angry. Only two had sold, and they had been sympathy purchases. These were women who had never learned the basics of business. They didn't know that success relied on their coming up with a product that was market-driven. And now they felt bitter that they'd been led down a dead-end track.

Then I heard about Mahreen. I knew I had to meet her but it was a long journey to Baltistan, a conservative area in the Northeast corner of the country. With its soaring peaks and glaciers the area was a climbers' paradise in more stable times. A hauntingly beautiful place – almost unearthly – it is the home of the legendary snow leopard. And of Mahreen, an equally rare beast, I was to discover.

I had to travel via Shandur Top, a high mountain pass which can only be crossed between late April and early November. There, on a lush grassy plateau, I almost wondered if I had stumbled upon a film set. A huge crowd of people had gathered there for a polo match. Famous, apparently, for being held on the highest ground in the world – and for its lawlessness. The teams, from the towns of Chitral and Gilgit, battle it out without umpires or rules. It is not uncommon for horses or players to die of exhaustion.

I heard the horns before I saw the crowd. It was an incredible sight. Handsome, muscular men were striding about the field in tight white jodhpurs, taut with anticipation and excitement. A cacophonous band of tabor players and drummers, dressed in white military uniforms, were tuning up in readiness for the match.

And, all around, as far as I could see, were hundreds and hundreds of men. Not a woman in sight.

Meeting Mahreen, after witnessing such a surreal scene, felt equally strange. She was sitting in her office, behind a heavy oak desk. She greeted me warmly, with great poise. I noticed she was wearing a soft mauve shalwar kameeze – no black burkha for her – and a daring wisp of hair peeped out of her *hijab*. Queen of her small kingdom and loving it. The room was sparsely furnished. Three tall bookshelves held neatly-labelled files. Centre-stage was a white board covered in dates, sales projections and graphs.

Mahreen's story was atypical in every way. As she told me, women in Baltistan are '*not* seen and *not* heard.' She placed a heavy emphasis on 'not'.

'So how come you were able to start a sewing business?' I asked her.

'Allah has blessed me with a good husband.'

'What does he do?'

'Javed works for me,' Mahreen said, watching my reaction. Delighted to catch my surprise.

She smiled at me. 'It's not always been like this. It's taken him time.'

Mahreen told me she had had almost no education. Girls weren't offered much in the way of schooling, and she was married off at twelve. She couldn't have stayed at home any longer as she was the oldest of four girls and a drain on the family purse.

'It was an unhappy time. My husband was away for weeks at a time. My mother-in-law worked me hard. Always finding fault. I was rarely allowed outside.'

Ultimately, this hadn't stopped Mahreen. As a child she had been called 'Little Miss Chatterbox' by her mother, always asking questions. She had listened to women bemoaning their husbands' dreadful taste in clothes. As they weren't allowed on the streets, their menfolk had to buy clothes for them. And how the men complained at having to take the long bus ride to Karachi to buy their children's school uniform.

'I remember thinking at the time how odd that was,' said Mahreen. 'That there weren't any uniforms made locally.'

We finished our chai and biscuits and Mahreen took me to see her workroom. She walked slowly, through a shady courtyard and along a dark corridor, holding herself with dignity. Inside the room I saw ten women, aged between sixteen and sixty, seated at their workstations, operating sewing machines, ironing and pressing, and cutting cloth. The moment they saw Mahreen they stood up.

'This is my team,' she said proudly, motioning for them to carry on with their work.

'School uniforms. That's how I started out five years ago,' She picked up a navy pleated skirt and scrutinised the stitching.

I longed to know how she made the leap from Cinderella to

business owner. We sat on a small sofa in the corner of the workroom and she told me.

'An elderly uncle visited often,' she said. 'He was a tailor. Went everywhere with a tape measure around his neck and a row of pins stuck in his waistcoat.'

12-year-old Mahreen would dance around him, picking brightly-coloured lengths of cotton from his clothes and measuring things with his tape.

'It took me weeks to pluck up the courage to ask him. So scared my dream would be lost forever.'

'You asked him to teach you to sew.'

'That's right,' said Mahreen. 'I begged. I pleaded. I was told to leave uncle alone: "Know your place, girl," my aunts said. "This is men's work."'

Eventually Mahreen's uncle persuaded her mother-in-law that sewing would be a useful skill for the household, one which would save them money.

'He took me through the backstreets to his tailor's shop.' she said.

'Did it have to be a secret?' I asked.

'My family didn't want to lose face. People talking. Asking questions.'

The dark, dusty room was paradise to her. In the centre was an ancient Singer pedal machine. Hour upon hour her uncle taught her everything he knew: how to measure accurately; how to make a pattern; and finally, how to use the machine. Shortly after the birth of her son, her second child, when she was sixteen, Mahreen was allowed to attend a three-month professional tailoring course, organised by a local charity. This time, her mother-in-law encouraged her.

'Nine months later, my business was producing school uniforms for five villages!'

As we discussed her business plans, I was delighted to find that Mahreen was increasingly looking outward, with a natural pull toward corporate responsibility. She was already donating uniforms to divorced and widowed mothers and she was bursting to tell me about her big idea. Her dream.

'What is your idea, Mahreen?' I asked. 'We can help you with it, I'm sure. Pair you with a business mentor if that's what you need. Give you help with financial planning, accounting, marketing.'

'My idea is to create a women's centre. No men allowed inside,' she said, her brown eyes glowing.

Mahreen's dream was to create a space where women could develop small businesses – services that women want: clothes shop; tailor; beauty parlour; restaurant; photo studio; slimming and exercise centre; and crèche. Something which gave women the freedom to enjoy their day out. Without brothers, uncles, fathers, or husbands telling them what to do or how to behave.

'The key is to persuade the men that it is a good thing,' Mahreen said. 'And once we have their confidence, women can set up their own businesses there.'

Mahreen was keen to see widows and divorcees given a leg-up. 'That way, they can support their own family. No more handouts.'

I was reluctant to leave Mahreen, as I felt so fired up by her vision, but I had to catch a plane that evening. I promised that I would find her a business mentor and the next morning I was straight on the phone to a successful entrepreneur in Karachi. Mahreen was subsequently given small loans and enterprise training by HH The Aga Khan's First Micro Finance Bank. Her mentor supported her in creating a business plan, and guided her in accounting, marketing and management.

The women's centre was created exactly as Mahreen had dreamt. On average, it is used by sixty women a day. And, in turn, it has spawned ten more budding entrepreneurs, many of them divorced or widowed women. Mahreen is their mentor.

Six months after the earthquake in Pakistan, many of the affected areas were beginning to get back on their feet but others were still suffering badly. The last thing anyone needed was another disaster. But on June 23 2007, Cyclone Yemyin tore through Sindh and Balouchistan. It was followed by torrential rain. The result of the subsequent flooding was disastrous: many villages were completely marooned, with roads and railway lines blocked by landslides, water systems and wells destroyed, as well as houses, crops and livestock. Nearly four hundred thousand people had lost their homes, with hundreds dead or missing. And to make matters worse, the weather pattern was set to continue for another two to three months.

In Islamabad, for weeks now, intense storms had turned the streets into a river of swirling muddy debris. Moving around the city was difficult but that was nothing compared to the images we had seen of the cyclone-affected area: people wading waist deep in water, suitcases on their heads; families perching on the roofs of mosques or in trees. I knew that I needed to go to the flood-affected area, and without delay.

The government of Pakistan had chosen not to make an appeal for international assistance. To make matters worse, international charities were asked not to travel to the disaster areas, which they badly needed to do in order to assess the situation. Foreign journalists were told to stay away so the news getting through was patchy. As I was employed at that time by a national Pakistani NGO, funded by the World Bank, the directive didn't actually apply to me. I went straight to the charity's director, requesting their backing. I wanted to conduct an assessment mission to evaluate the needs of the victims and see how we might help. Thankfully, he was used to me by now, and I was given the green light.

On July 19, I landed in Sukkur and was met at the airport by Mahdi.

'Linda, it's terrible. The aid isn't getting through quickly enough.'

He gave my arm a squeeze. We didn't hug – it was too hot for that. I was cursing my headscarf and long-sleeved top.

'It will reach nearly 50 degrees by lunchtime. The flood victims are camped out on any piece of remaining high ground. No shade at all. Can you imagine?'

He opened the car door for me. 'Excuse the mess. I've been living in it for days.'

The backseat was packed to bursting: a jumble of water bottles, first aid supplies and food leftovers. The smell was rancid but I could tell that Mahdi was oblivious to it. He had more important things on his mind.

'Where are we going first?' I asked, climbing into the front seat.

'If the roads are not yet submerged, we'll hopefully get as far as Dadu and Shahdadkot,' he said. 'First I want you to get a full briefing from my army contacts.'

We sped off along a highway. I expected to see lines of relief trucks heading to the area but the roads were eerily deserted. After a while, on either side, the fields were disappearing, drowned in floodwater. Soon, our single raised road became the only remaining structure in sight. It was as if the Arabian Sea had exploded and moved inland.

Mahdi started talking again, filling me in on the situation. 'The people are angry. It's not a pretty picture,' he warned me. 'Riots are breaking out all over. They're desperate for aid. Water supplies are contaminated and there's no electricity.'

I looked up at the blackening sky and wondered how much

more rain it would take for the road to be devoured by the flood waters. I shuddered, wondering how deep the water was. There was the odd tip of a corn stalk poking its head above the surface. The only sign there had ever been a crop growing here.

I grabbed my camera. 'I've got to keep a record of it all, Mahdi. Please, you will remind me if I forget to take pictures. It's really important.'

We were met by Captain Walim at a makeshift army base. He was bowed over a map with his fellow Pakistani rangers when we drove up. Tracing lines with a stick; giving orders. He stood up straight when we walked up to the group, a tall man in khaki and a wide-brimmed hat. He asked me to sit down.

'What are you doing here?' He wasn't hostile, but definitely suspicious. 'Journalist?'

'No,' I replied. 'I'm working for a local charity, based in Islamabad.'

Mahdi stepped forward, speaking to the captain in Urdu. As he explained, the other man's face softened a little.

'OK, young lady. Here it is.'

I got out my notepad to take notes.

'We are battling against the floodwater. It's moving south from Dadu at speed; it's already covered twenty-five kilometres. My men are trying to keep one step ahead to evacuate people in its path but it's almost impossible. So many people are getting stranded on the bunds.'

He showed me the map, pointing out where the bunds, or levees, had been sufficient to hold back minor floods. But they weren't able to cope with something on this scale. 'Right across this area,' he said. 'All of them. Washed away.'

'Can you advise us where we should be visiting today?' I asked him.

The captain spoke to one of his men, then turned to us.

'Follow Corporal Sheeha,' he said. 'He'll take you there. Keep it brief if I were you – the sun is a killer. It's bad enough in daylight. After dark it's treacherous – and there are riots breaking out everywhere.'

We promised we'd be back by nightfall.

Corporal Sheeha was a short, stout man with a John Wayne swagger who seemed delighted to be coming with us. I felt instantly at ease with him.

'Let's go. Stay close to me.'

He jumped into a big green army truck and we followed in Mahdi's car, keeping close, bumper to bumper. Soon the already narrow road became even narrower as makeshift shelters on either side encroached, jostling for space. It was a pitiful sight. We came to a halt next to two baby girls, who had been placed under a ragged sheet, draped over two wooden bed-frames turned on their sides. The girls lay motionless, staring into space without blinking. Legs as fragile as twigs. Next to their shelter, a seemingly dead infant lay between the wheels of an upturned cart. I gasped at the sight.

'Take a picture,' said Mahdi. 'Let them see how dreadful it is.'

We moved slowly along the track, witnessing one dire scene after another. Family after family, crouched, hiding any way they could from the baking sun. Up ahead, I saw a man in the water. I could just make him out. It was up to his nose and he was still managing to wade, his right hand stretched high above his head holding the last of his possessions: his sandals.

We turned a sharp corner and the army truck came to an abrupt halt. Mahdi and I jumped out of the car to see what had happened. The road ahead had crumbled under the pressure of water. There were at least ten metres missing. The other side, families, carts, men on bicycles were gathered, marooned.

Corporal Sheeha reached for his walkie-talkie. 'This must have just happened. I must alert Captain Walim.'

The crowd was screaming, jumping up and down and waving their arms. The captain raised a hand, indicating to them to wait; be calm. I grabbed Mahdi's arm. A man had leapt into the water in a frantic attempt to swim the gap. He had no chance. In seconds he was dragged downstream by the fast-flowing water. I breathed again when I saw that he had managed to grab hold of a tree branch.

Corporal Sheeha shouted to the man. 'Hold on! You'll have help soon!'

He turned to us. 'Captain Walim is sending our one and only hydrofoil. It should be here soon.'

We stood at the water's edge, feeling helpless.

The Corporal checked to see if I was okay. 'Please go and drink some water,' he said kindly. 'It looks like you're about to faint.'

I did as I was told. Then I made out the hum of the hydrofoil, getting louder as it approached.

'Let's go now,' the captain said. 'Under control now.'

It looked far from that to me.

Dodging the ever-growing crowd who were watching the rescue, we reversed a kilometre, turning off onto an even narrower side road. The sights continued to appall me. Occasionally we would slow down to allow a trail of barefoot women and children to pass. They did not even turn to look at us but moved along slowly, faces a mask of pain and despair. Many of them were carrying an infant on their hip, while on their heads they were bearing huge bundles: pots and pans; a bag of rice; bedding. We peered at them through the sizzling heat haze that engulfed the scene.

We passed a boat, full of men, standing so as to cram as many in as possible. It was barely above the water line.

Above left: Tsunami survivors' camp.

Above right: Phi Phi island.

Below: Displaced family.

Above left: Art therapy.

Above right: Even the circus came to help.

Below: Visit to Royal Thai Navy with David Arkless, Manpower (*left*), and David Fall, British Ambassador (*right*).

Above: Small rubber producing business.

Below: A surprise thank you from Thai fishermen – a boat with my name on it!

Above: Paul Choong, Thai Beverage (*left*) distributing Everton FC-donated footballs to children in Khao Lak.

Below left: An innovative Thai's solution to a future tsunami!

Below right: Thai fishermen experiencing their first Christmas.

Above: Flooded family in Sindh, Pakistan.

Below: Women and children leave flooded area with their few remaining possessions.

Above: HH The Dalai Lama and Nelson Mandela. My constant inspiration during the dark moments in Pakistan.

Below: Sindh province. Listening to local farmers' challenges.

Above left: Finally, my own burkha!

Above right: Fastest seller on the Afghan border.

Below: Homeless earthquake family in Pakistan.

Northern Pakistan. Loaded up and heading for home.

'Look! Mahdi,' I said. 'That boat doesn't have a single woman or child on board.'

I felt outraged. They had left their women and children to fend for themselves. 'Slow down. I need to take a picture.'

The men suddenly noticed me and whistled and cheered lecherously. My blood boiled.

A little further along we stopped.

'This is the end of the road. We need to walk from here,' the Corporal told us. 'Captain Walim wants you to see where the people are stranded on bunds. Still with no shelter. We can't get tents or water to them fast enough.'

I braced myself for the next circle of hell.

As we walked, painfully thin boys came to join our group, running and screaming and circling around us. Soon there were fifty or so following. The pied piper had arrived.

Corporal Sheeha was amused. 'You've caused quite a stir. Nice to see them animated for a while.'

Finally we reached a makeshift medical tent. 'We cannot move anyone for the moment so we've brought doctors and social workers here,' the Corporal said.

Inside there were six camp beds; on them patients were lying, hooked up to IV drips. Around the tent, a crowd of hungry, bewildered people hung about.

'Stand back please,' the Corporal said. 'Let the sick get some air.' The crowd edged back reluctantly.

The Corporal led me into the tent. 'Come and meet Dr Azam.'

I waited as the doctor performed the difficult task of inserting an IV drip into the back of a severely dehydrated boy's hand. The infant's body was in a state of collapse, no veins visible. Dr Azam tried many times before he finally succeeded. It must have been painful for the boy, but he didn't move or cry. Just stared with glazed eyes at the needle and bandage strapped to his sparrow-like hand. He was so badly malnourished that although he was probably four years old, he looked two.

'Come and sit in the shade,' Dr Azam said, handing the limp child back to his mother. 'I need a break.'

Dr Azam looked at the end of his rope. His face was haggard and he was pencil thin. His unwashed hair was sticking to his scalp and his clothes were stained with a combination of blood, dirt and sweat.

'We're trying to do our best. But it's not enough,' he said. 'Our biggest problem is the lack of clean drinking water. You saw the boy.'

He explained that the children's bodies had little strength to hold out against diarrhoea, dysentery, respiratory diseases or malaria attack. 'Trouble is, they were already half-starved before the floods.'

'How many of them are orphans?' I asked.

'A lot,' he said. 'It was only the lucky few who managed to scramble onto the bank when ten feet of water rushed in. Many got swept away.'

Dr Azam looked helplessly at the growing crowd of people outside the medical tent. 'It's only going to get worse. When the flood recedes, the stagnant water will bring in malaria. And more cases of snakebite.'

'We'll have to get you more help by then,' said Mahdi.

'Let's hope so.'

A young social worker came over. She was wrapped like a mummy in reams of cloth. It must have been unbearably hot for her. She handed Dr Azam a bottle of water. He thanked her wearily.

'There aren't many women in the queue,' I said. 'Why is that?'

'Mahdi, you'll need to take Linda to see the women.' He turned to me. 'They're the most vulnerable of all. You'll see.'

The doctor pulled himself up and we said goodbye to him. He was the only medic here, and was working round the clock. I couldn't bear to think what would happen if he got sick. We wished him luck.

Mahdi and I walked slowly on, without speaking. The heat bore down on us like a hammer driving into our skulls. I loosened my *hijab*. My throat was bone dry but with so many people around me desperate for water, it didn't feel right to take out my bottle. A little way ahead I could see a small island of mud, bulging out like a carbuncle from the main bund. On it I could see what looked like an abandoned heap of colourful clothes, discarded at the side of the road. As we drew closer I realised that it was a group of women and children, huddled together on the dirt. They were out in the open, without shade.

Mahdi told me that physical hardship was only part of their problem. 'They're so traumatised at being visible. The whole family honour is wrapped up in their keeping purdah. Being shut away.'

We approached the group cautiously. They were clearly terrified; washed up by the floodwater and left at the side of the road like some flotsam that could be picked over by anyone who passed by. Never having been seen by men other than those of their family, they bowed their heads.

Mahdi spoke soothingly. 'We are here to help you. Please do not be afraid.'

The group huddled even closer but two of the older women stood up. One of them stepped forward. Her cheekbones stuck out sharply from her sunken face. She looked like one of the walking dead.

Her voice was thin but she radiated anger. 'Look at us! I am a widow. My children have no food.'

Mahdi spoke to the woman in Urdu, then translated for me.

'She says that when the truck came yesterday she wasn't strong enough to fight for her ration. The men got it all.'

The other woman spoke in a trembling voice. 'We are scared for the safety of our children, especially the girls. We hear stories. Children going missing in the night.'

I looked at the women. Some of them were pregnant. I thought what a hellish situation it was for them, or for those menstruating. No water; no sanitation.

Mahdi spoke calmly in a strong voice. He told the women that he, personally, would come back the next day with tents and ration packs. Each pack would contain enough rice, ghee, candles, soap and water purification tablets to keep them going. The women nodded their thanks.

'Inshallah – you will return.'

They stood like statues, watching us leave.

'Come on, we need to hurry,' Mahdi said. 'We need to get back by dark.'

When we reached Corporal Sheeha my head was throbbing.

'You don't look at all well,' he said, fussing over me like a mother hen. 'Time to get some fluids into you.'

He looked at the sky. 'Rain's on its way. We need to get going.'

As we set off, the rain started to fall. Very soon it was a torrent and our windscreen wipers were useless against it. Mahdi huddled over the wheel, peering through the blur of rainwater. We were making almost no progress. Heading in the direction from which we had come, a convoy of water tankers, trucks and tractors, loaded with sacks, bedding and mattresses, was making its way to the flood survivors. Going our way, in an exodus of misery, were those determined to leave. We crawled along behind an old wooden cart, piled high with the remnants of people's lives: clothes, cooking pots and bedding. Women and children were perched precariously on top, drenched to the skin. A couple of times I wondered if we would have been the last vehicle to get through: the fragile roads were crumbling all the time under the pressure of water.

When we reached the army base, Captain Walin was waiting for us. He wasn't happy.

'You should have got back hours ago, Corporal,' he said. 'What were you thinking of?'

Before the other man could answer I spoke. 'I'm sorry. It was our fault,' I said. 'The good news is that we've got the pictures. We've seen enough.'

I told him that Mahdi would drive me immediately back to Karachi where I would take the first flight to Islamabad. There I would head straight to the World Bank for a debrief.

'This needs to be told.' I said. 'I promise, your time with me hasn't been wasted.'

Captain Walim was torn. He was keen to see me off his patch, but he also felt responsible.

'You're crazy,' he said. 'It's an eight-hour drive from here to Karachi.'

He looked out from under the tent canopy at the rain, sheeting down in the darkness. 'We've just had news it's happened again. Kashmore district is now under water. Should have been safe. Surrounded by bunds.'

Mahdi asked what had happened. The Captain explained that one of the government ministers had ordered his people to cut a hole in one of the bunds to stop his own land getting inundated. The villagers were given only two hours' notice to pack their things and clear out before the bund was breached.

I looked at the Captain, shocked. He shrugged his shoulders. 'That's life,' he said. 'Survival of the fittest.'

We drove slowly, for hours. I was worried Mahdi might fall asleep at the wheel. I looked out at the straggly lines of people and animals, trudging through the rain: farmers with a couple of buffalo, searching in vain for an inch of pasture on which they could graze; and shepherds with shotguns strapped to their backs to ward off bandits.

Mahdi dropped me at the airport; there was a 6am flight available. I called Faisal, my trusty driver, with my arrival time and told him I needed to go straight to the offices of the World Bank. He told me to wait inside the terminal building if I couldn't see him. I did as instructed, then after a minute I ventured a peek outside and saw him running towards the airport building in a fluster. He hadn't been able to park as there had been a stepping up of security around the airport. The Red Mosque siege had been going on for weeks, totally disrupting the city.

'Madam, please hurry,' he said, grabbing my suitcase and heading back towards the main road.

In front of us I could see a commotion – a small crowd was watching a police fork lift truck clearing a car from a restricted area. I realised, to my horror, that it was ours. Faisal was wide-eyed with panic. I ran at the policeman, without stopping to think, the combination of tiredness and desperation propelling me forward.

'Put it down!' I said, pointing at the car, which was suspended in the air above us.

The man looked at me in disbelief.

'Put it down!' I said again, pointing first at the car, then the ground.

'This is my car, and I am late.' I tapped my watch.

'I need to leave now. Put it down.'

My voice was as commanding as a head-teacher's. Out of the corner of my eye I saw Faisal, moving nervously from one foot to the other. The policeman was still staring at me, goggle-eyed.

He held my gaze a moment longer, then turned, gesticulating for the fork lift driver to lower the car.

'Thank you.' I said, still maintaining an air of authority.

We leapt into the car and shot off. My knees were shaking. I had to acknowledge that there was the odd occasion when the shock-factor of my being a foreign woman in Pakistan worked to my advantage. This was certainly one of them.

Faisal dropped me at the World Bank. I met with my contact there, Farhan Khan. He asked me to set up my computer while he gathered the team. 'We all need to hear this,' he said.

Minutes later, a group of executives were seated at a table, watching one picture after another of the suffering and desperation that I had taken on my trip with Mahdi. It needed no commentary; they were shocked.

'There's no doubt we have to move fast,' said Farhan Khan.

The Director of the World Bank immediately started issuing instructions. 'Before we do anything else, we need to show this to parliament. Give the presentation to the General in Charge of Relief at the NDMA [National Disaster Management Authority]. Let's hear what he has to say. Then we can plan our action.' He turned to his PA. 'Frida, please call the General. Say it's urgent. We need a meeting within the hour.'

I went to the bathroom and splashed cold water on my face. If it hadn't been for the adrenalin coursing through my system, I didn't think I would have got this far.

We arrived at the NDMS less than an hour later and I gave the same slide show to the General and his disaster relief team. When the General had viewed the last image he turned to me. 'When were these taken?'

'Yesterday,' I said. 'I was there yesterday.' I kept my voice calm. There was no need for histrionics – the photos said it all.

I waited in the room with the three World Bank officials while

117

the General had a word with his colleagues outside. When he returned he spoke to us with sincerity.

'Thank you,' he said. 'It's very clear that we need to get extra relief to the area. We'll get on to it at once.'

He shook my hand warmly as we left. 'I will keep you all informed of our actions.'

Farhan said goodbye in the lobby. By now I was desperate to lie down but before we parted I had one more thing to ask of him.

'Could you come to the same slide presentation in Karachi next week? I need to brief my business supporters and mentors.'

'You can count on us,' Farhan said.

A week later, at the Pearl Continental Hotel in Karachi, the same slide show was played to a room packed with heads of business. National and multinational companies were there in force, including Standard Chartered Bank, ICI, Unilever, Dupont, I-Textile, Citibank, Telenor, and Engro. They all wanted to help, to create an emergency relief team. Everyone was buzzing with ideas: the pharmaceutical companies discussed which medicines they should send first; the mobile phone companies suggested how they could boost communication in the area. Each company decided how they could use their core business to help to mobilise food rations, tents and water.

At the end of the session the Director of the World Bank stood up. 'Linda went to the heart of the disaster,' he said. 'She took enormous personal risk to bring us this presentation. It's not her people. Not her country. The least we can do is help.'

Pleased as I was at what we'd been able to achieve in Pakistan on a practical level, on a personal level I was lonely. The truth was, I was desperate for some female companionship. Every day I met only men, whether they were wearing Armani suits in city boardrooms or grubby shalwar kameeze in humid villages. I missed women's conversation, the type of emotional intimacy you naturally get in their company. I knew that to help women effectively I needed to wear their moccasins, hear their stories, understand their situation. I was acutely aware of my limitations: however much I felt I might have succeeded in understanding a situation there would always be a layer of me that was thinking from a European perspective.

I was well into my second year in Pakistan – almost a year after the cyclone hit – before a perfect opportunity arose. I didn't usually bother to open the online newsletter for ex-pats that announced the forthcoming events. I was so rarely in town to attend anything but this happened to be a week when I was under a lockdown in Islamabad, and I felt like a caged animal pacing my apartment. I needed to find something interesting to do. I scanned the list without much hope – our movements were so restricted at that time that most events, I guessed, would be cancelled. Then one of the items caught my eye: a stress management course at the Women's Centre. And boy, did I need stress management. For months now I hadn't been sleeping well. I had got used to living with high levels of tension but it was taking its toll on my body. A couple of months before, on 15 March 2008, a group of us, journalists and UN security friends, had decided to go out for dinner to a favourite restaurant, the Luna Caprese. We hadn't gone out for ages and thought we would risk it as there hadn't been a bombing for the past three months. We had booked a table for 8pm but we were running late. We were a few streets away when we heard an almighty explosion. Minutes later, we received a text on our phones: 'Bomb blast in F6 – Luna Caprese Restaurant – situation unknown – AVOID'. Instead of returning home, a couple of us rushed to help. The place was in smithereens. We learned later that the casualties were mostly non-Pakistanis and included a

Turkish nurse, seven Americans, a Chinese national, a Briton, a Canadian and two Japanese journalists. That night we steadied our nerves with a bottle of Chivas Regal and for many minutes sat in silence, staring into space. There was a sense that the tide had turned and things were going to get a lot worse.

I hoped the stress management course would be a welcome relief but when I got to the women's centre I thought I must be in the wrong place. The lobby was packed with jostling men. Then I remembered that if you were a woman in Pakistan, a male member of the family had to accompany you to a venue and stay until you left.

Adding my purple ankle boots to the pile of ladies' shoes left outside the hall I pushed open the swing door and entered. The room was large. Cushioned mats lay scattered on the floor. The curtains were drawn – to keep out men's prying eyes, I guessed. Candles flickered from the stage. A divine scent of jasmine filled the room. Music played quietly in the background. I looked around me hoping to make eye-contact with someone. I was the only foreigner. The other women were mostly wearing burkhas and *hijabs* so it was difficult to guess their age. A few sat in pairs, heads close together, whispering. Most of them sat quietly, eyes down, lost in their own world. I found a mat near the back and got out my notepad and pen.

A few moments later, our teacher breezed in. She had an energy about her that was enchanting. The group followed her every movement, spellbound. Pakistani ladies almost always keep their black hair long, tied back severely in a ponytail. Hers, however, was short and wavy, a light-brown bob that bounced as she walked. She was wearing a white cotton full-length dress with a shawl around her shoulders, embroidered with pink roses. Amongst the black burkhas the contrast was striking. She looked like an angel.

She stood with arms wide open and spoke in a warm, low voice. 'Welcome ladies, and thank you for coming. My name is Jeannie.'

She introduced our session acknowledging how hard it must have been for many of the group to come.

'Weeks of gentle persuasion at home...our menfolk very protective of us, yes?' She sought their eyes. 'So...well done, I applaud you. You did it, and now you are here!'

She told us that in this room we were sisters, that there was no need for shyness or fear.

'Anything that is said in this room is confidential. It will not be repeated to anyone. This is a rule. We must have absolute trust.'

Jeannie scanned the room, looking into the eyes of the participants, getting each one's silent promise. Once she was satisfied, her serious expression fell away and her playfulness returned. She asked us to give our names, one by one, and say a little about ourselves.

She suggested I went first. 'I would like us all to welcome Linda, a guest from our foreign community. It is so nice to have you with us.'

Twenty pairs of eyes gazed at me. I couldn't read their expression.

Words tumbled out. 'Salam Alikum. My name is Linda. I am a social worker from England. I have been living and working in Pakistan for over a year. With the recent bomb blasts I can't get to my projects in Sindh. I have come here to relax and make new friends.'

One by one the women were called upon to introduce themselves. Silence hung heavy in the room following each intense outpouring.

Priya, from Rawlpindi, spoke first, explaining that her husband was a bully and her in-laws wanted her to give up her job in the bank.

'I have no freedom...I just want to die.'

'This is not going to be a light relaxation class,' I thought, as Priya started to sob quietly

'Thank you, Priya,' Jeannie said tenderly. 'And can you tell us what you hope to gain from the course?'

Priya swallowed her tears with difficulty. 'I want to learn how to survive my situation.'

Priya's honesty encouraged other women to open up. One by one, bursting with pent-up anger and bitterness, they shared their tales. These were women who were sufficiently well-off to pay the course fees, but their lives had many of the same restrictions as the villagers' I had encountered.

Nida, a thirty-year-old, desperate for a divorce, spoke of eight years of hell. 'I am being suffocated day by day,' she said. 'I do not believe this is the life Allah wants for me!'

When she was asked what she wanted to get from the course, she spoke passionately: 'Courage not to give up. Strength and encouragement from other women. Who know what it is like to suffer every day.'

I was shocked by the amount of pain each of the women was carrying. I thought of the group of men, waiting in the lobby. *Their ears must be burning.*

The introductions completed, Jeannie asked us to get to our feet and find a space. 'Time to get your bodies moving!'

She asked us to breathe deeply, to feel the music in our bodies. She suggested we keep our eyes closed as she realised so many of us would feel self-conscious. I began to move to the music, dropping my shoulders, feeling my body grow lighter as tension ebbed away. I hadn't danced like this since the wonderful evenings at the Marley café in Thailand. After a little, I ventured a peep at the other women, curious to know if they were joining in. It was a surreal and beautiful sight. They had thrown themselves into the dance with abandon. Burkhas were whipping round and billowing like the robes of whirling dervishes. Hips were swaying, arms moving as expressively as in a Hawaiian hula dance. It spoke of a feeling of safety. Of freedom. Of birds escaping their cages and flying free.

Afterwards, there was clapping and laughter; an exchange of smiles. Then, as we lined up at the water dispenser, I was brought sharply down to earth.

'You hate us!' A woman, in front of me in the line, almost spat the words.

'Sorry?' I said, completely taken aback.

'What are you doing here? Are you a spy?' she asked, eyes narrowed. 'The mullah comes to our university most days. He tells us. He knows.'

'He knows what?' I said, indignant.

'You have no respect for us.'

'Would I be here if I felt like that? It's dangerous for us. I'm risking my life here.'

Tears welled in my eyes. The girl glared at me, silent.

I took a breath. Decided to change the subject. I asked her what she was studying at university. She told me she was a medic. Then her frustrations came pouring out. I guess she had decided I wasn't a spy after all.

'It's a waste of time. When my parents find me a husband he will never let me have a job,' she said bitterly. 'It's a joke.'

Jeannie called us together again. This time she wanted us to sit facing a partner, cross-legged. It was an exercise in love, she told us. The love that connects each one of us, every second of every day. A feeling of unease once again filled the room.

'I don't know anything about love,' one of the youngest girls said. 'I can't do this.'

'Yes you can,' said Jeannie. 'Just think of a newborn baby in your arms. What would you feel then?'

'Love,' the girl replied reluctantly.

'Please take your partner's hands and look into her eyes. That is all I want you to do. Don't talk. Just look into her eyes,' Jeannie said. 'Get comfortable. You'll be doing this for ten minutes.'

My partner's hands were calloused. She had dark circles under her eyes. At first, we were both embarrassed to look at each other. We glanced sideways, up and down, anywhere but straight ahead. Many of the women shuffled around or giggled nervously. Jeannie asked for quiet.

Then the magic began. Our inhibitions fell away and we did as we were told, imagining the word love, the essence of love, in our mind's eye. I felt a connection with my partner that went way beyond the physical, breaking through any boundaries or barriers. We were merely two human beings connecting, soul to soul.

'Now drop your hands,' Jeannie said.

I couldn't believe that ten minutes had passed already.

'If you feel like it, you can give each other a hug.'

All of us hugged and most of us wept a few tears as well.

'You are never alone,' Jeannie said quietly. 'All you have to do is look into someone's eyes. Then you don't see strangers around you. You see friends.'

We finished the session doing shoulder stands. As the women raised their legs in the air, their burkhas tumbled over their heads. Everyone was giggling.

Later, when I was sifting through the piles of shoes to find mine, I felt a light tap on my shoulder. It was the medical student.

'Sorry,' she said. 'I know what I said isn't true. Do you think we could meet up for a cup of coffee?'

We hugged and exchanged phone numbers.

'Do you know much about Islam, Linda?' she asked.

I shook my head. 'Not much. Only a little.'

She dug in her bag and brought out a book. 'Please accept this gift,' she said shyly.

I stammered my thanks.

'It's an English translation of the Koran,' she said. 'I would like you to have it.'

I walked out into the cool night air and watched while the men bundled their women frantically into waiting cars.

'Did you have a good evening, Madam?' Faisal was holding open the car door.

'I did, thank you, Faisal.'

Faisal beamed and gave me a double thumbs-up, a gesture he had caught off me.

I felt suffocated in Islamabad. I couldn't move. I couldn't work. I was desperate to get out to Sindh. There was so much I wanted to do. I knew the risks and sometimes I took them, partly out of defiance, partly for my own sanity.

Then, on 22 September 2008 the Marriott Hotel was bombed.

It was the final straw for many of us. The hotel was believed to be impregnable, its security so tight that it was one of the only two places in Islamabad where Western diplomats were allowed to dine. Inside the hotel's plush interior we could relax, forgetting for a short while what was happening on the other side of the door.

The blast was the biggest Pakistan had ever seen. The device was carried on a truck packed with 600kg of RDX and TNT explosives. The bombers had packed aluminium powder around the explosives to accelerate the fire which reached 400 degrees, making the sprinkler system useless. Every one of the Marriott's 290 rooms was gutted by fire. The bomb left a crater 59ft across and 24ft deep and a death toll of fifty-three.

Ever since Benazir Bhutto's assassination the previous

December, the writing was on the wall. It was becoming increasingly difficult to work in Pakistan. I had escaped death a few times but I didn't know how much longer my luck would hold. It was time to leave.

Back home in England, I found it difficult to adjust. I kept looking at people, especially women, going about their everyday lives with a freedom they took completely for granted. My first day home, I headed out to the shopping mall. Delighted not to have to wear a *hijab*, and free to do whatever I pleased, I felt relaxed for the first time in ages. I was in the pharmacist's browsing at the cosmetics counter.

Suddenly there was a loud crash behind me. I threw myself under the counter, my hands over my head. Where I'd just come from, if you waited a split second to find out where a bang came from, the one after might get you. Fortunately, this time there was no second bang. Just the voice of a kindly shop assistant.

'Can I help you?' The woman was looking down at me, concerned. 'Are you alright?'

I could hear her voice but I dared not move.

A hand gently touched my shoulder and I flinched. 'It's just one of our delivery trucks.'

She helped me to my feet. I was embarrassed to find that a curious crowd of onlookers had gathered.

'I'm sorry – I thought it was a bomb. I have just come from Pakistan…I thought…' the words tumbled from my mouth.

'Can I get you some water?' the woman asked.

'No.' I smiled to reassure her. 'I'm fine now.'

I hurried away, my knees still shaking from the shock. I could feel the cool rain but did not notice how wet I was getting. I just needed to walk.

The experience of Pakistan has never left me. To this day when

I enter a hotel room, I move the bed away from the window and draw the curtains. Some reflexes are simply hardwired in me now. It was a difficult time – an ugly time in many ways – but I wouldn't have swapped a minute of it. I still live life on the edge and regularly take risks, but after Pakistan my appreciation of life, of human rights, is much higher. I savour the freedom I have, knowing that millions have never known it.

Pakistan taught me some of the most important lessons of my life.

PART 2: IN AN ALIEN LAND

Working with Refugees

'I've learned that people will forget what you said
People will forget what you did
But people will never forget how you made
  them feel.'

Maya Angelou

CHAPTER FOUR

INTO THE FIRE

India

Moving from China to India felt like going from a boarding school to a brothel. The two countries have the largest populations in the world, with China just a nose ahead, but otherwise they couldn't be more different. Diving into the chaos of India made me long for the order of China, although when I had been living there I had felt stifled by it.

I had spent a year in southern China – my first placement – as a volunteer teacher in schools and hospitals. The places I worked were deep in the rural interior, where I had to adjust to the locals screaming and running away at my approach, and being called '*guilo*', the foreign devil. There was never a problem with discipline in my classroom: secret policemen invariably sat at the back, checking that I didn't step over the line. I didn't need an alarm clock: the pounding feet of the local schoolchildren did the job, as they jogged military-style around the village to the regimental cries of their sports coach. All day it was a tight structure of rotas, regimens and regulations. At 10am and 2pm every day, music would come on over a PA system and the children would break from their lessons to perform a programme of eye exercises: 'Eyes left! Eyes right! Eyes up! Eyes down!' Everything was designed to make the nation strong and healthy, right down to their eye muscles. And everyone complied, without question.

It brought out the rebel in me. In China, where religion had largely been stifled, issues of faith consumed me. I had never really thought about the role it played in my life until I lived there. The average person didn't believe in anything other than the Party. The communist regime only permits religious practices in a controlled and heavily monitored way. I wasn't allowed to discuss politics or religion in the classroom but it was clear to me, especially after talking with some of my more depressed university students, that in a country where religion was frowned upon, hope seemed to have drowned along with it. Even in a relatively apathetic Christian country, like the UK, there is a sense that something bigger than yourself is present in our everyday lives, where 'higher power' doesn't simply mean 'State'.

In China, their spirit seemed squashed. Dressed in shapeless trousers and tunics, in the same shades of grey and brown, the mass populace go about their business, androgenous and quietly stoical. In this atmosphere of utilitarian conformity I tended to butt the ceiling, like a jack-in-the-box who had been squashed down in his tin. I read and asked questions in a quest to understand more about the country and its people. Increasingly, Tibet was an issue that fascinated me. Why did China invade it? Why did the world not react? Why was China so threatened by his Holiness the Dalai Lama? What happened to the fleeing refugees? It wasn't easy or safe to research on computer. Many search engines were blocked – due to 'the great firewall' – and if I ventured to tap in the words 'Tibet' or 'Buddhism' I spent the next few hours wondering if police would come banging at my door.

Once back in the UK, I started my research in earnest. Everything I had read or heard about the plight of Tibetan refugees made me keen to know more and I was increasingly determined to find a way to get work, either as nurse, teacher or social worker, in one of the camps in India. The story of the refugees' flight from their home country began over sixty years ago, in 1949, when the People's Liberation Army of China marched into Tibet's eastern provinces of Kham and Amdo. It seized control of the eastern Tibetan headquarters of Chamdo the following year. In 1951, the so called '17-point Agreement on Measures for the Peaceful Liberation of Tibet' was forced upon the government of Tibet and its people. In the succeeding years the Chinese advanced further west and eventually crushed the Tibetan national uprising of Lhasa in 1959.

That same year, hot on the heels of their beloved Dalai Lama, 80,000 Tibetans abandoned their homeland and sought refuge in India. The Indian government, led by Jawaharial Nehru, generously absorbed the mass migration and agreed to provide assistance to the refugees until the situation was safe for their return to Tibet. A year later, it became clear that this wasn't going to happen in a hurry, so permanent facilities were constructed. It was a challenge to find space in this highly populated third world country so it was in some of the least accessible and developed areas that the camps were eventually built.

I tried to imagine how the Tibetans had fared. Coming from their cool mountain dwellings, and resettled in far-flung rural areas of India, many of which were impoverished parts of the south, in Karnataka State, where temperatures soared to fifty degrees and stayed at that level for months.

Today the vast majority of Tibetans living in India are still living in inhospitable areas of the south. Around 50,000 of them have adapted to the harsh weather conditions, the unfamiliar diet, the alien language. Over the past 60 years, 150,000 Tibetans have set up home in India. His Holiness the 14th Dalai Lama, in one media interview, described India as his country, rather than Tibet: 'I refer to India as my country because I have spent half of my life here,' he said.

His Holiness the Dalai Lama established the Tibetan exile administration in the north Indian hill station of Mussoorie in 1959. Known as the CTA (the Central Tibetan Administration), it is a continuation of the government of independent Tibet. In 1960 it was moved to Dharamsala.

For weeks I did my homework, pouring over research papers, reading conference reviews, studying the focus of the Tibetan NGOs and learning the goals of the Tibetan Government in Exile. I turned over stones repeatedly in the hope that I would come across some area of need that might secure me funding. Keen to actually meet some Tibetans, I contacted the Office of His Holiness the Dalai Lama in London. There I hit the jackpot. They suggested I meet a British volunteer, Marsha, who had just returned to the UK from a Tibetan camp in the north of India where she had been teaching for over a year.

Marsha confirmed what a few research papers I had read had alluded to: there was a problem with drug and alcohol abuse among the young people in the camps. She said that it had not been a focus of aid, largely because it was very much a taboo subject. I pricked up my ears. This was potentially where I could make myself useful to one of the aid agencies.

'I had been asked to work with a group of unemployed school leavers,' she said. 'But it was hopeless. Hardly anyone turned up for class.'

She told me that she had been a social worker back home, so it was second nature to dig a little deeper. She talked to the village leaders and the parents but failed to get satisfactory answers.

'It was like I'd hit a brick wall,' she said.

'What did you do?' I asked, sensing Marsha wasn't the sort of woman who'd give up.

'I had to try something else to lure them out.'

Marsha started a small youth club in her apartment where the students could listen to music and play games. The relaxed atmosphere brought them out of themselves, got them talking and sharing their problems.

'A lot of them were on drugs,' she said. 'In despair at being addicts.'

'Who could you refer them to?' I asked.

'It was really hard. There weren't any rehab programmes or anything,' she said. 'And because the subject was taboo, if they admitted they had a problem they were expelled from class.'

'So you became the resident counsellor?'

'I did. It was one sorry story after another.' Marsha gave a frustrated sigh. 'To be honest, I barely scratched the surface.'

Buoyed up by Marsha's heartfelt desire that something should be done for these Tibetan youngsters, when I got home I contacted a small Buddhist centre whose flyer I'd seen at my local library. The manager advised me to call the Tibet Relief Fund.

I didn't get anywhere on the phone. I knew I had to meet the Chief Executive face to face or I wouldn't stand a chance of getting funding so I looked at the Tibet Relief Fund's website to see if there were any events coming up at which she might be present.

I finally got to meet Philippa, the CEO, at the end of a long evening at a community centre in central London. I had sat through a lecture on Tibetan medicine given by a doctor from Dharamsala and now I was the last in a long line of people waiting to talk to her. I was panicking that I might not get the chance to say my piece before she left.

Finally, I was at the front of the queue and introduced myself to her, gabbling. I didn't pause for a moment, fearing that if I did so, she might shove a fundraising pack at me and flee for the exit. I explained that while so many Tibetan charities were raising money to help children, women and old people, there didn't seem to be anyone focusing on the group I had identified as needing help.

'I was hoping that I might be able to meet with you in your office,' I said. 'I have been researching the Tibetan cause for months.'

She smiled, looking at the enormous file I was carrying and my desperate expression. I don't know whether it was out of politeness, curiosity, or simply a desire to make a break for the exit at the end of a long evening, but she said, 'Look, why not come to my office on Thursday. I can give you 20 minutes and you can run through your research then.'

Soon after, I was on a plane to Delhi. I had researched the history, now I was itching to see the reality of life for Tibetans living in India. Philippa had listened to my proposal and had persuaded her colleagues at the Tibet Relief Fund that it was a good idea to send me on a recce to the refugee camps there. My task was to find out how widespread the drug and alcohol problem was among the younger Tibetans before coming up with ideas to prevent it escalating or happening in the first place. My brief was to meet officials at the camps and ask questions. Once I had presented my findings to the Tibet Relief Fund, they would decide how funds should be spent.

I only spent a short time in Delhi as I was due to head out to Dharamsala, where the Central Tibetan Administration was located, just a few days after my arrival in India. During those first days I felt almost overcome by the heady, full-on chaos of the city but I was never without help. The unofficial welcoming committee, headed up by two friends Tsering and Sonam, made sure I never felt out of my depth. They found me a room at Majnu Ka Tilla, the Tibetan camp just outside Delhi, where they both lived.

Sonam in particular took me under his wing. A young man with a long ponytail and a charming, easy-going manner, he wore his jeans and T-shirt with a natural elegance. He told me he was trying to carve a living as a graphic designer, although he took on work as a guide and general fixer to make ends meet.

Sonam insisted on putting me on the train to Dharamsala. There the Tibet Relief Fund had arranged for me to meet Samdhong Rinpoche, the Tibetan Prime Minister.

'Let me take you. Otherwise the touts will have fun with you. I will help you get a ticket and a good bunk,' he said. 'It's a sleeper so you need to be in First Class.'

It is hard to describe to those who haven't been to Delhi how overcome by the sheer volume of people you feel when you visit the city. Within a few hours of being there I was exhausted by sensory and cultural overload. You walk out of the airport and all of a sudden you are on a frenetic fairground ride. And at the station the chaos was so intense that I hesitated for a second, not knowing if I could manage it. The train had come in and a seething mass of people were dashing for the unreserved third class carriages in their worn-out flip-flops, somehow managing to step over the homeless children sleeping on the station platform.

Sonam took my arm gently. 'Come on. I will get you to your bunk and Karma will meet you at the other end,' he said. 'It looks worse than it is. If any of the guys start to touch you, look them in the eye and shout. They will soon run away.'

He told me that there would be a scrum for my suitcase at Dharamsala so I should hold on to it tightly.

'I've got you a top bunk,' he said, showing me into a small

cabin with four bunks and a dirty curtain for a door. 'Don't let anything leave your sight.'

I hugged Sonam and wished he was coming with me. In his company I had felt safe and protected during my time in Delhi and now I was setting out on my own for the first time. He understood my fears and said reassuringly before he turned to go, 'Let me know what day you're coming back. I will be here waiting for you. Don't worry.'

I sat on my bunk, feet dangling. I wasn't alone for long. Three smartly-dressed men in their forties came in. They greeted me and I didn't know whether to be friendly or cool, whether I was safe with them or not.

'Are you travelling alone?' one of them asked.

'Yes...' I knew I sounded nervous.

'Your first time in India?'

'Yes.' Immediately I wished I hadn't admitted it.

They told me that they were engineers working on the big dams in the north and that this was their commuting route.

'We know all the best food sellers,' one of the men reassured me. 'You'll be safe with us.'

I wasn't sure about that. The youngest man was looking at me with a little too much interest.

It wasn't until I was tucking into some dal, chappati, onions and chilli – the men were as good as their word and helped me buy food from one of the hawkers – that I finally relaxed. I took a bite of the chilli and my eyes almost popped out of my head. On fire, I lunged for my water bottle.

'Kill the fire with the chappati!' The engineers laughed, and a moment later I joined in, eyes streaming. After that, I happily took their advice and we got along fine.

'Do you have your own chains and padlock?' the older man asked me.

I shook my head.

'You must buy them,' he said. 'Chain your things to your bunk. Here.' He showed me what to do. 'If you take your shoes off and sleep, they steal them.'

I slept in my boots with my rucksack for a pillow. It was a long night. The train, which was making its way to the mountains of the north, stopped at every village along the way. Each time it screeched to a halt I was nearly thrown from my bunk. I had restricted my water intake, hoping that I might last without having to go to the toilet but I finally had to give in. I carefully got down from my bunk and made my way along the corridor. There was a group of men, dressed in blue uniforms, blocking my way. Railway workers, I guessed.

'Is this the toilet?' I asked them, trying not to breathe through my nose, the stench was so vile.

They laughed and beckoned me through, standing aside to make space. I must have cut a strange figure, wearing my rucksack and sunhat in the middle of the night. One of them pinched me hard on my bottom. I swung round and yelled at him, my rucksack almost knocking the smallest man off his feet. They laughed again, but walked off, leaving me alone.

Karma, Sonam's contact, was at the station to meet me.

'Everything is organised,' he said cheerily. 'I will take you to Samdhong Rinpoche. We need to allow a lot of time to get through security.'

Dharamsala is considered the heart of the Tibetan world in exile. It is fondly known as 'Little Lhasa' and Tibetan and Western tourists alike flock to it, in the hope of catching a glimpse of His Holiness the Dalai Lama, whose portrait adorns every restaurant, shop window, and bus. He smiles at you from necklaces, T-shirts and postcards and from market-sellers' tables crowding the narrow streets. Around the monasteries, maroon-robed monks and devout laypeople move in an endless, slow-moving tide.

I was excited. Professor Samdhong Rinpoche is known in India as the 'Tibetan Gandhi' due to his belief in peaceful activism. Meeting him, I knew, was an enormous honour.

'Please, sit down,' he said, after shaking hands.

I took a chair and sat opposite him. He appeared quite frail and in his saffron-coloured monk's robe he looked almost out of place beside the huge pile of official papers that lay on his desk.

He had been briefed about my project and was more than aware of the problems faced by young Tibetans. The CTA's agenda had been focused, in large part, on promoting education among the exile population. Money had streamed in from donors and over half was funneled into education. There were now 106 kindergartens, 87 primary schools, 44 middle schools, 21 secondary schools and 13 senior secondary schools catering to 25,000 students. For Indian youngsters there was nothing like this ratio. Only 65 percent of them came out of school able to read and write whereas over 90% of the Tibetans in India achieved these skills. Strangely, in terms of the youth problems I was looking at, this was at the root of the issue. At eighteen years of age, these educated Tibetans were released from their well-ordered institutions and left to sink or swim.

After leading a sheltered life in the camps, with little attempt at integration, they were released into the outside world to compete with the more streetwise Indians. There was little vocational training on offer and unless they were to become more commercially savvy, they hadn't a hope of competing in the job market. The situation needed to change or else the endless cycle of education-disappointment-boredom-drugs would continue.

'It is a great worry to us,' Rinpoche said. 'We try to preserve our culture and values inside the camps but this must be balanced with integration.'

I could see that they had been faced with a challenge. How do you maintain the voice of 80,000 Tibetans in a sea of 1.3 billion Indians? Creating 'mini Tibets' within the confines of the camps had worked to preserve their culture, but isolating themselves from the 'madding crowd' that would have gobbled them up in a heartbeat, created its own problems.

'Let me show you where the camps are,' Samdhong Rinpoche said, taking out a large map of India.

He showed me where the first group of settlers had built a camp in the south of India. 'The government of Mysore gave them 3000 acres of land. That was in 1960. The Tibetans named it Lugsung Samdupling.'

'What about the south?' I asked.

'That was a few years later,' he said. 'The first in Karnataka State was Tibetan Dickey Larsoe. And then three more settlements followed. Now the south has the biggest Tibetan population in the country.'

'I'm thinking I should visit the larger camps first. Then move on to some of the smaller ones in the centre.' I said, peering over the map as he pointed them out.

Rinpoche looked at me appraisingly. 'You know it is called the Stove of India?'

'I had heard that. Yes.'

'When my people first settled there, many of them died from the heat,' he went on. 'We had to clear great areas of jungle. Fighting for territory with the wild elephants.

'Few of the aid agencies get to visit those camps. They never have time,' he said. 'They're too far away from any airport or railway station.'

'Are you sure you want to go?' He looked at me intently again.

'It's not a journey for the faint-hearted.'

I nodded vigorously.

'Remember to take a fan and plenty of water.'

I promised him I would.

'And tell the camp leaders when to expect you. They will send people to meet you and guide you in,' he said. 'We don't want you getting lost.'

Samdhong Rinpoche asked if I could meet with Kesang, coordinator of their career counselling programme before I left Dharamsala. An hour later I was sitting with him in his tiny office. On the wall, six passport-sized photos were pinned to a board.

'Our Fulbright scholarship students,' Kesang said. 'It nearly didn't happen this year.'

'Why not?'

'We sent five students to the USA last year and three asked for asylum,' he said. 'Tore up their passports. The Indian government was angry. It made them look bad.'

'Are there a lot of young Tibetans leaving the country?'

'Not so many. They aren't given passports, only a stay permit,' he said.

We spoke about the difficulties the Tibetan school leavers faced. They were used to learning by rote, handing over responsibility for their learning to their teachers for whom they had absolute respect. They emerged from this sheltered world timid, and lacking in self-assertiveness. They didn't have a clue how to create relationships outside their own pool.

'Most of them don't live with their parents, so have no one to guide them,' Kesang said. 'They are used to living away from home in boarding schools.'

He was obviously passionate about his work but frustrated that he could not do more.

'My patch is so big that I cannot visit each camp every year,' he said. 'I run career opportunity programmes in Dharamsala once a year but most students can't get here. It's too far.'

Like Samdhong Rinpoche, Kesang was delighted that I was to visit some of the more isolated camps. I had sensed that it would be better for me to strike out from the more well-trodden paths and now I was convinced. I would go where I was likely to be of most use to my sponsors: to the Stove of India.

In the shade of a big oak tree outside Ambikapur station in Chattisgargh, a group of taxi drivers had gathered round a chai wallah and were sipping tea. Used to having people falling over themselves to offer their services, it hadn't occurred to me that I might be turned down.

'I want to go to Mainpat camp,' I said. 'Can anyone take me?'

Not one of them moved a muscle. They carried on sipping their tea, shaking their heads, sighing and tutting. It took me an hour of cajoling and offering increasingly large amounts of money before finally one of the older men capitulated. I shouldn't have been surprised at their reluctance: after all, the camp was an eight-hour drive away. I had heard that the last three hours of the drive would be on very poor roads, deep in the interior, and the driver would have to stay overnight.

Finally, in desperation, I blurted out a sum which was ridiculously large. One of the men paused a moment, then rose stiffly to his feet.

'You pay all the money now,' he said.

'I will pay you half now, half when we get back here,' I said firmly. There was no way I was going to risk being left high and dry in the wilderness.

We stocked up with water and snacks from the village shop and set off in his ancient Ambassador taxi. Five hours into the drive, we passed the last village and from then on there were no further signs of human habitation. The dirt road was full of potholes and my driver cursed and hissed as he tried to negotiate them. Occasionally, when we hit a particularly big rock, he unleashed a furious stream of invective, threatening that if there was any damage to his tyres I would be paying for new ones. Other than the odd soothing word, there was little I could say to console him so I sat in silence, gazing out at the parched land, thousands of acres of scorched and withered wheat and maize fields, and our cracked and pitted road stretching into the heat haze. The land had a jaundiced kind of beauty but I was feeling too nauseous from the potholes to appreciate it.

At one point I wondered what would happen to us if we broke down and once the thought had entered my mind I was consumed by it. I had heard that if you got lost in this vast, sun-baked interior you would either die of thirst or be consumed by the wild animals that roamed these flatlands and vestiges of jungle. Other than the Tibetan settlement I was heading for, I had been told that the only people who were mad enough to live in this 'stove' were fugitives or bandits. My mind played a morbid game, tossing up whether it would be better to die of thirst, be bitten by a cobra, or torn to bits by a sloth bear.

When we caught sight of a ramshackle group of buildings up ahead I felt dizzy with relief. My driver, who had been anxious as well as tetchy, smiled for the first time in three hours.

'This is Mainpat,' he said.

He followed the road, past broken down outbuildings and scattered pieces of rusted farm machinery. We pulled up outside a group of one-storey wood and stone buildings. The place was like a ghost town, metal shutters pulled down on its one shop, the odd dustball bowling half-heartedly along the dirt road, borne on an intermittent breeze, so scorching that it only served to make the camp feel even hotter. As I stepped out of the car, I had the horrible sensation of being in a fan oven. With the sun bearing down like a mace, it was only a few seconds before I felt faint. As we got out of the car, a smiling, rotund man emerged from the largest building. He introduced himself as Dawa, the camp leader. His welcome, so wholehearted, managed to dispel the last of my anxiety.

'We don't get many visitors,' he said. 'They call us the Forgotten People.'

He ushered me quickly inside his office. It was a simple room, simply furnished, the starkness broken by little colourful reminders of home. There were two pictures on the walls, one of His Holiness and the other a large map of old Tibet. Little rug squares on the chairs were woven with images of the Himalayas, nomad tents and yak. We pulled our chairs as close as we could to Dawa's noisy, ancient fan, so that we were almost sitting on top of it. I noticed a rifle propped against the wall and wondered whether it was to protect the townsfolk from marauding animals.

I know the English are famed for always talking about the weather. At Mainpat it was difficult to talk about anything else. The heat bore down on you so that you found it hard to concentrate on anything else. It was like an adversary that dominated your every waking moment. I drank glass after glass of water, wondering if it would ever quench my thirst.

'It is 30 degrees by six o'clock in the morning,' Dawa said. 'We have to get up very early to get any work done.'

'I didn't see anyone in the street.'

'They hide indoors. Anywhere they can keep cool. You are lucky my fan is working. We have power cuts all the time.'

He asked me if I would like to take a look around the camp.

'Take your water bottle with you,' he said, although I didn't need reminding.

As we walked along the dirt road, I saw that Mainpat wasn't

completely deserted. A few desiccated elderly men and women sat in their doorways, snoozing. With their eyes closed their faces looked like prunes.

'Only the very old and the very young live here,' he said. 'The children are sent away to school. Once they have flown the stove, they never come back.'

'What jobs could they get if they did?' I asked.

'There's nothing for them,' he said. 'Some people sell traditional Tibetan sweaters ... but the cold season is very short. There's little work to be had on the farms.'

I looked at this lively, bright man and wondered how he had come to be here.

'People joke that I must have done something wrong to be posted here,' he said.

'So will you leave?'

'Camp officers stay for three years at each place,' he said. 'I have been here for four. No one has offered to take over.'

'Have you got family?' I asked him.

'My children are at a boarding school in Dharamsala,' he said. 'My wife stays with them.'

'How often do you see them?'

'Only once a year.'

I said that it must get lonely for him. Dawa gave a small nod, but his cheery expression did not waver. 'We make our own fun. Dances...competitions. A trip once a year to the forest.'

He paused, then added, 'I want to do my best for the people here. They have so little.'

We walked over to one of the two water pumps in the camp. Dawa told me that they dried up regularly. I asked him what emergency services they had.

'There aren't any,' he said. 'If we do get a volunteer teacher or nurse they never want to stay.'

We stopped outside the shop and Dawa rapped on the metal shutters. A couple of mules were tethered to a post outside. Against the wall was propped an old-fashioned black bicycle. I guessed there was little in the way of motorised transport. We had seen a graveyard of rusty motorbikes on the outskirts of the camp, long since discarded through lack of spare parts or fuel. I had seen only one car, which was Dawa's. It was covered with a dust sheet.

'Is that you Dawa?' a voice called from inside the shop.

'Yes it is. Open up. You have a customer.'

The shutters gave a metallic groan, opening to reveal a slight man, wearing an oversize white cotton shirt, baggy trousers and braces.

'Well, well,' he said, looking at me with interest. 'How did you get here? Magic carpet?'

'Come on,' said Dawa. 'Are you going to leave us standing out here?'

I was desperate to get out of the sun. My lips were cracking and my lungs were on fire. As soon as we were inside, the man pulled down the shutters. He introduced himself as Kelsang and called out to his wife to bring us tea. He caught me looking at the shelves which were empty except for a few neatly stacked tins of meat and soup, a little stationery, and some basic toiletries.

'We are a bit low on stock at the moment,' Kelsang said.

'You always are,' teased Dawa.

The men had an easy, playful way with each other. Until now, I had been increasingly depressed by Mainpat, the 'forgotten' place. But seeing these two laughing and teasing each other was instantly cheering.

In the far corner of the room was a barber's chair in front of which a cracked mirror and a small table stood, covered in a white cloth and a collection of implements: scissors, a razor, and a pot filled to the brim with bright green disinfectant.

'He will pull a tooth if you want him to,' laughed Dawa. 'He's done it before.'

I looked at the small noticeboard on the wall. Meditation group at Lopsang's house, Tuesday 6–7pm. Trip to the forest, October 8th – sign up by September 8th so we know numbers for the bus. A child's handwritten letter, which had been sent from boarding school, was pinned there for everyone to read.

'This is the centre of all gossip,' said Dawa. 'If I want to get a message out, I just tell Kelsang.'

Kelsang nodded. 'We do a lot of talking here,' he said. 'Although news from the outside world is never very fresh as it takes the postman three days to walk here.'

'So you are shopkeeper, barber and agony aunt?' I said.

'Not just that,' he said. 'I am also electrician and carpenter. I made this chair and the shop counter.'

With so few customers Kelsang had to be a jack-of-all-trades to have a sufficient income. I asked him why he didn't move to another camp with better amenities.

'It's not that simple,' he said. 'When they built the camps they kept communities together. Everyone here is from the same area of Tibet. We stick together.'

Kelsang's wife came in to the room, bringing the tea. She was very tall and thin. Her hair was worn in a braid, wound around her head, and she wore traditional Tibetan clothes.

'Come and sit down, Dolma,' Kelsang said. 'I want you to meet Linda.'

She poured the tea, and when she had finished, I asked her what occupation she had in the camp. She explained that she was head of the Tibetan Women's Association at Mainpat. The women in the camp had formed support groups who helped out the pregnant mothers. With no doctor or nurse in the camp, they had to see them through to the birth, and deliver postnatal care themselves, as well as making sure that there was a crib, nappies and any other items a mother might need. Like everything else, it was difficult getting hold of baby equipment and they had to start sourcing it months in advance.

'That must keep you busy,' I said.

It turned out that that was only a part of her work. Dolma was also the kindergarten teacher.

'I ask anyone who is artistic to make the teaching materials,' she said. 'And I have a rota of mothers who help out at the school.'

There was an energy about the three Tibetans which, in large part, stemmed from the pride they took in being self-sufficient. Left to sink or swim, they had come through triumphantly. It was strange that their isolation had not had the effect of making them introverted and inward-looking. They were the opposite, quizzing me about everything going on in the world and the places I had visited, from Paris to Peru. It was wonderful to find such a positive and self-motivated group in a one-horse town, barely marked on the map.

That night I stayed in a bedroom which adjoined the community hall. I was alone in the building. There was no electricity after 11pm so I had to use a candle. I looked out of the window. Outside it was as black as pitch. Nothing pierced the darkness: there was not a lighted house for miles around. I had felt relaxed and expansive earlier in the evening, laughing and chatting with Dawa and his friends, but now that feeling had ebbed away. There was a bucket of water in my room and I washed as best I could, then lay down on the rickety wooden bed. I was feeling jittery. At one point a giant shadow was cast on my wall as someone walked past with a torch. My ears listened for the slightest sound. A dog howled. Then something scratched at the window. My mind went wild, imagining all kinds of horrors. I rummaged for my earplugs and put the bedsheet over my head. In the early hours of the morning I finally drifted off to sleep, only to be woken again soon after. The people of the camp were getting ready to start the day.

I have a nasty habit of overdoing things. When my body screams for me to stop, I continue to push on when it would be much more sensible, and possibly more productive, to take a rest. In India, the distances I was covering – bumping along in taxis, battling through the crowds at railway stations and taking frequent internal flights – soon took their toll. I lost weight and my blood pressure dipped so that I often felt weak and faint. I was having to get used to a whole host of unfamiliar stressors, many of which I found intimidating: never having any privacy; having to fight my way through crowds to get anywhere; being stared at constantly; and being pestered and touched inappropriately. India is a frenetic place, and yet when you are trying to make something happen it often feels as hopeless and as if you were trying to run a race in water up to your neck.

I was often lonely. There was a level of politicking among Tibetan aid agency workers for which I had been totally unprepared. It wasn't how I had imagined it would be. Not knowing how to play the game, I blundered into this new world, very much a greenhorn, no doubt stepping on a few toes as I went. As a result, I lacked for friends among the community of aid workers, which sometimes made it feel like I was scaling a mountain on my own.

Every couple of weeks, I was knocked down with 'Delhi belly'. Not giving myself the time to recover fully, I grew steadily weaker. Not long after my trip to Mainpat, I fainted at the airport in Delhi.

'What's happened this time?' the doctor asked, as he took my blood pressure.

'I'm not sure,' I said. 'I fainted when I got off the plane.'

'Well, your blood pressure is in your boots,' he said. 'It is time you had time off. You are no good to us dead, young lady.'

It was a timely warning, and after that I did try to pace myself a bit better. Sonam, my Tibetan friend, was my saviour when things got too much. He always seemed to know when I was feeling lonely and had an attack of the blues. Then he would pitch up, like a good genie, to spirit me away. One day he asked me if I wanted to go out that evening with him and a couple of his friends, Tsering and Diki, whom I had got to know over the past weeks. I was longing for some friendly company and thanked him. He told me he would pick me up from my guesthouse at midnight.

'Where are we going at that hour?' I asked, wondering if I would be able to keep my eyes open until then.

'It's a surprise,' he said. 'Wear trousers and I'll see you then.'

At midnight, as promised, Sonam and his friends Tsering and Diki, the school nurse at the Tibetan children's village, were waiting for me on the main road. They were astride two Hero Honda motorbikes, Tsering and Diki on one, Sonam on the other.

'Here, put this on,' Sonam handed me a helmet.

For a split second I hesitated. The streets of Delhi were alarming enough in a taxi. What it would be like on a bike, I hardly dared imagine. 'Oh, what the hell!' I thought. 'You only live once.'

We shot off, chased by a pack of wild dogs barking at our heels. It was lovely to feel the cool breeze as we whizzed along. We wove our way through Majnu Ka Tilla, the Tibetan colony on the outskirts of Delhi where I had been staying. In the night sky, Tibetan prayer flags fluttered, orange and red, criss-crossing over the high rooftops. We wove our way through narrow streets lined with guesthouses and restaurants, curio shops and beauty parlours. Books of the Dalai Lama's teachings were displayed in several shop windows. And every café owner, stall holder, and shopkeeper had proudly pinned up the Tibetan flag.

I didn't know where we were headed. All I knew is that I had started a love affair – with motorbikes. At one point Sonam swerved the bike as a rickshaw driver next to us spat a great red wad of betel juice in my direction. He turned his head to me and raised his helmet, laughing. 'You OK?'

In the distance I could hear the rhythmic beat of the all-night wedding drummers. I was bewitched by Delhi at nighttime. It was only now, once the day was done and most workers had shut up shop, that its romance was fully revealed. And nowhere more so than at India Gate where a fiesta was in full swing. We parked the bikes near the enormous 12 foot statue of Hanuman, the monkey god. All around, sitting on the grass at the foot of the monument, families had gathered and spread out their picnics. Vendors were out in force, selling food and balloons.

'Is it always like this at night?' I asked Sonam as the four of us wandered up to India Gate.

'Always. Every night it is a party but it doesn't start till late.'

We paused at the red sandstone and granite monument which had been built to commemorate India's dead from the First World War. At the tomb of the unknown soldier we stood for a moment in silence, watching the eternal flame flickering in its sconce.

Sonam was longing to eat. 'Come on guys,' he said, hustling us along. 'Let's get some chaat masalas!'

We stopped at a stall and sat down on a patch of grass with our food. I bit into the crisp pastry shell, yogurt and chutney dripping down my chin. Tsering asked Diki how her week had been. She lived at the hospital, hardly ever taking a break, and was nurse, doctor, and surrogate mother in one. The children who had survived the journey through the Himalayas from Tibet arrived in a very bad state, malnourished, often with frostbite, and very traumatised. Most would never see their parents again and Diki had to provide a good deal of psychological counselling.

'We had a very sad case yesterday,' she said. 'An eight-year-old boy. His frostbite was so bad we had to amputate both feet.'

I asked what they thought they would gain by risking such a journey.

Tsering explained that as well as seeking to escape oppression they hoped they would learn English in India, as there were few English teachers in Tibet. They saw it as their passport to getting on in the world. And here in India they could lead a Tibetan way of life in freedom.

'But it's not just that,' said Jampa. 'Many just want to be close to His Holiness. They are prepared to risk their lives for that.'

'So what had happened to the boy?' I asked her.

'His family had paid a professional guide to draw a map. That was all they had to guide them through the mountains,' she said. 'They didn't even have a compass.'

Diki told us that the boy, Tenzin, and his older brother, accompanied by a monk, set out taking little food with them and only the clothes they stood up in. They could only travel by night. In the day they had to hide in ditches and caves. Walking for days in knee-deep snow, Tenzin's feet in their running shoes soon began to swell. Then the final straw. Chinese troops set up camp near their hiding place. They were there for two full days, during which time the Tibetans could neither move nor speak. They were forced to pee, sit, and sleep in the same spot.

'When at last the troops left, Tenzin's brother managed to

make a fire. Tried to warm his brother's feet,' Diki said. 'But it was too late. He had to carry Tenzin after that.'

'How long did it take them to get to India?' I asked.

'Forty days,' she said. 'They begged a little food but for half of that time they lived on a cup of tea a day.'

She told us that by the time Tenzin had arrived at the hospital the previous day, he had lost two of the toes on each of his feet. The bone was visible, from his big toe to his ankle, and the skin around it was blue and dead. Diki took a pull on her beer and closed her eyes a moment. When she opened then again she gave a tired smile.

'What would I do without you guys?' she said, and Sonam slung his arm around her shoulders and gave her a hug.

'Come, I'll get us a paneer tikka,' he said. 'Cheer you up.'

We followed the paneer tikka with an egg paratha, by which time we were so full we could do nothing but stretch out on the grass. There was something I was longing to ask. 'What do the poorer Indians think about the relative wealth of the Tibetan refugees?'

It is obvious, when you visit the larger camps, that there is no shortage of aid money flowing in. Dharamsala is full of gilded monasteries and monuments. Westerners fall over each other to help these gentle, peace-loving Buddhists and their revered leader. Free Tibet is a popular cause. Many of these spiritual tourists, after having visited Dharamsala, empty out their suitcases, giving away fleeces and boots. Some of them go even further, offering to marry Tibetans to give them a passport. It is a cause that brings up strong emotions in people.

'A fight broke out today,' Tsering said. 'Indian and Tibetan boys. The poor are drawn to Dharamsala, knowing there's money there.'

'Tibetans tend to trade with their own people within the

camps,' Sonam said. 'That doesn't help relations. We do need to integrate more.'

'Tell you what,' said Tsering, pushing himself up and into a squat. 'Let's go integrate. Do you play snooker, Linda?'

I said I did, but rather badly.

'Come on then,' he said, getting up and putting our rubbish in a bin.

'OK,' said Diki. 'But I don't want to be too late.'

We jumped back on the bikes and made our way to the narrow lanes of Old Delhi. Tucked into the shadows of its ancient rotting buildings I caught glimpses of groups of men drinking tea or playing dice. Sonam carefully manoeuvred his bike, avoiding potholes and sleeping dogs who barely troubled to raise their heads as we passed. The stench from sewage running down the gulley in the middle of the road, combined with the smell of rotting fruit, was overpowering. I had heard that the streets of Old Delhi had been designed like a maze so that people could escape from invaders and hide out in safety. Sonam seemed to know his way but some of the alleys were so narrow that there was barely room for his bike. I felt suffocated as if the rickety buildings on either side would tumble in on top of us. I sensed movements in the shadows and pulled my hood over my head, zipping up my jacket to cover most of my face. It was no place for a blonde-headed foreigner.

We came to a halt in front of a small wooden building, the low tiled roof sagging so badly it looked like it might cave in at any moment. Tsering knocked on the metal door, three fast raps, then a pause, followed by three slow ones. The door creaked open a couple of inches. A voice barked a question gruffly. Tsering answered. The door remained shut.

'Hurry up, Asif. Let us in.'

Asif opened the door and ushered us quickly inside. He

enveloped Tsering in a huge hug, almost smothering him with his bouncer's body. Tsering explained to Asif that he was here to give his foreign friend a good time. I thought he was probably wasting his time. I felt sick from the food I had consumed earlier and the stench in the streets and I was nervous. We were led through a pitch-black, damp corridor. I held on to Sonam's arm tightly. Then another door and more knocks. When we walked in to the small dimly lit room I blinked as my eyes adjusted to the light and the thick eddies of tobacco smoke. Tsering led the way to one of the snooker tables and Sonam ordered beers at the bar.

The two men were in their element, chatting and laughing as they chalked their cues. Diki must have been to the snooker hall before as she took it in her stride, even though the punters looked a disreputable bunch and were casting sly looks in our direction.

'Who are these guys?' I asked her in a whisper. 'They look like gangsters.'

'People do hide from the police here,' she said, which made sense to me. 'Some will be undercover. Those are Gurkhas,' he pointed at a couple of men at the next table. 'And Sonam says he's seen Two-twos here.'

'Who are they?' I asked.

'Sonam knows all about them,' she said. 'His brother served in the Indian army for years. They are Tibetan commandos. Mostly Khampas.'

'Highly classified, Linda,' Sonam said with a wink as he neatly put a red ball in the pocket. 'Armed by the CIA.'

I had never heard of a Tibetan regiment in the Indian army. Sonam explained that Establishment 22, as they were more properly known, was a Special Frontier Force who had been around since 1962 when Nehru decided to create an elite group of rugged highlanders to fight the Chinese in mountainous and difficult terrain. This was not stuff for the ordinary Indian army. These were men who were tough enough to survive high altitudes and tackle the enemy on glaciers.

'Anil, my brother, got to know some of the old Two-twos in a bar,' he said. 'When he was stationed at Dehra Dun. It's a barrack town. He'd buy the beers. They'd talk.' Sonam told me that one of the Two-twos' most valiant operations had been in the war against Pakistan in 1971. I asked how the Indians had managed to persuade the Tibetans to get involved in their war.

'Indira Gandhi didn't force them to join up,' he said. 'She just told them the Bangladeshis were being treated as badly as the Tibetans by the Chinese. That got their attention. Clever lady.'

The Tibetans agreed to get involved in the war and Operation Mountain Eagle was launched. The Two-twos became the unsung heroes of the campaign when they secured the Chittagong Hills. After that, they were nicknamed the Phantoms of Chittagong by a Pakistani special service group under the command of General Musharraf. These 'phantoms' formed a silent, deadly, preemptive strike force, sweeping the hills and valleys of East Pakistan, taking many key Pakistani posts before the regular Indian army moved in after the rainy season.

'India won that war because of our Tibetan fighters,' Sonam said, eyes glowing with pride.

'And they never got any recognition,' said Diki. 'Officially they do not exist.'

'The only time they ever came out in the open,' said Sonam, 'was on the Chittagong road when victory was announced. But they are still being trained.'

'How many of them are there?' I asked.

'I think about 10,000. Although forty years ago there were double that.'

I asked why Tibetans in India didn't seek to employ this elite force against the Chinese.

'The young ones want to,' Tsering broke in.

He explained that His Holiness's 'middle way' of peace couldn't satisfy their anger.

'You wonder why they sit around all day drunk? They want to walk tall. Fight for their homeland.'

I sensed Tsering felt the same way.

Other than my patchy health, everything else was coming together well. Prime Minister Samdhong Rinpoche, who I had met at the beginning of my trip in Dharamsala, had been a powerful ally, his name opening doors wherever I went. I had talked to camp leaders in the large and small camps and everywhere the message was the same: eighteen-year-olds, once they were no longer being cared for in school, generally sat idle about the camp. In their depression they were being drawn increasingly towards alcohol and drugs. It was a hidden plague, one that was having a steady and insidious effect on these communities. It was not easy to find out who needed help. The young people kept behind closed doors where no one could witness their shame. Their families did everything they could to hide what was going on.

On one occasion, after a youth meeting at one of the southern camps where I had raised the issue of drugs and alcohol with the youngsters, a young man named Pesang approached me. In the session, he had bravely admitted to having been addicted to prescription drugs at school. After he had done so, the discussion had flowed much more freely and I was grateful that he had spoken so boldly. Pesang asked if I would come with him to visit the home of one of his friends, Kulu. The boy was in a dark place and he was concerned about him.

Above: Tibetan refugee camp in India. Visit by HRH Prince Charles.

Below: Presentation of gift to HH Dalai Lama, India.

Above: Road into Burmese refugee camp on Thai border.

Below left: Blind amputee Burmese refugee.

Below right: Life in the camp.

Above: Burmese refugee preparing to be resettled to the USA.

Below: Enthusiastic Manpower employees from Bangkok inspired by volunteering in the camp.

Above: Elderly yak herder, Nepal.

Below: Nomad children from North West Nepal.

Above: My journey with Tibetan nomad caravan.

Below: A break in the journey for butter-tea and prayers.

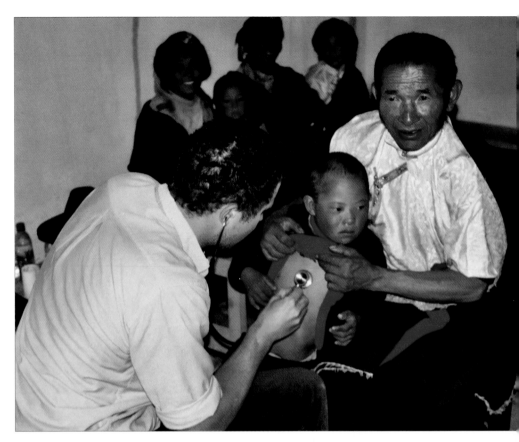

Above: British medical student with Tibetan nomads.

Below: Tibetan nomad mothers learn babycare.

Above: Tibetan nomad family.

Below: Throwing paper wind-horses in thanks for safe passage over a high Tibetan pass.

Above: Hameed the nurse (*middle*), Abderahim the driver (*right*) and the wonderful Hajj Maurice (*left*).

Below: Volunteer paramedic trains Berber girls in first aid at Education For All boarding home.

'Kulu's parents say he has been possessed by an evil spirit,' the boy told me as we walked to his house in the cooler air of the evening.

'Is he on drugs?'

'It is better his brother explains,' Pesang said.

We were ushered into the house quickly by Kulu's brother. The living room was stuffy and dark. The curtains were drawn, the only light coming from a lamp on a table and two butter lamps on either side of an altar. The air was thick with incense. I had the almost irresistible urge to pull back every curtain and open the windows wide.

'Pesang tells me that your brother might need help?' I said.

There was no mention of drugs, nor did I probe the man. His concern was that Kulu was worshipping Dorje Shugden. This is a Buddhist deity, the worship of whom is believed to bring material gain. So many of the other Buddhist practices promise a better life in the next world or on a higher plane of existence. Dorje Shugden, by contrast, promises wealth in the here and now, clearly an attractive proposition for people at the poor end of society. The Dalai Lama had issued a ban on anyone in the exile community worshipping this 'worldly' dharma protector, believing that it would increase sectarianism, a new stress fault in an already fractured community. The deity belonged to the Sakya and Gelug traditions and had been worshipped for over three hundred years. It was known to have a powerful and malign influence. Many people, it was said, had killed and lied in the name of this deity, causing devotees to become fearful and confused. However, the ban had not managed to wipe out the practice completely. The promise of worldly wealth was far too tempting. I could see how appealing it would seem to an out-of-work youngster like Kulu.

'Kulu left school and could not get a job,' his brother said. 'He met a girl but with no money he got angry with life.'

'So he turned to Shugden?'

'Yes.' The man hung his head.

He told me that Kulu was upstairs in his room. He rarely left it. The boy had given up the will to live.

'He is possessed by the spirit,' he said. 'He wants to die.'

I promised that I would call Kesang, the counsellor I had met in Dharamsala. This was a complex case but I had no doubt he would find a way to help the boy.

In the session earlier that same evening, the youngsters had vented their frustration at not being able to get jobs. As aliens, they did not have the right to seek work in the Indian civil service and they could not see how they would be able to penetrate the Indian job market. I thought about what might be done and arranged a meeting with Colonel Singh from the Mysore Indian Chamber of Commerce. Together we discussed the possibility of arranging a job fair. If those businesses which were open to hiring Tibetans could be persuaded to attend then the fair might create a useful bridge. The Colonel agreed that there was a need for new channels to facilitate the Tibetans getting jobs. Like many Indians I had spoken to he had nothing but goodwill towards the Tibetans. He knew them to be honest and hardworking. The problem was that he never saw them. He could see the need for new initiatives.

Samdhong Rinpoche had received my field report which suggested setting up formal links with Indian business groups who were receptive to hiring Tibetans. He discussed it with his teams to work out how this would be sustainable across India, linking to each of the camps. In the meantime, I continued to talk to local businesses. One of the most important links happened quite by chance. On my frequent taxi rides across Delhi, a poster kept catching my eye. It featured the supermodel face of Shahnaz Husain, with her enormous mane of hennaed hair and equally impressive diamond stud in her nose. Curious to find out more about her, I did some research. Shahnaz's story was legend. The founder of Shahnaz Herbals, an ayurvedic range of beauty products and chain of salons, she had managed to convert a teenage passion into a multimillion pound beauty industry with an empire that stretched from Seoul to Dubai. Shahnaz, an Iranian muslim who had moved to India at the age of 13, was engaged at 14 and a mother at 16, had built up the business until it was the largest organisation of its kind in the world, with a chain of over 400 franchise clinics worldwide and 375 formulations for beauty and health care.

As I trawled through Shahnaz Herbal's website, something caught my eye. Shahnaz Husain had received the 'World's Greatest Entrepreneur Award' by Success Magazine in the States. She had been the first woman in 107 years to receive it. I gave her a call.

When Sonam heard that she had invited me to her house for a meeting he was impressed. 'She's like royalty here,' he said. 'People think of her as their princess. They love her.'

'Well that's what your cause needs,' I said. 'If she likes the project she'll have the power to move it along. That's what we need, entrepreneurial types with spirit.'

What I couldn't have foreseen was that, not only did they take up the Tibetan youth cause and ran with it long after many other businesses and agencies had dropped off but Shahnaz and her daughter Nelofar would become two of my greatest friends and supporters.

I was met at her house by a friendly army of security guards and servants and led to a palatial sitting room. It had deep-piled white carpets, walls and furniture, and there were flowers everywhere. It looked like someone had designed a movie set for heaven. Shahnaz made a magnificent entrance, an imposing figure in a floor-length leopard-print Louis Vuitton robe. She must have been six foot in her heels. Her personal photographer and videographer followed in her wake.

'Do sit down, Linda,' she said. 'You look exhausted.'

I did as instructed and almost disappeared in her pillowy sofa. I was all prepared to pitch my project to Shahnaz but she was well-briefed already that I let her do the talking.

'I know all about what you are trying to do,' she said. 'I want you to meet my daughter Nelofar. She's the one leading our community development work.

And then, before I could say anything, she continued: 'I know exactly how we can help you. But first I want you to do something for me.'

'Of course. What would you like me to do?'

'Take a day off,' Shahnaz said. 'You look very tired.'

Before I could protest, she had picked up the phone and booked me a full round of treatments at her spa downstairs.

'You, my dear, need pampering,' she said. And she was off, telling me about everything that would be done to my body, including an oxygen facial where my skin would end up being infused with diamond dust, crushed pearls and flecks of 24-carat gold. I was speechless, having recently come back from Mainpat, where there had been no running water and I had to wash using a bucket.

Shahnaz read my face and hers scrunched up in displeasure. 'You must never neglect your femininity.'

I had to concede that pampering myself hadn't exactly been high on my list of priorities. And I had got run down. She had a point. I decided to go with the flow and found myself asking her how she made her hair look so gloriously lustrous.

'Twice a week I treat it with 16 egg whites mixed with lemon juice and olive oil,' she told me. 'And for my colour, a blend of henna powder, ground coffee beans, lemon juice, tea, and as many as 20 eggs.'

Goodness, I thought. It was like listening to a chef. An equal mix of passion and obsession.

'You see, Linda,' she said. 'I take care of myself, and so should you. Now off you go. No more talk.'

As I said goodbye to Shahnaz, I had a sudden desire to cry. It had been a while since I had last been cared for. In the new life I had embraced I had chosen the job of looking after other people's needs, but in the process had forgotten to care for myself. Shahnaz had clocked my situation in a millisecond.

The next week I met with Nelofar, an equally stunning woman with the same extraordinary hair as her mother's. We got on immediately. She asked me how much I wanted her to donate.

'Well, actually, nothing,' I said.

She looked surprised. It wasn't often that someone turned down the offer of money.

'What I was hoping,' I went on, 'is that you might be prepared to offer an apprenticeship to a girl from one of the Tibetan camps in one of your beauty salons.'

I explained that our programme was all about offering empowerment and creating independence in these young people. Nelofar listened carefully while I outlined my ideas, nodding thoughtfully, never once interrupting.

'I know they can be very timid but that will not matter,' she said. 'The important thing is that Tibetans have a reputation for being caring. And that is just what we need in the beauty business.'

She told me what the training would entail and I jotted down the details. 'It will take six months,' she said. 'And will cover hairdressing, skincare, haircare, manicure, pedicure, bridal make-up, waxing, threading and health and wellness.'

I was excited. The girl I had in mind, Dolma, would be ecstatic when she heard what would be in store for her.

'Bring her to my Khan Market salon on Monday,' Nelofar said. 'I'll speak to my salon manager right now.'

I rushed off to break the news to Dolma, but she wasn't so much ecstatic as terrified.

'I don't think I can do it,' she stammered. 'It is the top salon in India. They are all Indian.'

We talked it through and I promised to come with Dolma and introduce her to the staff. I would pop in regularly to check she was okay.

The following Monday, Nelofar herself was at the salon to greet us. She welcomed Dolma warmly and her Indian staff followed her lead. I sat in the corner of the salon chatting to Nelofar as Dolma assisted in her first cut and blow dry, sweeping the floor, folding the towels, and bringing the clients coffee.

'She will be fine,' said Nelofar. 'I've given her to my best manager. I'm in here most days. I'll see she's OK.'

I thanked Nelofar and left the salon feeling reassured. I had arranged to meet Dolma regularly in the camp so that we could talk over any problems she had. At our initial catch-up she spoke tentatively at first, explaining that the travelling was tiring and the local buses were crowded. It wasn't long, however, before her enthusiasm took over, and she described her work with pride.

'A client asked specially if I could do her manicure and pedicure,' she said. 'They tell me that I am good at varnishing.'

'That's wonderful,' I said. 'And how are you getting along with the other girls in the salon?'

'They like me, I think,' she said. 'They help me if I don't know how to do something.'

'Excellent,' I thought.

Nelofar called me shortly before Dolma's six-month training was due to finish.

'Let's meet up,' she said. 'It's time to celebrate.'

Nelofar was very pleased with Dolma's performance, pronouncing her ready to return to her mountain village to start up her own business.

'The girl's a natural entrepreneur!' she said. 'We'll miss her and so will the clients.'

'Do you think she's ready for that?' I asked.

'Don't worry. We'll keep in touch with her and keep her training updated,' she said. 'Now it's time you bring another Tibetan girl to us. We've got work to do!'

Nelofar, true to her word, supervised the 'hand up' of one Tibetan girl after another. She wouldn't take any thanks for her generosity. Instead, she thanked me.

'As one of my favourite Chinese verses says,' she said, putting her hand on my arm. 'A little fragrance always clings to the hand that gives you roses.'

If you are trying to move mountains it certainly helps to have someone powerful on your side. I was no 'Two-two' capable of lifting boulders on my back. And in the summer of 2002 I was given just the lucky break our project needed. I made a call to Youth Business International, one of Prince Charles's charities in London. They sounded interested in what we were doing. What I didn't know when I made the call was that the Prince of Wales himself would be visiting Delhi later that Autumn.

When I received a call from the British High Commission suggesting that the Prince should meet some of our Tibetan entrepreneurs I panicked. Our project was in such a fledgling state that I feared our efforts to impress him would appear derisory and that our young Tibetans might feel exposed. I knew I had to swallow my fears though. A VIP visit would give the Tibetans just the boost they needed.

I said we would be delighted to receive a visit and phone calls went back and forth to London for a week or two. Then we hit a snag. Eric, my friend from The British High Commission, called me.

'The Indian Government aren't happy,' he said. 'They say it's not safe for the Prince to visit Maj Nu Ka Tilla.'

'Oh no,' I groaned. I couldn't see how Maj Nu Ka Tilla, the camp outside Delhi which had been my base throughout my time in India, would pose a threat to his safety.

'That's so unfair,' I said, hot with frustration. 'Dirty and smelly, yes. But not unsafe.'

'They are suggesting that you bring the Tibetan entrepreneurs to meet the Prince at a five star hotel in Delhi,' he said cautiously, knowing that I'd erupt.

'You know that won't work,' I said. 'He needs to see that these businesses are being run from a refugee camp. That's the whole point. They don't live in a bloody five-star hotel.'

I could sense Eric trying not to smile on the other end of the phone.

'Look, calm down. I've got a suggestion,' he said. 'Some guys from Scotland Yard are coming out on a recce. Let's ask them to assess the site and we can take it from there.'

'And let the Prince decide,' I said.

'Exactly.'

Weeks went by before Eric called me with the news that a group of plain-clothes policemen and the Prince's private secretary would be paying us a visit the next day. The visit was quick and efficient. The police spread out to check out the camp and we met up an hour later at the playground where I planned we would showcase the Tibetan entrepreneurs' work.

Tim, Prince Charles's bodyguard, was relaxed and efficient. 'The Indian Government are insisting that we place some armed police on the rooftops,' he said. 'To be honest, I think it's a bit over the top but we can agree to that.'

'That's wonderful,' I breathed with relief.

'I think the camp will be a good place to visit,' he said. 'The "boss" is keen to meet the refugees on their own turf.'

He had a quick word with one of the policemen then turned back to me. 'One last thing,' he said. 'We just need to identify a place where you can escort the Prince in an emergency.'

I looked around helplessly. There weren't any rooms that had direct access onto the playground. Tim and the policemen walked around the perimeter of the playground.

'Hang on. What's this?' Tim opened a small wooden door.

He reared back quickly. 'Ah, a rather dirty toilet.'

I looked apologetic but he smiled, wiping his hands on his trousers. 'Perfect. If you clean it up it will be fine'.

'Really?' I said with disbelief. Pray God the Prince won't have to go there.

I was relieved that The British High Commission had requested that the Tibetan event be very low profile, with few guests and no speeches. The Prince wanted to meet the young people themselves, and for that to happen we couldn't have dozens of officials crowding the place. The press would be allowed to attend but would be kept in one small area.

We had a month to get organised. Five Tibetans were selected to showcase their businesses and products: Pema – beauty treatments; Dawa – event management; Kesang – IT; Dorjee – graphics and signwriting; Norbu – fashion. The latter would have his work cut out as I had tasked him with creating a catwalk fashion show.

Dawa, the event manager, was in his element, rushing around having meetings to organise the running order and how the stage, lighting and seating would be erected. I didn't imagine everything would run to plan: orchestrating any event in India was always unpredictable.

'Just remember, India runs on "Indian Standard Time"', my friend Jan told me when I called for our weekly chat. 'Don't expect things to happen on schedule. They will eventually, but not in the way you planned.'

'Yes I know, Jan,' I wailed. 'But we have so little time and so much to do!'

'It doesn't help to get angry or frustrated, Linda,' she said soothingly. 'India works in its own special way and there's absolutely nothing you can do about it.'

I thought of Jan's words standing in the playground in the midday sun. It was the day of the event. The stage was still being built. I wanted to stomp around cracking my whip but when the chai wallah arrived announcing a tea break I decided to let it go. Everyone downed tools and took out their steel tiffin boxes. I sat down with Sonam and the workers. They had been doing a sterling job and I didn't want to spoil the day by shouting at everyone. I just had to trust it would all come together.

As the chai wallah poured my tea, he asked a flood of questions: 'Are you married Madam? How much money do you make? Do you sleep with your boyfriend?'

This last comment gained him a slap from Sonam. 'That's enough, my friend,' he said. 'Back to work.' We all fell about laughing.

HRH was due to arrive at 1pm and with only an hour to go we still had a lot to do. There were still a few nails to be banged in to the wooden stage; the red carpet needed to be laid and water splashed on the dusty trees. Most importantly, I needed to light the incense sticks we had positioned in buckets behind the Prince's chair. I was worried that the wafts of sewage coming from the nearby river might make him retch.

The clock was ticking and I realised that Norbu still had not arrived with my outfit. I had lost my hairbrush in the melee and had the sickening thought that I might have to welcome the Prince of Wales in my dirty black trousers, looking like I had walked through a hedge.

'Linda, time to get changed,' Sonam emerged looking handsome in his dark black *chuba* and white silk shirt. 'Your dress has arrived.'

I looked wildly around, taking in all the things that still needed to be done. 'Can you light the incense,' I bleated at him. 'There's still so much to be done.'

'Yes. Go, go, go!'

Norbu had done me proud. I threw on the dress and it fitted perfectly. It was a wraparound Tibetan *chuba*, made of peacock-blue silk, which shimmered all the way to the floor. Around the neckline there was intricate and sparkly embroidery in contrasting shades of blue. Norbu had chosen a pair of beautiful Rajasthan slippers and a turquoise necklace to match. I could have wept.

'Shame there isn't time for a shower,' I thought to myself, running my fingers through my hair as I dashed off to the transformed playground. I was about to clear away the tea cups that had been left lying around when my mobile phone rang.

'Hi Linda, Eric here. We are running a bit early – can we bring the Prince now?'

'Now?' I squeaked.

I looked at the men still laying the red flooring. 'Please,' I begged. 'Can you take one more trip around the block? Please…?'

I waited on the roadside, outside the gates of the school for the Prince and entourage to arrive. My phone rang again. This time it was one of the Scotland Yard officers.

'Two minutes and the Prince will be arriving,' he said. 'Are you in position?'

Prince Charles, dressed in a double-breasted navy pinstripe suit with a Remembrance Day poppy on his lapel, stepped out of the British High Commissioner's car into the heat and noise and chaos of a three-lane highway. Amazingly, he looked totally at ease.

I had rehearsed my curtsy and welcoming words: 'Your Royal Highness – thank you for coming,' but when the moment came, I opened my mouth but nothing came out. I gaped like a fish.

The Prince beamed at me. 'What a delight to be here. Thank you for inviting me.'

A moment later my wits returned and I was able to chat to the Prince as we entered the gates. Once inside, he moved from one entrepreneur to the next, asking questions and looking thoroughly engaged. I could tell he was enjoying himself. He stopped at Norbu's display, particularly taken with the unusual design on Norbu's shoulder bags, made of layer upon layer of silk. He showed them to his private secretary.

'These will make lovely presents,' he said. 'Well done. Stunning!'

Norbu beamed with pride. He had been working around the clock, not only on the clothes and accessories for his stand, but also on my dress and the outfits for the catwalk models. Five ultra-shy Tibetan office girls had been taught by Dawa, the event manager, how to move along the stage to music. It hadn't been an easy job. I had watched him earlier in the day calling out, 'Lift your heads! Stop looking at your toes! The Prince wants to see your beautiful smiles!' His tutelage had not been in vain. Now the models were smiling for all they were worth as they sashayed down the catwalk and I could tell the Prince was charmed.

As a grand finale we had laid on something very special. I had had to keep my surprise a secret as the Chinese had a habit of putting on pressure so that such events never happened. I asked Miss Tibet to come to the show. The Chinese, having occupied Tibet, don't recognise it as a country so they try their best to delete Miss Tibet from any global parades or competitions, putting pressure on the organisers to drop her from the pageant. I wasn't going to let that happen. We wanted to make a statement and what better way than to invite Miss India along with Miss Tibet for the event? I knew that if the beauty queens were seen together in fellowship the world would sit up and take notice. Now, as they walked along the catwalk, arm-in-arm like sisters, we all held our breath, mesmerised by their beauty and grace. They curtseyed to the Prince and he smiled, later standing to have his photo taken with the pair. The Tibetans cheered and the press went mad, camera bulbs popping furiously. The moment was captured forever in *Hello* magazine.

The Prince of Wales spent hours in the sweltering heat talking to each of our young Tibetan entrepreneurs. At one point a young Tibetan approached him, offering tea. We had been told he would not be able to accept any food or drink but he accepted the cup and drank. His interest and concern was evident in each conversation. Long after his allotted departure time the Prince finally took his leave. The inspiration and encouragement he gave to the group was priceless.

CHAPTER FIVE

IN GOOD COMPANY

Burma

In 2008, a global home furnishings company commissioned a report into one of its proposed supplier's factory conditions in Lahore, Pakistan. With its plentiful supply of timber and cheap labour, Lahore made perfect sense. But, when the report revealed that the factory employed workers under the age of sixteen, the company was thrown into a dilemma. On paper, the solution seemed obvious: only use business practises of which shareholders (and the Western world in general) would approve – get rid of all underage workers. Instead, the company decided to take a hard look at what effect doing so would have on the local community. What they discovered was that many of the children, if deprived of their livelihoods, would turn to street crime, prostitution – or simply starve. The company realised, although it seemed counterintuitive to do so, that acting responsibly meant employing these twelve- to sixteen-year-olds. But only for a limited number of hours a day. The other half of the working day would be spent at school. Strong and effective measures were put in place to protect these vulnerable youngsters. They are committed, in a joint project with Unicef and Save the Children, to help tens of thousands of children a year.

Knowing the troubled situation in Pakistan, I applauded the company's responsible attitude. I wasn't involved in the project but I do think it provides a good example of what many companies are trying to do. In the past three years I have been asked increasingly to help multinational companies set up community projects. These are companies who have a clear ethos: they intend to 'put back'; to support those people who live and work locally; to be sensitive to cultural issues; and to keep their own employees motivated. A company with the right ethos and a committed vision is a happy one.

In autumn 2008, I met up with David Arkless, Manpower Group's President of Corporate and Government Affairs. He needed my help to set up a project for Burmese refugees, in camps on the border between Thailand and Burma. I didn't hesitate to get involved. I would be working alongside Simon Matthews, Country Manager of Manpower, Thailand. He and I had worked together post-tsunami and on Princess Sirindhorn's project the year before. British by birth and married to a Thai woman, Simon is a charismatic leader with a powerful gift of inspiring others.

Manpower is a company committed to helping vulnerable communities across the world. In 2006, as part of The Council of Business Leaders that included Nike, Microsoft, Merck and Price Waterhouse Cooper, it made a commitment to partner with the UN Refugee Agency (UNHCR) to provide education to nine million refugee children, exiled in camps across the world. Simon's task was to involve his own staff in the education and skills training of Burmese refugees in Thailand, to prepare them for a new life in the USA, part of a large resettlement programme. We had already had a meeting to discuss some of the complex issues faced by the Thai and overseas governments and the aid agencies. There was little hope of repatriating the refugees in the near future and the situation in the camps wasn't ideal. There were few opportunities for work and education – basic human rights – in the camps. Resettlement to another country has become one of the best options. The Thai government agreed on a resettlement programme in 2005 as a form of 'burden-sharing' with the West. Currently, up to 20,000 are resettled in the USA every year.

As I walked into the lobby of the gleaming tower block in Bangkok which housed the Manpower offices, I wondered how Simon's staff would cope in the mud and squalor of the refugee camps. It was beautifully cool inside. There was a small coffee shop just inside the entrance where smartly-dressed office workers were chatting and sipping cappuccinos. I took a lift to the first floor and walked through the electric glass doors. Inside, all was quietly efficient, hushed and carpeted, a relief from the buzz and bustle of the busy city streets. An organised, high-tech world of computers, multi-media projectors and whiteboards. Rows of white tables and coloured chairs, a touch of dynamism to inspire the team creatively. The receptionist beamed at me.

'Linda, we've been expecting you. Let me show you to the meeting room.'

A minute later, members of staff began to gather in the room, bright-eyed with anticipation. It was a young team, dressed in fashionable clothes, the men in pastel shirts with contrasting ties, the women in pretty summer dresses and high heels. They brought with them the whiff of expensive aftershave and perfume.

Simon strode in and called out, 'Saw wa dee ka!' to everyone, then shook my hand warmly. 'What a great turnout. I'm delighted!'

After introducing me, Simon asked if any of his employees could tell him what Manpower's four pillars of social responsibility were. Eee, the marketing manager, called out from the back of the room.

'Workforce development. Disaster recovery. Reaching out to refugees. Combatting human trafficking.'

'Correct,' said Simon. 'And this project will come under reaching out to refugees.'

Simon had already told me that we'd have our work cut out to gather a team. Because of the difficult economic times, they would only be able to work on the project outside office hours. It was an incredible commitment. Many of them worked a twelve hour day, and now we were suggesting they gave up precious hours on the weekend. We weren't going to strongarm anyone – it wasn't worth it. If the project was to work, it needed a group prepared to make a commitment for a decent period. It needed enthusiasm as well as consistency. And it is true what they say: 'One volunteer is worth ten pressed men'.

Simon went on to remind the group of one of Manpower's main mission statements: to connect an individual to the dignity and independence of work. This is of particular relevance to the refugees who were not permitted to work inside or outside the camps.

For the past two decades Burmese refugee camps have become a fixture on the Thai-Burma border. They are now the second longest standing refugee settlement in the world. Since 1962 Burma has been a military dictatorship. Many of the refugees who fled to Thailand are the Karen people, an ethnic group which had experienced myriad human rights violations, including torture, rape and forced labour. Most came over the border, picking their way through landmines, only when they had exhausted all other means of survival. They are unwilling guests, hating that they've been forced to leave their country. Patriotic, they fight to retain their own identity, customs and religion.

The Thais are generally unwilling hosts, seeing the Burmese as a drain on their resources: either lazy and dependent on handouts or providing cheap labour and taking their jobs. Either way, they are unpopular. The refugees form a significant minority in Thailand. About 150,000 reside in nine camps, Mae Sot being the largest. Some have lived there for over 20 years. As Thai policy forbids refugee labour, only by going under the wire and working illegally outside the camp can additional items be purchased to supplement the camp rations. So it is that there is a willing pool of 80,000 under-paid and exploited migrant workers in the Mae Sot region alone, where factory owners see no need to pay a minimum wage or provide acceptable working conditions. It is ironic that the Thais think of the refugees as a drain on their resources. In fact, they make a significant contribution to the Thai economy. One visible result is that Mae Sot, over the years, has been transformed from a small trading post into a sizeable industrial zone.

After Simon had described the refugee situation briefly, he handed over to me. I sensed the mood had dipped so I decided to throw some questions to the floor and make the presentation more interactive. However powerfully Simon had introduced the project, the fact was that his employees were now faced with the idea of losing their free time as well as working with the Burmese, whom they neither trusted nor liked.

'What are you going to do today when you leave the office?' I asked. 'Chirawat. You start.'

Chirawat grinned at the group. He was an extrovert and a sharp dresser. 'I'm going to the mall to buy some sports shoes.' One of his friends gave a wolf whistle.

I went quickly round the group. 'Going to the movies'; 'Seeing my boyfriend' (another whoop from the crowd); 'Planning my holiday'; 'Playing on the internet.'

'Do you feel safe when you're doing these things?' I asked them.

'Of course!' came the chorus of replies.

I then asked them what they knew of the Burmese.

'My family always have Burmese maids,' a young woman said.

'And how's that been?' I asked.

She shrugged. 'Some are great. Like they're part of the family. Some unreliable. Steal. Disappear without warning.'

There were sounds of agreement from the group. I asked another what he knew of the refugees.

'They're cheap labour,' he said. 'I see it all the time at work. We try and place Thai people in a company and find it's full of illegal Burmese. Being paid half the salary. It's not right.'

'But why are the Burmese here? Why aren't they at home in their country?' I asked, scanning the room.

'Better conditions here,' one of the group spoke up. 'Life is easy.'

'All true,' I said.

Simon caught my eye, knowing I was on sensitive ground, encouraging me to go on. I told the group that I was going to show them three pictures that I had taken at my recce at the Mae Sot camp the previous week. I paused while they absorbed them, the cramped living conditions, the sea of mud.

'Can you imagine being born into such a situation and never knowing any of your freedoms?' I asked them. 'No trips to the mall? No popping to the supermarket to buy your favourite snack? No chance to watch the TV?

'There's an old Cherokee Indian saying: Before you judge a man, walk a mile in his moccasins,' I went on. 'Now I would like you to close your eyes for a moment. Imagine you are a Burmese refugee. Wear their shoes. See how it feels.'

Four months earlier, in October 2008, I had made my first reconnaissance visit to the refugee camp at Mae Sot. I was still over an hour's drive from the Thai Burmese border when my car was stopped at a heavily armed military checkpoint, an elaborate affair of barriers and barbed wire. It was to be the first of many. I had never seen such a high level of security around refugees. Sniffer dogs with their handlers patrolled the cars which were searched thoroughly, every bag opened and scrutinised. A tailback stretched out in each direction.

'What are they looking for?' I asked my driver.

'Stowaways, weapons, drugs,' he said. 'Much illegal traffic on this border. Army very busy.'

I looked at the powerful spotlights and cameras surrounding the interrogation area. The driver read my thoughts.

'They don't come through in cars,' he said. 'The jungle is very thick. Easy to hide. Many snakes.'

I shuddered, looking out at the lush jungle on either side of the road. It was like something out of *Jurassic Park*. The plants were on an epic scale. Giant tree ferns waving fronds in the breeze, looking like fingers waiting to catch you. We set off again and I held my breath as we climbed steep hills and hurtled down the other side, a combination of hairpin bends, blind corners and sheer descents. The driver drove fast, overtaking struggling lorries on the hills which belched out great clouds of black smoke. I was relieved when we parked up outside the offices of ZOA, the charity with whom Manpower were proposing to team up.

I was met by Ka, one of the key people at ZOA. I warmed to him immediately. He was a handsome man in his thirties, with soft features that looked more Tibetan or Mongolian than Thai. It turned out that he was Karen Burmese, married to a Thai woman. I quickly came to see what an asset he was to the charity, able to speak the Karen dialect as well as fluent Thai and English.

He led me to his jeep. 'Your permit slip is only for today,' he said. 'No time to waste, I'm afraid.'

It was an hour's drive to Mae La Camp, the largest of the seven camps dotted along the border. Ka briefed me on the way.

'We get a lot of flare-ups along the border between the ethnic armies and the military,' he told me. 'Mae La is only eight kilometres from Burma.'

He told me that any minute now I might catch a glimpse of the notorious Thahan Phran – or Black Rangers – a paramilitary light infantry force that patrols the borders of Thailand. Part of the Royal Thai Army, the name means 'hunter soldiers' and, unlike the Border Patrol Police, they are trained for combat.

'It's a very porous border. We get new arrivals most days,' he said. 'Many of them injured by landmines.'

We talked of the resettlement programme and I asked him, 'Don't you think it will only serve to sweep the refugee problem under the carpet? It doesn't exactly keep up the pressure on the Thai government and Burmese junta to work out a solution nearer to home.'

'Certainly a valid point,' he said. 'It's not going to help the democracy movement if the resistance to the junta is taken away.'

He went on to tell me about one of the most pressing problems in the camps. Certain Western nations, including Finland and Canada, would only take in the more educated and skilled refugees. As a result of this brain drain, there were few teachers or medics left to work in the camps.

'We've got as many as 20,000 uneducated refugees, without language or local knowledge, being dumped in the States with little support,' he said. 'That's where we need help.'

'So you're hoping Manpower staff can create an education package?' I said.

'What teachers we have don't have the skills. They're barely trained,' Ka said. 'This needs to be efficient. We only get three or four weeks warning when a refugee's name comes up.'

I had heard some of the stories. The Karen people had no idea how to perform the most basic of tasks in their new country. They had no notion of saving money, having existed always on a hand-to-mouth basis. The Western notion of timekeeping was a mystery to them, which had proved a problem with employers.

'It's terrible, Linda,' Ka said. 'Even on the plane on the way to New York they get into difficulties. They worry that they will have to pay to use the toilet. So they hold on, the whole flight. One of the older women collapsed.'

My mind boggled. I tried to imagine the refugees, one moment in a jungle war zone, the next in an urban metropolis. 'Culture shock' isn't enough to describe it. Things would have to change.

After driving for an hour, the jeep rounded a bend and there I saw it, nestled at the base of a beautiful green mountain, thick in vegetation. An endless floating canopy of overlapping sundried brown leaves, crisp and curled up at the edges: the roofs of the camp dwellings. They lined the road on one side, right up to the wire of the camp boundary. We passed small groups of children, jumping up and down and waving, behind the fence. Then, after one last checkpoint, we were through the high iron gate of the camp's main entrance.

Ka jumped out of the jeep and went over to report in at the Camp Commander's office. He had told me that foreigners were forbidden to stay overnight at the camp – even the ones working for the aid agencies – so I would have to be signed out by nightfall.

He got back in the car. 'Apparently there were some gang fights last night,' he said. 'They are a bit twitchy. Scared you might be a journalist. The army hates to lose face.'

I asked Ka what the gang fighting was about. He told me it

was an increasing problem with sixty-five per cent of the population in the camp being under twenty-five years of age.

'You can imagine what happens,' he said. 'All that boredom and lack of hope. Fighting is a release. They pick on the new arrivals. Easy prey.'

We drove down a rough dirt road lined with deep, muddy furrows. The brakes groaned as the jeep slid its way down the hill.

'Lucky you've got four-wheel drive,' I said.

'One of our jeeps got stuck here last year. We had to get an elephant to pull it out. Very embarrassing!'

The mud was all-pervasive. It stained the bodies of everyone living in the camp. At a water pump, rows of buckets were waiting to be filled and taken back to the little shelters built on stilts. I doubted the women bothered to wash their children. They would be fighting a losing battle.

We pulled up outside the Camp Leader's house. As I picked my way carefully to the steps, I was touched to see that they had made me a welcome sign which was hanging on the porch. 'A warm and hearty welcome to Linda Cruse.' Standing in front of it was the Camp Leader, Dee, a short, stout man with receding grey hair. He greeted me warmly. I added my shoes to a mountain of muddy flip-flops at the doorway and went through. Inside, the Camp Committee were sitting cross legged on the bamboo floor, each wearing the Karen traditional dress of red and blue woven shirt or tunic, a matching woven shoulder bag, containing their most treasured possessions, on their laps. I joined them and we spoke of the main issues affecting the camp.

One of the unforeseen problems that had emerged in recent months was that the influx of aid money from overseas and the resettlement programme had drawn the poor from other communities to the camps. Many Bangladeshis and Indians had made their way through Burma on foot, with the hope of being resettled.

'It's one of the reasons that the refugees are not allowed to work,' Dee told me. 'The government doesn't want to encourage more of them to cross the border.'

Ka had already touched on the sensitive political situation with Burma, made more so by the presence of the refugee camps. Thailand had to play a careful game if it was to preserve its relationship with Burma, an important trading neighbour. Burma is a country rich in mineral deposits, natural gas and timber. Some nations – Russia and China especially – compete for these commodities, while others favour a boycott, outraged at the military junta's brutal suppression of pro-democracy advocates.

We didn't stop long. Soon I was being taken on a tour of the camp. Everywhere we went the story was the same. No work, low self-esteem, and boredom that spread like a deadly virus, infecting everyone, especially the young people. Parents worried about their children. One woman described the sex trafficking that was rife in the border area. She said that the Thai and Burmese drug lords were becoming richer and more powerful by the day, growing opium and churning out methamphetamines. She feared for her teenage daughter. So many girls, with little to keep them in the camps, were being lured into sex work.

I met some of the students at the community centre. Ka told me to be prepared for a bombardment of questions: 'Time is one thing they have way too much of.'

Ka was greeted by friendly boos and a football thrown directly at his chest. There were over twenty students in the centre. He took me over to meet one of them, a boy of sixteen, with dyed red hair and elaborate tattoos.

'Linda, this is Idy,' Ka said, patting the boy on the shoulder before disappearing to the back of the room to see how the food was coming along.

'I love your tattoos,' I said to him.

'The monks gave them to me, for protection,' he said. 'I move around a lot so I need it.'

I asked Idy how he'd come to be here. He told me he was the oldest boy in the family. His father had been killed by a landmine whilst trying to reach the camp. It was up to him to provide for the family now. They couldn't survive on camp rations so he had to go under the wire and earn some extra money in town.

A boy in a red bandana with an angry knife wound on his cheek, who was sitting next to Idy, said, 'If they catch him, he'll be sent back over the border.'

'The Thais know it, so they do what they like to us,' Idy said. 'I had one boss, didn't give me anything at pay day. Said if I made a fuss he'd report me.'

He told me that they were offered vocational training in the camps: weaving, stove making, basket weaving, car mechanics, haircutting, cooking.

He finished the paper aeroplane he had been making and launched it into the air. 'It keeps us busy. But for what? Most of us don't bother to go any more.'

I could see his point. Khun Ka was right. Resettlement must be the best option these young people had. Otherwise it was a downward spiral.

As if he knew I would need to see something uplifting before the day came to a close, Ka had left the best for last. A pilot project, funded by ZOA, it allowed a group of refugees to work outside the camp. Ka was hugely heartened by its success.

'Come, I'll show you.' he said. 'It's a small farm, just one plot of land at this stage. Across the road from the camp. It's amazing. Only a few steps away, but it's given them such a morale-boost, having to leave the camp to go to work.'

We signed out and left the camp. I followed Ka up a steep dirt track to where a small group of men were sitting under a tree. They were painfully thin. Ka told me each was blind. Three of them were missing limbs and were wearing old-fashioned prostheses, flesh-coloured above the ankle, but with black feet with mock toes below. It looked sinister, as though the foot was rotting. But what seemed strangest of all, considering what poor shape the group was in, was the joking, laughing and sheer joy that emanated from it. They called out to us as we approached and Ka introduced me.

One of the group, a man missing most of his fingers, said to Ka, 'Take her to see our work. We've cleared a big patch, ready for planting tomorrow.'

Ka joked with him, and all the men laughed uproariously. Once we had walked on and were out of earshot, I asked what had happened to the man.

'That's Saw,' he said. 'Amazing man. Former freedom fighter.'

'What happened to his fingers?' I asked.

'He was tortured. They were chopped off. That was before a landmine blew off his leg and blinded him.'

'I can't get over how happy they seem,' I said.

'They love the project. It's given them a purpose,' he said. 'They're great workers.'

We climbed further up the steep dirt slope until we had a view of the whole area. A large chunk of the hillside had been cultivated.

'Over there is the frog farm where we harvest the legs for sale to restaurants,' Ka pointed to two big concrete tanks. 'And in the shed there, we've started a mushroom farm. A high-value crop. We're hoping it will fund a lot of new projects.'

'How many have you got working here?' I asked.

'A hundred and sixty,' he said. 'We've chosen them carefully. Women-headed households, the disabled and sexually vulnerable. We've allowed them to choose what they grow,'

This was music to my ears. I asked him whether this had sparked a real entrepreneurial spirit in them.

'The latest new business idea is to grow flowers,' he said. 'It's been brilliant. They're selling them in the camps for weddings, funerals and birthdays.'

He told me that the success of the flower business had fired up the refugees. Now they were asking to set up worm farms, hives, and wanted to plant more high-value vegetables. A true sign of the success of the project was that twenty-seven of the initial eighty who started the project saved their 1800 baht per month salary given by ZOA and went on to invest it in their own business within the camp. The latest initiative was chilli growing.

'The aid agencies could no longer afford to give them chillis so, guess what, they're growing their own.'

We walked into a small office and sat near a fan. Ka took a couple of cans from the fridge and we drank, thirsty now.

'In January we had the first sign of growth from the land,' he said, clapping his hands together, delighting in the memory. 'Our greatest joy was to hear the refugees singing in the fields.'

ZOA had been careful not to step on the toes of the Thai locals, many of whom are very poor. The pilot project outside the camp involved both Burmese and Thais and the charity did not want to create any more animosity or jealousy than there already was. Dissolving barriers between the two races, both fiercely patriotic groups with many reasons not to like each other, would be an important factor in the Manpower project. We would be bringing together rich city kids and traumatised rural farmers and the only way we could bridge the gap of distrust that divided them was to have them meet, face to face. Simon Matthews had been certain that his staff, who had been under huge pressure of late to deliver in a tough economic market, would benefit from the diversion that this charity project offered. He was right.

Twenty-five Manpower employees signed up. Of those, Simon and I selected four team leaders whom we would take on an insight trip to Mae Sot. Their objective was to work out a plan, having met the refugees they would be helping, in line with their mission statement which was:

'To equip refugees with skills necessary to become socially and economically successful citizens in resettlement countries.'

The four team leaders were nervous at first, concerned that they wouldn't be able to communicate, and that the refugees might be hostile to them. I assured them that this would not be the case, telling them:

'Just be open-minded. Ask questions and then listen without judging. You may not agree with all you hear. Allow them to share their fears, their hopes, their dreams. Get to know them as people. See where they live, what they do, how they feel.'

At Mae La camp, the group was taken first to an English language class. The teacher asked them if they would like to sing an Abba song the Burmese students were learning. For a moment, I saw the team dither, looking at each other, embarrassed. Then a painfully thin Karen boy took Chanarat's arm, encouraging him to get to his feet and to join in. Soon we were all standing in a tight group, singing our hearts out.

UNHCR were impressed with the energy shown by the Manpower volunteers. It was agreed that, in partnership with ZOA and IOM, the volunteers would redesign IOM's current 25-hour orientation programme, including the English language skills component, and also develop a three-week to three-month curriculum, based on ZOA's current English language curriculum. For the pilot, fifty refugees would be selected, from the thousand whom had been formally approved and selected for resettlement to the USA, but who had not yet been given a departure date. Of that number, an initial group of fifteen would be trained.

Once we had listed the main issues: high teacher turnover; teaching methods; teacher quality; and lack of teaching aids and illustrations, the team set about coming up with standardised curriculum and lesson plans that any new teacher could pick up and run with, and teaching materials, including scrapbooks of pictures and flashcards. They had witnessed Burmese students learning by rote, and devised a new set of interactive, fun activities that would help them retain information more effectively.

My job was done. I was confident that my small group of four had everything they needed to empower their own teams which, in turn, would teach a new group – Burmese this time – to be camp trainers. It was a process, like wildfire, that spread – once started, difficult to put out. And with it, goodwill and understanding between two groups of people who had formerly been on different sides.

PART 3:
POVERTY AND AID

'Be the change you want to see in the world.'
Mahatma Gandhi

CHAPTER SIX

HELP IN THE HIMALAYAS

Nepal

In 1953, Edmund Hillary and his Sherpa companion Tenzing Norgay pitched their tent beneath the summit of Mount Everest, at 27,900 feet. On the morning of the climb, Hillary emerged from the tent to find that his boots had frozen solid. After two hours spent thawing the boots, the pair set out for the summit with 30lb packs on their backs. When faced with a 40 foot sheer rock face Hillary remained undeterred and edging himself in a crack in this great wall of rock, which was later named the Hillary Step, he began inching his way with his trusty companion towards the summit.

You only have to say 'Nepal' and people's eyes mist over with romantic stories of courage and adventure. They think of brothers in arms scaling the highest mountain on Earth. Or of Gurkha soldiers, wielding their terrifying *kukri* blades, striking terror in the hearts of their enemies. In more peaceful moments they might dream of Kathmandu, a city immortalised in the songs of hippy folk bands. Love and Peace.

Then other facts jostle for room. Hillary himself spent the rest of his days raising funds to help the Sherpa people of the Himalayas. This is revealing. As is the sheer number of young hopefuls wanting to join the Gurkhas. As many as 28,000 try out for only 300 places each year. As they battle to be selected, running uphill with a 70lb basket of rocks on their backs, each of them has one goal in mind: getting out of Nepal. Around thirteen hundred other Nepali men and women leave their homeland every day, bound for Malaysia, Qatar and other countries in the Middle East. Unless they find the means to feed their families they face starvation. The hard fact is that Nepal is one of the poorest countries on Earth.

There is also no halo of love and peace over Kathmandu. For the past fifty years political instability has brought the country to its knees. At the time I was working there, between 2001 and 2003, it was a dangerous place to be. Maoist rebels had stepped up their campaign of violence in a decade-long bloody civil war, seeking an end to the monarchy. In 2000, there was an attempt at peace talks but by the following November the Maoists ended a four month truce. In that same month, a State of Emergency was announced by King Gyanendra who ordered his army to crush the rebels. For the next two years it was all out war.

Since my first visit in 2001, I have continued to work in Nepal and my love for the country and its people deepens with every visit. Over the past decade I have helped numerous NGOs on all kinds of projects: anti-trafficking; refugees, schools, orphanages, HIV AIDS and women's cooperatives. A third of Nepal's 28 million inhabitants live below the poverty line. It is the poorest country in South Asia and over 70% of Nepalis live on less than $1.25 a day. Most households have little or no access to basic social services such as health care, education, clean drinking water and sanitation services.

In what I now see is a delicious irony, I first visited Kathmandu in 2001 for a rest cure. I needed to get away from the chaos of India for a while. My doctor had suggested a break after I had fainted at Delhi airport, suffering from burnout. There were two Tibetan refugee camps in Nepal and the Tibet Relief Fund were happy for me to visit them and add to their body of research. Although Kathmandu did not exactly spell love and peace in these war-torn days there was still something special about the place and I decided to stay on for a while.

Thamel, in the heart of the city, was a mecca for backpackers, trekkers and mountaineers of every nationality who headed there to shop and have fun. Shops and stalls selling Buddhist statues and shawls, puppets and paper lanterns shared space with trekking stores. Tourists happily picked their way through this shoppers' paradise of hippy souvenirs and the latest North Face climbing and camping equipment. In the evenings, on every street corner or crowded nightclub, bands played seventies classic rock covers until the small hours.

It was at a nightclub that I first met Karma. He came up to me, intrigued no doubt by seeing a Western woman in the crowd of jostling partygoers. Tall and broad, with flat, almost Mongolian features, there was something so confident about him that when he asked me to join his group of friends I felt compelled to follow him. I was quickly to learn that Karma's confidence was matched by a warm-hearted desire to do good. As soon as he heard that I was involved in a charitable project he made sure that I had all the help I needed. It turned out that he was one of a rare breed – a free spirit as well as being dependable. Over the years he was to become my fixer, requisition officer, PA and travel companion rolled into one.

Ours was a friendship which grew quickly, helped by the fact that Karma managed to save my life more than once. I could not have survived – and I certainly wouldn't have achieved very much – without Karma. His local knowledge and the respect others had for him was invaluable. Without him I would have come unstuck in the early days in Nepal. He took care of my health and safety, making sure that my street food was well-cooked and that my utensils were clean(ish). He tasted my drinks to check that they weren't 'duplicate' (chemically spiked). On his bike he took me to places others rarely visited, negotiating treacherous mountain roads and helping me to find, meet and talk to the people we both wanted to help. Karma taught me to see and honour the invisible poor in Nepal, not the beggars and refugees but a whole exploited and downtrodden underclass. People such as the lowly guard who stood all night at a car park. Karma would always go out of his way to shake their hand, say a kind word, give them a coin. He was a master at random acts of kindness.

At first, Karma's friends were wary. When he brought me over to their table at the nightclub the night we first met, they seemed uncomfortable. At one point, one of them took Karma aside and I could tell from the man's tense whispering and nervous glances that he was warning Karma not to associate with a Westerner. Karma explained to me later that in a country where the police and local government officials were invariably corrupt it was safest to keep your head down. Not get noticed. And then, a few weeks after our first meeting, something happened which helped me understand their point of view.

We were in the same nightclub at 11pm on a Saturday night and the dance floor was heaving. We were taking a break from dancing, drinking our beers at a table near the bar when the music suddenly stopped and the lights were thrown on. For a moment, it was like I was a teenager again; I half expected a teacher to step forward and read the riot act. Instead, six policemen barged through the swing doors of the club. Everyone stayed still, rooted to the spot. Apart from the noise of their heavy boots clattering on the polished floor, everything was silent. The uniformed men stood in a line and shouted, brandishing heavy wooden sticks at us. I could feel the tension in the room. Not fear exactly, but a kind of waiting as if a breath had been taken and not yet expelled. There was anticipation, as if each person was waiting to see which one of them would be picked out. I sensed that it had happened before and that they knew the drill.

One of the policemen saw me and a handful of other foreigners. In broken English, he bellowed at us, 'Get out. Go! Go now!' Then, when some of the Nepalis started sidling to the door, he barked, 'All Nepalis stay.'

A group of tourists stampeded for the staircase. I didn't move. Alok, the youngest of our group, said to me, 'Go with the others!'

I was furious. 'Why should I? They've no right...'

'They will get what they came for. Just go.'

When Karma saw that I was not getting up he pulled me to my feet and gently pushed me towards the door.

'Go' he whispered. 'Please. There is nothing you can do.'

I started heading for the door then thought the better of it. Instead, I walked up to the policeman who had been doing the shouting and stood facing him, eye to eye. He grabbed my arm and tried to push me in the direction of the door but I stood firm. His pungent body odour made me want to heave.

'I leave when they leave,' I said, fists clenched at my sides.

The more he shouted, the more I stood firm. By now, his colleagues had formed a circle around us, curious to see which one of us would break the standoff. The policeman looked away first. A moment later, with a quick motion to his men, they left.

Later, I sat with Karma and his friends at our regular roadside café, sharing a jug of beer.

'You're one crazy woman, Linda,' Karma said.

I sipped my beer as the guys chatted animatedly in Hindi.

'What would they have done?' I asked Karma.

Without saying anything Mingma, one of Karma's friends, bent to slip off his shoes and socks. He showed me the soles of his feet which were scarred with blackened puncture marks.

'First they tie our hands behind our backs,' Karma said. 'Then they put our ankles in...' He searched for the word.

'Stocks,' I suggested.

'Right.

'Then wood with nails in it. They beat us on our feet.'

'What are they wanting?' I asked.

'Money,' Alok said, giggling nervously. 'Money to buy tea!'

Karma explained that if someone was not able to give even the smallest bribe, enough for a cup of tea, they would be beaten. No one complained. To do so was seen as a sign of weakness. Anyway, the police stuck together. If anyone spoke out, they would simply make up a worse charge. Better to tough it out. I blustered about the injustice of it all and Karma watched me, smiling.

'Welcome to Nepal, Linda.'

He raised his glass to me and his friends joined him in the toast. I sensed that I was now a fully fledged member of their gang and I couldn't help blushing with pleasure.

It was while I was visiting Boudhanath, one of the largest Stupas in the world and one of its holiest Buddhist sites, that I spotted a small advertisement.

'Nathiagali School. We need your help. Volunteers required urgently. Tibetan nomad children from Dolpa. Please call Lama Tashi.'

Back at my Kathmandu guest house I called the number and spoke to Lama Tashi. The next day I paid the school a visit. At the gate he was waiting to greet me. He had an almost uncanny resemblance to images of a laughing Buddha, his smile so broad that his eyes were almost completely lost in the creases.

Welcome to Nathiagali School,' his deep voice boomed out.

At the sound of Lama Tashi's voice two little boys appeared through the door of the building behind and ran to catch hold of his legs. It was hard to tell how old they were. Their shaven heads looked too large for their undersized bodies and their eyes appeared old and tired.

'Come on, children,' Lama Tashi said, leading us to the doorway. 'Let's get Linda some tea.'

Inside, in a dimly lit, warm room a woman was standing by a small stove slowly stirring rice porridge in a large tin pot.

'Lunch,' Lama Tashi said. 'Fills the children's stomachs up.'

We sat down and one of the little boys jumped on his knee.

'This is Rinzin,' he said, squeezing the boy's hand. 'He arrived last week. Still feeling a bit homesick.'

'Where is he from?' I asked.

'The north of Dolpo,' he said. 'Most of the children are from there. North-west Nepal, bordering Tibet. I grew up there. In Lhori.'

'What's it like?'

'Big and high up,' he said, laughing. 'Upper Dolpo is one of the highest human settlements in the world. Perfect place for snow leopards, wolves and black bears to hide.'

Although it sounded a harsh place to live I could tell that Lama Tashi loved his childhood place.

'The houses have no windows at all. The villages look like forts.'

He glanced down tenderly at the little boy in his lap. 'They are a tough lot,' he said. 'This little fellow has tended yak for ten months of the year, from the time he could walk.'

I asked him if the same had been the case for him.

'Yes,' he said. 'But I was lucky. When I said I wanted to be a monk my parents allowed me to leave Dolpo and study.'

My tea arrived. Lama Tashi apologised that it wasn't butter tea, just hot water and herbs.

'We've run out of butter and tea,' he said, adding that getting enough provisions and making them last was a real difficulty for the school.

After the tea he took me on a tour of the building, starting with the boys' dormitory. Rows of bunk beds, with hardly space to squeeze between them, were crammed from wall to wall. Lama Tashi told me that little ones like Rinzin shared beds. It saved on space and gave them comfort as they were not used to sleeping alone. There was minimal bedding. Most beds had neither pillow or blanket, just an old, stained mattress.

A bell rang and suddenly the room was filled with children, most aged between three and six. They were dressed in a motley selection of ill-fitting clothes and were crusted with dirt. Lama Tashi read my mind.

'We have eighty children and one bathroom,' he said. 'We only have two *amalas* – house mothers – so it's quite a task to keep them clean.'

He told me that in Dolpa washing was considered an unhealthy, harmful practice. Some people would go through a whole lifetime without ever taking a bath. He waved his hand in front of his nose, eyes disappearing again in the folds of his face as he smiled.

A little girl took my hand. She told me her name was Dorjee and asked if I'd come and see their garden. Lama Tashi explained that they were in the process of making a kitchen garden as they wanted the school to be as self-sufficient as possible. The children had devised a rota and worked hard. I tried to imagine the average eight year old in the UK being responsible in this way. We walked outside. The courtyard was stony and dusty. Kathmandu suffered from clouds of pollution from the brick factories that surrounded the city and every time a motorbike passed by or a child kicked around a football clouds of dust were thrown up. Dorjee proudly showed me rows of carrots and potatoes, and the herb patch that had supplied my tea. The few plants that had managed to push through the stony ground were struggling for life in the dust. She bent to pick up some stones, removing them carefully, and we watered some of the shoots. I wished that the vegetable patch would do its job of feeding the children but I thought it might take rather more than a wing and a prayer.

We passed through a narrow alley and entered a large piece of wasteland bordered by a high red-brick wall.

'Our new playground,' Lama Tashi said. 'We are very lucky to have an outside place to play.'

It was empty – no swings or goalposts. Nothing.

'To be free to play...not look after sheep and yak all day...That's why my brother and I set up the school.'

'Do any of the children ever get to visit their homes again?' I asked.

'Some of the children are orphans but the ones with parents don't get to see them more than once a year, if at all,' he said. 'The journey is so difficult. The area is cut off by snow for half the year.'

I thought of those children destined never to see their parents again. It was a hard thought to bear.

'We can offer them a better life. Free education,' Lama Tashi said consolingly. 'Their parents are happy that their children will be well looked after.'

As soon as we were back inside the school a middle-aged Nepali man in jeans and T-shirt came up to us. He introduced himself as Kalden, a teacher who was responsible for several subjects: English, Nepali, science and art. He greeted me warmly then turned to Lama Tashi.

'We have a new arrival,' he said. 'A two-year-old. I don't know what to do. We have no room for him.'

Tashi Lama turned to me. 'Let's go,' he said.

He explained as we followed Kalden that word of the school was spreading quickly around Dolpa. Families just turned up. Sending them away would break your heart. They had a three-week gruelling trek to reach Kathmandu which cost more money than they could afford.

A wizened man wearing a tall dusty black felt hat sat on the bench. His head drooped with fatigue and in his lap a tiny boy wrapped in soiled rags lay sleeping. He saw us approach and made to stand up.

'The journey must have been exhausting,' Lama Tashi told him, motioning him to stay seated. 'Stay overnight and rest. Have some warm food.'

The old man thanked him, bowing his head. He said that he needed to get straight back as the main salt-trading season was about to start and he was needed at home. It was hard to think of him turning around and suffering another three weeks of hard travel without so much as one night's rest. He told us that his sister, the boy's mother, had died in childbirth and that the boy had no one to care for him now.

'We know Karma is safe with you.'

The boy looked severely malnourished. He certainly couldn't be turned away.

Lama Tashi was briskly efficient. 'The first thing we need to do is attack the lice,' he said. 'Are you any good at that?'

'No problem,' I said, rolling up my sleeves. 'I used to be a school nurse many moons ago.'

Lama Tashi handed me a bottle of fluorescent green liquid, a fine comb and some scissors. With my other arm I scooped up the boy. Two hours later Dawa was dressed in fresh clothes, clean and deloused. I left him being fed porridge in the warmth of the kitchen and made my way to Lama Tashi's office. There I asked him what other help he needed and whether he had specific projects in mind.

'I want them to learn how to be children, how to play,' he said. 'I want to see them singing, making paper planes, drawing and painting, hearing bedtime stories. You see, Linda, their childhood has not started yet.'

'OK,' I said. 'I'll see what I can do. Anything else on your wish list?'

'Pyjamas!' he said. 'The children have two sets of day clothes. They wear one set day and night for a week before they change.'

'I see,' I said, making a list. 'Anything else?'

'Food. If we can get funding for some fruit or eggs. A banana a week, maybe?'

I nodded. That was the easy part.

After I left I went back to my guest house and called my daughter, Gail. She's a natural carer and I knew she would be a real asset to the school if she could come out as a volunteer for a few weeks. She had worked on projects before and is enormously creative. Children have always loved being around her.

A couple of weeks later Gail struggled out of the airport with armloads of luggage and hand baggage. Tall and blonde, she towered over the Nepalis.

'I kept thinking of things we'd need!' she laughed as I relieved her of some of it.

Later, at the orphanage, we carried the bags into the room we had decided would be the playroom. It was empty, other than a threadbare carpet on the floor.

'Perfect,' Gail said. 'Plenty of space to play!'

She took a CD player out of one of her bags. Soon music filled the room as we unpacked the rest of her stuff; she had brought reams of coloured paper, crayons, glue and gold and silver stars. We laid them out and waited for the children to arrive.

When they came into the room their eyes were as big as saucers. They had no idea what to do.

'Tashi Delek. Namaste,' Gail said, smiling. 'Today we are going to make paper hats.'

Blank faces stared at her.

'We will cut them out, colour them in and decorate them,' she said. 'How does that sound?'

Still the children didn't move. Finally, one of the older boys spoke. He asked where she wanted them all to sit. Once Gail had told him that she wanted them in groups of four they started to move, slowly, not daring to touch anything. As we helped them cut and colour their paper hats, hardly anyone spoke. Instead of scribbling freely, they painstakingly coloured inside the lines. Little by little they relaxed into the task but there was a curiously work-like quality to everything they did.

'I see what Lama Tashi meant, Mum,' Gail said later. 'They do need to learn how to play. Right from the very beginning, as if they were babies again.'

Gail stayed for three weeks. Whenever she wasn't bent over the wash tub scrubbing the children or their clothes she was singing songs with them, doing face painting or teaching them games. I managed to organise funding for pyjamas and food. Karma was brilliant and set out to source everything the school needed. He even managed to find a Father Christmas outfit so that we could have a Christmas party at the school.

When Lama Tashi offered to dress up as Father Christmas I was a little taken aback.

'But you are a Buddhist monk!' I said. 'What would His Holiness think?'

'I would like to be Father Christmas,' he repeated. 'I will practice my "Ho ho ho"!'

I shrugged, laughing. 'Okay then.'

On the day of the party we secured cushions around his midriff and stuck on his beard. He made an excellent Father Christmas. All day long he 'Ho-ho-hoed' and laughed so much that his eyes disappeared into the creases of his round cheeks.

Three months after I arrived in Nepal, I set out with Karma to find a village in the east of the country, four hours north of a hill station named Hille. I had been tasked by one of the local NGOs to conduct a basic needs assessment as well as looking out for signs of human trafficking. The confusion of the civil war had led to an increase in the number of girls being drugged and kidnapped and the NGO wanted to know the scale of the problem. Most girls, I had been told, were taken to Mumbai and forced to work in brothels. Some were as young as twelve.

Before we left, Karma had suggested that it might be safer if we travelled in a group but I thought he was being over-cautious. Later, I wished that I had listened to him.

We had to go through numerous checkpoints. Maoist rebels usually armed their pillion riders as they could more easily wield a gun having both arms free. As a result I had to dismount and join a queue at each checkpoint for an arms inspection. As soon as the soldiers saw that I was a foreigner they brought me to the front of the line but it still slowed our progress. On the road, Karma rode fast and confidently, honking his way past huge lines of Tata trucks. Up front, the cabs of the trucks were edged with fairy lights and on their rear ends the all-seeing eye glared at us as we overtook. The drivers would flick a switch as we passed them and a vast array of trumpety horns on the roofs of their cabs would play a multitude of tunes. Although invariably drunk or buzzed on stimulant drinks to keep themselves awake, they were not half as dangerous as the drivers of the local minibuses who drove at breakneck speed, overtaking three abreast on blind corners. Karma told me that they were paid an attractive bonus, calculated on the speed of their journey, so were prepared to risk their lives. Every now and again we passed the crumpled shells of vehicles which had not made it.

Karma and I were on a trail bike so it was relatively easy to take a break from the chaos of the main road. Whenever he could, he turned off the highway, escaping onto rough, stony roads chiselled out of the mountainside. It was not much safer on these mountain passes but it was a blessing to be free of the pollution and noise. We stopped frequently to answer the cries of the troubled bike. Only a few army-controlled petrol pumps had clean, undoctored fuel. The rest, especially in the outlying areas, were invariably contaminated and clogged up the arteries of the engine. In a poor country like Nepal, people are used to fixing things with anything that comes to hand. Whatever can be welded, stapled, glued or nailed is repaired, however old or defunct. There was no shortage of mechanics to tend to Karma's bike and they would use a variety of makeshift tools. The funnel used to pour in the oil was a large rolled-up leaf and the humble coat hanger, manipulated into all sorts of shapes, turned out to be a most effective multi-tool. It was only ever a temporary fix and we always had to stop again after a couple of hours.

Because of the army roadblocks and repeated breakdowns, our journey took far longer than we anticipated. There was a curfew at 8pm and Karma decided we should stop at a friend's house for the night. It was a typical wooden farmer's home on stilts with the ground floor reserved for the animals. It was a simple but functional place with squat toilets across the yard. The men of the house greeted us with a warm Namaste, palms together with a nod of the head. The women hung back at first, their hands held up in front of their faces, giggling shyly.

We sat around a bonfire outside, eating dhal, vegetables and rice, while the men told stories. Later one of them played a guitar. In the firelight I could see the shadows of scars crisscrossing their faces. I noticed that one of the men was missing a finger, a calling card of the Maoists. At one point I heard the sound of what I took to be fireworks. I asked one of the men if the village was holding a festival. I felt very foolish and not a little apprehensive when he replied that it was gunfire. A raid on the local police station had been predicted that night.

The chilly air finally drove us all indoors and we climbed the ladder to the first floor. Once we were all inside, the ladder was removed and the trap door bolted shut. I hoped I wouldn't need the toilet before morning. As was the custom, all eight of us lay down together on the floor, lined up in rows like sardines in a tin. I was the last to lie down and as I carefully picked my way across the sleeping bodies I noticed that each man was holding his *kukri*. They were unsheathed. I felt both fascinated and repelled. I had heard that in times past if a *kukri* was drawn in battle it had to taste blood. If not, its owner had to cut himself before returning it to its sheath. I hoped it was just a myth.

The next morning the old man of the group saw me watching him clean his *kukri*. He did so with great tenderness. He asked me if I would like a lesson. Before I could respond he leapt nimbly to his feet and started to demonstrate the moves. He showed me that you had to first slap the knife against the skin of your opponent, next turning the blade quickly with a flick of the wrist, then slicing firmly downwards. He gave me the knife and my arm buckled under the weight of it. I remembered a British diplomat in Delhi once telling me a story. Apparently an angry crowd had gathered in the streets of the city, preparing to riot. The police and paramilitary had arrived armed with rifles, but the crowd refused to budge. Things were getting nasty, a powder-keg ready to explode. Then a group of Gurkhas showed up with their *kukris* drawn. In seconds the protesters stopped what they were doing and walked away in silence. I could well believe it.

We left later that morning, each man embracing Karma firmly. They warned him to be careful and I sensed that they were concerned that we were setting out on our own, without back-up. We travelled fast on the windy, mountain track. The small villages we passed seemed oddly deserted. I had a distinct feeling that we were being watched. I felt unnerved by the quietness and realised that my eyes had been searching continuously for signs of life. Occasionally, when we passed through a small settlement, I thought I saw something moving in the shadows – a flash of colour – but otherwise the only signs of life were the birds of prey circling high above us, occasionally diving to spear a small creature for dinner.

By late afternoon I needed a break. I desperately wanted to stretch my legs.

'Can we stop?'

'Not here.'

'Please Karma, my back is aching,' I begged. 'And I need the toilet.'

We continued to bump our way along the rutted track. 'I have a bad feeling about this place,' Karma said. 'It's too quiet.'

Karma was usually so self-assured. Nothing ruffled his feathers. I'd never seen him like this. I saw him glance at his fuel gauge; it was showing just over a quarter of a tank. The wind had picked up and I moved my body a little closer to his. Soon we entered a densely forested area and our track became narrow and overgrown. At one point we swerved to avoid a hare and I gave a little yelp.

'Keep quiet Linda!' I could feel the muscles in Karma's back, rigid with tension.

I was cursing the blithe and careless way I had laughed off Karma's fears. Before we had set out he had warned me that it was better to travel in a group. 'What if the bike breaks down?' he had said. 'How could I leave you alone if I had to get help?'

Karma took a corner too fast and we skidded on the damp undergrowth. We managed to steady ourselves and when we looked up Karma slammed on his breaks. A man blocked our path. We were looking straight into the barrel of a gun.

Karma shouted at me, 'Take your helmet off now!'

In a split second my blonde hair was flying loose. The man with the gun froze, shocked to see a foreign woman. Then he shouted furiously at Karma. I knew him to be a Maoist by the red bandana he wore. We were in a lot of trouble. The rebel soldier jabbed me with the steel butt of his gun, forcing me to dismount. My body was trembling. I was certain he would shoot me. As I stood whimpering, the gun barrel pointed at my chest, all I could think about was that it was my son's birthday the following day and that he would wonder why I hadn't called.

Karma spoke then, his voice steady. 'Do as he says. No sudden moves.'

The man led us at rifle-point to a clear piece of ground on a hillside which was the camp. There were about forty young men and girls, painfully thin. Each one held a bamboo stick. They looked like kids who had bunked off school and didn't quite know what to do with themselves. For a moment I wanted to go into headteacher mode and tell them off but then I remembered the stories I had heard. Only a week ago, a 32-year-old subsistence farmer from Western Nepal was singled out in a random night-time attack. Her attackers were similarly young. I read that they had taken her out onto the porch where they bound her hands behind her back and tied her ankles together. Next, they put a large rock under her knee. One of them showed her an axe, then while several kids held her down, three others took turns hacking at her knees. There were pieces of flesh and bone all over the porch the next morning.

The Maoist rebels had conscripted large numbers of teenage boys and girls. Although their real enemy was the Royal Nepal Army, who were on the receiving end of some of the most horrific acts of torture, including slicing off soldiers' testicles or tying the young men to electric fires and watching them burn, ordinary Nepalis were also at risk. The rebels wanted to be heard and acts of cruelty were a sickeningly effective way of getting a reaction.

I looked around the camp. The ground was heavily scarred, with large patches of burnt grass. The trees were split and blackened. All around us were torched vehicles, piles of broken bricks, and empty tear gas and landmine shells. I wondered if this was where the rebels made their infamous pressure cooker bombs or the lethal homemade grenades that they filled with bits of rusted metal.

Now that Karma knew what he was up against he took a more commanding stance, speaking with authority. The rebels stopped talking and whacking their sticks. My friend looked at me with feigned disgust and indicated to the others that they should take me to the edge of the camp where I would be out of the way. I could think clearly but my legs were shaking so hard that I could barely walk. With a rifle pushed into my back I managed somehow.

I crouched alone at the cliff edge, staring blindly out at the terraced rice fields on the far side of the gorge, wishing I could disappear into the ground. I forced myself to keep calm, taking deep breaths. It felt like my vision was blurring but then I realised that was already nearly dusk. Realising that if Karma and I were to make our escape it would be better if I had some idea of the camp layout, I looked carefully around me in the fading light. Then I noticed some small sharp stones near my feet. I grabbed them quickly with trembling hands and pushed them deep inside my pockets. Pathetic weapons but they were all I had.

I could see Karma in the distance, sitting on the grass in the shade of a tree, relaxed. He was telling the rebels a story and being the children they were, they were gathered around him, mesmerised, to listen, weapons lying next to them on the grass. For the first time, I started to feel that we might have a chance.

A girl approached me. She was hardly distinguishable from her male fellows, with the same wiry body and uniform. I had heard that girls were recruited by the Maoists and were trained to kill, just like the boys. The younger ones were used as messengers, cooks and porters. Apparently they were paid in food but it didn't seem like this girl had eaten in days. She couldn't have been more than twelve years old although her half-starved body made her look even younger. She circled me a few times, scrutinizing me from every angle, then stared into my blue eyes without blinking. She might have held my gaze forever had she not been summoned by one of her comrades. As she walked away she turned and spat at me.

Now that I was alone again I forced myself to concentrate, making a detailed mental note of the route we had taken, etching a map in my mind. I hated being cut off from Karma and prayed fervently that he had a plan. I knew no one would come looking for us and I berated myself again for my foolishness in setting out without letting anyone know when we were due to arrive at our destination. We were a long way from the safety of a town and miles from the nearest army outpost. There was nowhere we could run. If we were to get out of here I knew we would need the bike.

Karma's group were growing louder. They were drinking *rakshi*, a home-brewed firewater which stripped your throat raw. The girls had started a fire. I shivered in my lonely spot and drew my scarf up to cover most of my face. A heavy mist rolled over the mountains. I had used up my last drip of adrenalin and my body felt limp with fatigue.

Night set in, the sky inky black. It was now bitterly cold. I reckoned it must be 2am. My eyes strained to pick out anything in the darkness. What was Karma doing? The camp was quiet. Desperate for a pee, I felt my way on my hands and knees to a tree and went behind it. As I did so bursts of automatic gunfire split the air, explosions shaking the ground. I could smell smoke and burning rubber. There was the sound of running feet and screeching which broke into peals of raucous laughter. I breathed again.

Reportedly no foreigner had ever been killed by the rebel army, although many had been asked firmly at gunpoint for donations. Somehow I could not see this mob of stragglers being organised enough to use me as PR to wake up the international community. It was much more likely I would be killed by a stray bullet from one of these drunken kid's guns. I rolled onto my back on the damp grass and stared up at the murky sky. I must have fallen asleep.

The next thing I knew I was being shaken awake. I felt warm breath on my cheek and inhaled the strong smell of *rakshi*. Karma spoke softly into my ear. 'Quick! Get up. Don't ask questions.'

He held my hand firmly as we slowly and carefully crept through the camp. I held my breath and willed my heart to keep calm. Karma moved with the confidence of a cat in the darkness. The bike was where we left it. I prayed that no one had drained the fuel from the tank. We would only have a split second to find out.

'Get on, he whispered. 'Don't worry – I drive better when I'm drunk.'

I climbed on behind him and, with a sharp downward thrust on the starter, the motor roared. We had no time to look over our shoulders but scrambled, zig-zagging through the forest, skidding on the mossy paths. Branches tore at my hair. Karma didn't dare put on the headlight. Gunshots blasted the air. We heard screams and yells of fury, but we didn't stop to look back. I steeled myself for a bullet but mercifully nothing hit home.

After crashing through the foliage, we bumped down onto a paved road, zipping past a burnt-out police station. Its walls were plastered with Maoist graffiti: red hammer and sickle flags and 'Long Live People's War' splashed in black paint. Karma drove until his tank was nearly empty. We didn't speak. Dawn was breaking now and there were a few signs of life. We passed an overladen truck with six men standing on the bumper and a group of early risers drinking tea. It was a comfort to see the world ticking along as usual.

We stopped for a liquid breakfast at a roadside café – a couple of shots of cheap Indian whisky. Alcohol was our saviour now, as I realised it had been the night before. I thought my relief was going to explode as floods of tears but when I looked at Karma we both burst out laughing and were unable to stop.

Administering aid to countries where corruption is rife does put governments and aid agencies in a quandary. Senior donor officials say that working in such countries as Nepal always involves the risk of fraud but they claim it would be ineffective to push anti-corruption measures on the government any harder than they already do. And to withdraw from a difficult working environment would betray the poor people who depend upon their support.

My own view is that we should support smaller, sustainable initiatives. I have spent the past decade watching how powerful they can be, where 'hand ups' rather than purely 'handouts' are offered. It is a view held by many. In an *Observer* article from July 2011, John Sentamu, the Archbishop of York, is quoted: 'Small, relatively low-cost initiatives can radically alter the future for local communities,' and he refers to some of the imaginative solutions coming from within Kenya, 'often piloted by women's groups.' He speaks passionately about involving people to be 'part of a global community', helping members of poor communities to 'take a series of small steps to raise themselves out of poverty.'

I'm aware that my solution requires more volunteers and that more volunteers means more money. But it need cost nothing extra to think a little bit harder about to whom and to what we are funding, before signing cheques. I have no wish to become embroiled in the politics of aid. My aims are simple: to help where I can; to report what I have witnessed; and to inspire with a testament to what has already been achieved.

CHAPTER SEVEN

MONKS, MEDICS AND MAGIC

Tibet

My extraordinary friendship with Tibet and the Tibetan people began in 2001 when for six months I travelled the length and breadth of India visiting remote and scattered Tibetan refugee camps. The problems faced by the young people in these camps had become so serious that HH The Dalai Lama himself was keen to hear the results of my research. That meeting was to have an extraordinary effect on my life.

On Saturday 26th October 2002 I travelled to Mindroling monastery, near Dehradun in the Northwest of India. I was greeted by the sight of a joyous carnival, a bobbing sea of burgundy and saffron. A gathering of monks, meditating and reciting sutras with a musical accompaniment of sacred horns and cymbals, had gathered there to catch a glimpse of this revered man of peace.

Inside the monastery I was taken to an austere office with dusty, dilapidated furniture, where I waited for two hours whilst an Indian official performed the necessary procedures. I watched him moving piles of paper painstakingly from one place to the next, pausing a moment to study one and occasionally asking me to sign another. This was followed by a close scrutiny of every page of my passport, with a great deal of head-scratching and 'oohs' and ahhs'. I understood it was a serious business: the Indian police were responsible for the safety and wellbeing of the Tibetan leader so it was no wonder that I was asked to answer a multitude of questions about my background and give my reasons for wanting to meet him. But, as invariably happens when I'm with police or uniformed officials, I had an uncontrollable desire to laugh. I tried as hard as I could to keep myself under control but every now and again nervous giggles burst out as hiccups.

At last, the moment came and I was escorted to His Holiness's private chambers. We waited in a glorious glass conservatory. My senses were almost overwhelmed with the beauty of the place; the enchanting sounds of Tibetan bowls; and the strong smell of yak butter candles. I felt the power of the mysterious symbolism of the thangkas, the brocaded pictures hanging on the walls. Through the glass of the conservatory, I could see the glorious gardens outside, in the centre of which was a breathtaking dome-shaped stupa, a dazzlingly colourful and gilded monument at least 150 feet high, built to house sacred Buddhist relics.

I stood in that beautiful room, soaking up the moment and not wanting it to end, every cell in my body tingling. In the next room, I could hear the Dalai Lama giving an audience, his rich, hearty laugh punctuating the conversation. I waited motionless, a white silk scarf, the *kata*, held in my hands, in readiness for his blessing. Just then, quite suddenly, the heavy wooden door to his private chamber flew open and the man himself breezed in. I had seen his picture so many times and here he was, dressed simply in his monk's robe, with a grin so wide it seemed to stretch from ear to ear. I was instantly struck by the sheer charisma of the man: he positively glowed with the delight of being alive. He stood directly in front of me, eyes twinkling, his gaze so direct it seemed to go straight past my eyes to connect with my soul. There was something exuberantly, almost boyishly, playful as he greeted me, peeping over his heavy-framed rectangular glasses, eyebrows raised – clearly a man who delighted in meeting new people. Taking my hand in a firm grasp, he held it a while, enough to make a real connection.

Then he asked me if it was OK for him to take off his shoes. I nodded, surprised by the question, watching as he kicked off his blue plastic flip-flops and sat comfortably cross-legged on the sofa. As we sat there, he listened intently as I told him about my plans, explaining all about the research project and the many problems faced by the Tibetan youth in exile. As I spoke, he smiled and nodded many times, often interjecting with a 'well done' or 'very important work'. An hour sped by, both of us totally absorbed in the discussion.

It was only when I happened to mention that I used to be a nurse, that the conversation swiftly took a new turn. With the agility of a politician, His Holiness changed tack, as he realised that here was something useful for the cause, something that might give a whole new benefit to his struggling people. Was there any possibility that I could look into a grave problem within Tibet itself, he asked? Then he explained that Tibet was experiencing the highest infant mortality in the world – and for a moment, the smile was gone and I saw real grief in his face. This was a serious concern for him. Of course I said I would go anywhere he felt I could best be of help. At that, he leant over and gave my arm a squeeze. Then, with a beaming smile, he said that he would fully support my work. And I realised I'd just been talked into a whole new job!

Realising that my audience was nearing its conclusion I dived into my big red carpet bag to give His Holiness the presents I had selected for him. Choosing a present, particularly one for a man, is never easy at the best of times. But what on earth do you give the self-labelled 'simple monk' with no need of possessions and no attachment to material things? It had been a question that had plagued me for weeks. I had pondered it over with friends and none of us had come up with anything that felt right. I had been brought up always to take a gift when visiting a friend, but – flowers, chocolates? Everything felt ridiculous but I knew I could not visit empty-handed.

I had rummaged through second-hand bookshops, grabbing any books I could find that covered the young life of the Dalai Lama. I was hoping to glean some small piece of information, just one clue that might inspire me in my search for a small present.

'I have a few small gifts for you from England. Can I give them to you now?' I asked.

His Holiness, an avid gardener, looked at the selection of old English seed packets, and studied them lovingly one by one. He held up the packet of Larkspur seeds, announcing excitedly, 'This packet I will send to Ladakh, it will grow particularly well there.'

The next gift, a pen-sized telescope, confused him; he looked quizzically at it for a moment, then suddenly understood its significance and burst into hysterics. He held it to his eye and told me how, as a child, he used to spy on the soldiers using a telescope, when he lived high up in the Potala Palace in Lhasa.

The final present was a tiny wind-up musical box. In my research I had discovered that another great hobby of His Holiness was to take apart and repair small mechanical items, such as watches and musical boxes. My gift filled the air with music. We swayed for a moment to the tinny strains of 'Singing in the Rain', tapping our feet to the rhythm. The feeling was magical.

'Now it's time for a photo,' His Holiness exclaimed. Without any stiffness or formality he put his arm around me and took my hand in a firm handshake.

After that, we bade our farewells and I tripped out of the room on cloud nine. And in that moment, I think my smile managed even to outstretch his own. In fact, it felt like every cell in my body was grinning.

'How can I help with the medical problems in Tibet that His Holiness was so concerned about?' I turned the challenge around in my head as I bounced along in the crowded bus back to Delhi.

Tibet was a notoriously harsh environment, especially in the High Himalayas where the worst of the problems lay. The locations that needed help were almost inaccessible: far away from towns and villages with even the most basic resources. Food supplies, medical back-up, or communication was scarce or non-existent.

I knew what I wanted. Medically-skilled and adventurous young people who would be sensitive to the Tibetan culture and the complexities of the Chinese occupation. By the end of my bus trip I had it. Second year medical students from training hospitals who were searching for overseas placements for their final year would be perfect. There would have to be a careful selection – I'd need to find individuals who were tough, resilient and resourceful.

I was keyed-up with excitement, planning the future of our project, and could hardly wait to start organising things. Just then a cow strolled into the road and the bus swerved violently to avoid it. I was jolted back to the present. I caught the eye of the lady sitting next to me, dressed in a colourful sari and nursing her chicken lovingly, and I smiled.

Over the next few weeks, it became clear to me that if I was to go ahead with this project I would have to assess the situation thoroughly before letting students loose in the Himalayas. My only knowledge of the area had been gleaned from some of the first great explorers of Tibet – inspirational, intrepid figures like Alexandra David Neel. They had coped so admirably with the challenge of that harsh, inaccessible terrain without the most basic comforts, but would I?

The more I researched the medical problems Tibetan women faced the stronger my determination to help them grew. Tibet has one of highest newborn and infant mortality rates in the world. Women are three hundred times more likely to die than Westerners from complications due to pregnancy or delivery. Postpartum haemorrhage is the leading cause of death. Likewise, babies are far more likely to die in Tibet than anywhere else in the world. But what really fired my determination to help was the fact that most of these deaths are preventable with minimal technology and simple interventions.

The vast majority of births take place at high altitude, in a cold environment and without access to electricity or healthcare. Over ninety per cent of women give birth at home. Of those, fifty-four per cent are attended by female relatives, while only thirteen per cent are attended by healthcare providers. Curiously, Tibetan society is one of the few in the world in which there is no tradition of trained midwives who facilitate the delivery process. Poor nutrition and the lack of trained health personnel or emergency services combine to place Tibetan women and infants at high risk for labour-related deaths.

A Tibetan mother's death is devastating to her family: it often threatens the health of her children and can impact the family for generations. The mother is considered the thread that holds the family together. When she dies prematurely, her surviving children are three to ten times more likely to die within two years. And they are less likely to attend school or complete their education. Many Tibetans believe that a mother's death during childbirth is ominous: a sign of bad spirits congregating to wreak misfortune on her family and community.

In Tibetan nomadic communities, most babies are delivered with only the help of the pregnant woman's mother or mother-in-law and then the only assistance they give is in the cutting of the cord. I was horrified to find out that many Tibetan women deliver their babies completely alone. The cold statistics pointed to an urgent need for action.

The following account of a Tibetan woman's labour was typical of the stories I came across in my research:

'She had been in labour for four days. I found her alone in a cold, dark shed, while her family huddled around a warm fire in the kitchen. Four hours later, the exhausted woman delivered a healthy baby boy into my bare hands. Tragically, just a few days earlier, another young mother in the same region bled to death during childbirth. There was one overseas experienced doctor living in the area but stretched so thinly over a huge area'.

My eagerness to jump straight in and get on with it, combined with my belief that 'everything will be all right' meant that my first trip to the High Himalayas nearly ended in disaster. It had taken me two days in a jeep, mostly 'off-roading' on dirt tracks, to reach my mountain guides. I was inappropriately dressed, had never ridden before and was sorely lacking in sensible provisions and medical equipment.

We set out with the rain beating down on us. Our jeep snaked its way along the road, driving precariously around piles of mud and stones from rockslides, past overturned trucks, tractor accidents, and vehicles bogged in mud. Halting often when sheep and wild yak crossed its path.

As we started to climb into the mountains the scenery morphed and changed countless times. We passed through dramatic blood-red cliffs, and wove our way around vast barley fields. In the villages, outside the two-storey mud-brick whitewashed houses, colourful prayer flags fluttered in the stiff breeze. Then we entered a vast and empty landscape, a forbidding place that looked as if it were caught in a medieval time warp where mysterious fortified castles jutted bleakly from the rock. Who knows what they were built for? A defence against enemies, perhaps, or wolves; or simply as a barricade against the howling, freezing winds.

The Tibetan caravan was waiting for me. It was the team that would lead me to the nomads I would be working with who were camped in the high mountains. My guides were enjoying the afternoon sun, their yak and mules grazing around them. They were chatting contentedly, drinking cups of oily Tibetan tea laced with salt and yak butter and eating *tsampa*. *Tsampa* is quite delicious and is the staple dish of the region, made of salted tea pounded together with yak butter, to which toasted barley flour is added and mixed by hand.

Tibetan life still revolves around the yak, which the people have herded and placed at the centre of their culture for at least two thousand years. Tibetans are warmed by yak-dung fires and lit by yak-butter lamps; they eat yak meat and yak blood, butter, cheese, and yoghurt; they use yaks for transport and weave clothing, blankets, shelters, and even boats out of yak hair. Baby yak are such a precious commodity to the nomads they sleep inside the tents with the humans, cherished and protected.

I looked at my assembled guides: a mixture of tall, dust-stained, dark-skinned women with sturdy limbs and wind-scoured faces, wearing deep-hued homespun robes bound with rainbow-striped aprons; and tall stocky men in dirt-stiffened *chubas*, their braided hair rolled into a bun. There was nothing extravagant about the harsh lives of these gentle souls, living in a most inhospitable land, but as if in mockery of that very idea, I was dazzled, as always, by the sheer brilliance of their coral, turquoise and silver jewellery.

My arrival caused a buzz of excitement as the horsemen and women made final preparations for the journey. Scruffy-maned, unshod horses and yak stood docile whilst an enormous number of items was thrown onto their backs. First of all, a crude wooden frame lashed together by rope was perched on top of the animal and tied firmly under its belly. On top of this odd-looking saddle went layer after layer: large hessian sacks of provisions such as tea and wheat; then blankets, rugs and a sleeping pad.

'How on earth am I ever going to straddle all of that?' I thought to myself. 'Great padding for my posterior – no chance of saddle sores – but I may just dislocate my hip.'

'Jump on board,' said my guide.

We edged the horse close to a large boulder which I used as a mounting block and then I was pushed and pulled until somehow I reached my lofty perch, my legs dangling over the many layers with the horse somewhere underneath. We set off in bright sunshine, strolling along the side of a gentle babbling brook. Within a short time I felt totally at ease. My horse was sixth in the long caravan train and I felt safe and secure. With the sun warm on my back and lulled by the hypnotic sound of the Tibetans chanting, I nearly fell asleep.

All of a sudden, I sensed a change of direction and I looked around to orientate myself. The gentle stream to my right had become a Himalayan torrent, fast-flowing and fierce. I pushed myself up on my stirrups so that I could see over the shoulder of the horseman in front of me. In horror, I watched as the horse leading the caravan plunged straight into the river.

My mind was in turmoil: 'No, I can't do that!' I looked up and down the river in desperation. There was no bridge in sight.

I needed to get somebody's attention. I swivelled round but my eyes were met by the nonchalant gaze of the heavily-laden yak behind. I bellowed, trying to get the attention of the rider in front of me. Nothing. The noise of the river smothered everything but the pounding of my heart.

My turn had come. We slid sideways into the icy-cold mountain water with a frightening splash. I shut my eyes and held on so tightly that every muscle in my body tensed. My horse lurched downwards and struggled to find his footing. My boots filled with icy river water.

I started to repeat the Tibetan mantra that I had heard so many times: '*Om Mani Padme Hum*' – 'Praise to the jewel in the lotus'. I prayed like never before.

The current was so strong, it was taking my legs, dragging me from the horse. Somebody was shouting something but, with the rush of the river and the seething panic in my head, I couldn't make it out. I held on with all my might, my mind focused intently on just two things: protecting my camera and passport; and remaining on the horse.

Then it was over. I was thrown sharply backwards as my trusty steed scrambled up the bank, gurgling and spitting water. I had survived. The shouting changed to clapping and I opened my eyes. Dry land. I felt as high as a kite, sailing on the crest of an adrenalin rush. Indiana Jones...on a clop-foot nag.

After that we climbed so steeply that we had to dismount from our horses. I lost my footing on the loose gravel. A firm, rough hand grabbed mine, pulling me along. Still feeling relieved after the river crossing and now comforted by my companion's strength, I had no idea how much worse things would get.

As we reached the rise, the blue skies began to turn black. There was no shelter nearby. We resumed riding as if trying to outpace the storm. Then it came upon us: the wind whipped up furiously followed by the rain, battering down in unforgiving and ice-cold sheets. With visibility now at zero, the caravan did not stop. There was nowhere to hide from this. We had to keep moving forwards.

By now I was slumped on the back of my mule, wailing. My head was pounding from altitude sickness and I was shivering uncontrollably. I was wet all over, my yak-hair blanket doing nothing to stem the flow of the icy water running down my back. I was pleading, although no one could hear: 'Please let me get off. Please just let this be over.'

I remember then that the horsemen tied me down and put a heavy blanket over me but after that I must have lost consciousness.

'What is happening to me? Where am I?' My numbed brain was confused.

I could feel my naked body being rubbed vigorously by several pairs of rough hands. I breathed in the pungent smell of rancid butter and I heaved. My body was so stiff and bruised that it felt like I was lying on a bed of stones – I could feel a thousand sharp edges digging into me. I tried to sit up but hadn't the strength to lift my head. In the feeble glow of butter lamps I saw the faces of women peering down at me. By their clothes I realised that they were nuns.

One of the nuns had lit a fire in what looked like a small saucepan, and was wafting it continuously up and down over the length of my body. They did not speak to me and never once did they stop the rhythmic rubbing of my body. They chanted, very quietly, as they worked. I slipped in and out of consciousness but at no point was I afraid. I felt, instead, a profound sense of peace and a relaxed acceptance of fate. I drifted off to sleep to the sound of thunder and the rattle of hailstones pelting the tent.

As dawn broke, I woke to the sound of giggling young nomads who were peeping curiously into my tent, excited to know what the night's activities were about. It was obvious that they had seen few white faces in their lifetime and this was too good an opportunity to miss. I found out that our caravan had stumbled across a small settlement of *drokpas*, nomadic shepherds living in black yak-hair tents. They had taken us in and saved my life. To my complete surprise I felt completely better that morning. Their medicine had been extraordinarily effective.

'Can you ride?' my guide asked me in sign language. I nodded.

Ignoring the Tibetan custom of making only the most conservative of farewells, I gave each nun an enormous Western hug before mounting my horse. Words could never have expressed what I felt. As our caravan of yaks and mules set off, I turned and looked for a final time at the small group gathered by the tents. I knew I had experienced the most precious of things: love bestowed by people who gave freely, without expecting anything in return.

The experience had made me more committed than ever to bring the medical students here to work with these compassionate people, who were surviving against such heavy odds. We would do our bit to help the Tibetans, one birth at a time. I started to formulate a better plan, one which would ensure that my team would be well prepared with the right resources and adequate backup. I was already making the lists in my head:

1. *Layered clothing works best – thermals, polar fleece vests, cotton T-shirts*
2. *Yak-hair poncho – to be ordered from Tibetans in advance – one per person*

3. *Head torch (need hands free!)*
4. *High-energy snack foods*
5. *Toilet paper*
6. *Warm sleeping bag*
7. *Waterproof bags for passport/camera/dry socks*
8. *Sunscreen – waterproof and highest factor available*
9. *Industrial-strength lip gloss (to avoid sore lips from the sun and wind)*
10. *Silk long johns and underwear, for anti-chafing*
11. *Talcum powder also to help with chafing*
12. *A waterproof hat (one you can tie on in the wind)*
13. *Sunglasses*
14. *Wet wipes (washing is usually not an option)*
15. *Perfume or essential oil such as lavender – calming and disguises a multitude of unwanted smells (see 14!)*
15. *A towel that packs and dries quickly (highly recommended)*
16. *Sense of humour (the most important)*

Six months later I returned to Tibet with two medical students from England, Steve and John. I knew that this trip would be out of their comfort zone but having done my own recce I felt sure that they weren't going to die of hypothermia. My interviewing technique had been unorthodox – instead of firing them up with descriptions of all the wonderful things they would see and experience, I painted an exceedingly bleak picture. The intention being to attract only those with the bravest hearts and toughest bodies. And, in the event, I was right – Steve and John were up for a challenge and had the mental as well as the physical muscle for the job.

It had been the Clinical Dean's idea to paint a black picture. 'That way,' he said, 'you'll weed out those who might get there only to beg to come straight back, finding they're missing their home comforts and the football results too much.'

He had looked rather wistfully at me, saying that if he'd had the opportunity as a youngster he would have jumped at the chance of going to Tibet. 'After all,' he said, 'it's not often you get the chance to be a pioneer these days.'

Within a week of my placing my advertisement, five med students had replied and we arranged to meet in Starbucks for an initial chat. I realised that I was carrying assumptions and preconceptions of my own, having met many med students during my ten years as a nurse. Whether they were nervous or arrogant, team players or obnoxious know-it-alls, most were fairly well-off, from comfortable middle-class families. I knew it would require a special type of person to slip quietly and effortlessly into the 'raw' world of rural Tibet with its hardships and political and cultural sensitivities. Would any one of my five fit the necessary profile?

Alice was the first to arrive. A tiny, elegant girl with waist-length gleaming hair, she beamed at me and sat down, almost disappearing behind her enormous brown leather satchel as she did so.

The words tumbled out of her in her excitement: 'I am so excited to work with you in mainland China. I was born in Hong Kong, I speak fluent Mandarin, I am a great supporter of the Dalai Lama – I know all about the terrible atrocities afflicted by the Chinese, I am a very active human rights member of Free Tibet'.

Alice barely drew breath and although I liked her enthusiasm there was something that worried me. Then Steve arrived. He was a slender giant of a man, very different from the tiny Alice.

'Am I late?' Steve's green eyes looked anxious. From his sweaty forehead and flushed cheeks I realised he must have run all the way up the long steep hill to get here. He collapsed into the nearest chair, his long legs easing their way into the available space.

'John will be here any minute. We've been playing rugby and he's hurt his head,' he said. 'Probably did it to get some extra time with the nurse.'

I gave a sheaf of photos to Steve and Alice and they started to sift through them. I couldn't help thinking how very young they looked.

'Sorry I'm late.' John, an athletic-looking redhead, rushed in. He shook my hand.

I looked at my watch. It didn't look like the others were going to show. 'Let's get started. Thanks for coming today and for your interest in volunteering in Tibet'.

As I looked at the three eager young faces opposite me I tried to envisage how they would fit in in Tibet. They looked so at home in Starbucks. What on earth would they make of Tibet where their only snack would be dried yak cheese washed down with yak butter tea. No comfy chairs, no heating and certainly no western loos.

'Have any of you travelled in the Himalayas?' I asked. 'Been to India, Nepal or Pakistan?'

'No, but I climbed Mount Kenya last year. It was great!' Steve stretched his legs as if remembering the exercise and grinned.

'Well I'm going to give you as much detail today as I can so that you can make an informed decision. It's important that you feel that it's right for you. We're going on a mission to teach safe childbirth practices to villagers who have no access to medicines or midwives and who are used to using dirty knives to cut the umbilical cord. You will find their beliefs and the way they do things strange. You'll be in an alien culture and you're going to need to work sensitively within that. They can't speak English so unless you speak Tibetan, you'll be miming what to do. I hope you're as good at acting as you are at medicine.'

They laughed.

'How would you feel about having no communication with the outside world for a month – no phone; no TV; no internet; no electricity; no access to news or media?'

John looked shocked. 'You mean we cannot call home at all?' he said in disbelief looking at his cell phone on the table.

Alice leant forward quickly, almost knocking over her coffee. 'But how do we charge our computers and camera batteries if there is no electricity? How do we document it all for our coursework?'

It was going to take a while for it all to sink in. 'Well, it's probably not even worth taking your computer – the batteries may freeze in these conditions. It's back to basics, I'm afraid. Note pad and pencil is best'.

I ploughed on, although I could see the students were clearly a bit nervous, frowning and chewing their lips.

'Look, if you decide to come you'll have no running water, very basic food, no salad, no fruit, no vegetables. You'll be sleeping in basic shelters, often tents, sometimes with the goats and yaks.'

At that, their eyes widened but they didn't interrupt.

'You'll be living and working at an altitude of over 5,000 metres. Steve, you may have some idea of what this will feel like, after Mount Kenya.'

He nodded, still silent.

'Basically, think of everything you take for granted in your day-to-day living and remove it. Your best friend will be your head torch when you're out on the steep gravelly mountainside in the pitch black trying to relieve yourself in the middle of the night.'

'I understand that we won't have our usual stuff, but how is it possible to actually work in these conditions?' exclaimed Alice.

I listed the things they would miss: basic hygiene; the easy access to equipment; senior staff to answer doubts and questions; nurses to assist them; the unlimited access to medicine; bandages; resuscitation equipment; diagnostic tools; X-rays; scans; path labs for blood tests. They would have none of these. I let the hard facts sink in. Then, feeling I'd listed enough of those, I reassured them that the people were lovely.

Alice was the first to speak up. 'I've heard that a Tibetan's pain threshold is extraordinary. They're not used to chemically-induced pain relief. Apparently they can break a leg and not even whimper. It's going to be exciting!'

I smiled at her, admiring that she'd moved so swiftly from trepidation back to enthusiasm. I looked at the other two, waiting for their reactions.

John was the first to speak up. 'Nothing I have heard has changed my mind', he said with a grin. 'I'll just have to fill my rucksack with Mars bars – and when they're gone I've got plenty of fat reserves to work on.' He turned to his friend. 'What about you?'

'I'm in! Sounds great.'

Oh, the optimism and flexibility of youth! I felt relieved. My time wasn't wasted.

'That's all for today. I'll email you the necessary forms and a packing list. By the way, you'll notice that I have written 'humour and flexibility' at the top – you'll need this most of all.'

Six months later I returned to Tibet with Steve and John. Alice had emailed to say that she had realised that her strong political beliefs might jeopardise our trip and I had to agree with her. My gut had told me much the same thing.

The lads arrived arrived at the airport laden with comfort food and thick novels, which they jokingly announced would double up as pillows. They were already growing beards.

'What's the point in shaving?' Steve said with a shrug. 'No running water in any case.'

I suddenly felt light-hearted. Yes, it would be a responsibility guiding these two young students but it would be fun too. We boarded the plane to Chengdu and by the end of the flight we had discussed a great deal and Steve and John were clear on all parts of our mission and what it would entail.

Guided by the brilliant work and research of 'One Heart', an American NGO, we would try and give the nomadic mountain groups self-sustainable and practical skills to keep mother and baby safe, knowing that in the absence of obstetricians, midwives, medicines or medical equipment, what they had available to them was limited. With the total absence of trained birth attendants in Tibet our task was to inspire and utilise whomever we had available – granddads, aunts, even nuns. I knew we could save lives.

I explained to Steve and John what we needed to teach. In each place we visited we would convey only three simple health messages:

1. A clean knife.
Problem: it was common for unclean knives to be used to cut the umbilical cord. For practical reasons, as these are a nomadic people, they have to carry everything about their person. Tibetan nomads own only one of each item they require for daily living: one cup, one knife, one purse, one matchbox – each dangling from their belts. The same knife was used to cut yak meat and, when needed, the umbilical cord. The local belief is that the birthing process and blood related to childbirth is polluted.

Thus they do not think it is necessary to clean the knife until after childbirth.

Solution: After lengthy discussions with the community elders and religious leaders, a practical and culturally sensitive solution was devised. When a mum became pregnant the family would buy a new knife and take it to the monk to be blessed, giving it a special reverence. It would then be wrapped in a silk scarf and kept in a safe place, unused, until the time of birth.

2. Inadequate management of babies who are not breathing at birth

Problem: research had shown that the Tibetan custom was for the mum to give birth outside and often alone. If the baby did not breathe as soon as it was born it was thought dead.

Solution: to teach mum what to do if the baby does not breathe automatically at birth. Teach her to check the baby's airways, how to clear the mucous from the nose and mouth and, if necessary, how to bring the amniotic fluid out of their lungs by turning the baby to its side to allow the fluids to drain out by gravity.

3. Insufficient protection from hypothermia

Problem: the mums had no understanding of the vital importance of keeping the baby warm just after birth. Babies, during the first few hours of life, have difficulty maintaining their body heat; newborn hypothermia can occur quickly and depress breathing.

Solution: to keep the baby warm, dry the baby, and place it immediately inside the mum's thick *chuba* next to the mother's chest. The mother's body heat will help keep the baby warm. They need to pay particular attention to keeping the head covered as heat loss from the newborn head can be substantial.

Three simple messages.

We parked our 4x4s on the hillside next to a flowing aqueduct of clear water…and waited. Steve and John took out a pack of cards and very soon they were rolling around the grass fighting and laughing. Neither of them were aware that I was on tenterhooks. In the back of my mind I had a nagging doubt that I dared not voice: 'Would anyone actually come?'

The high plateau was still; looking into the far distance it was empty and silent. No formal communication system operated here, no phone, no internet, no radio, no television – so perhaps no one had received the message that we were coming.

I quizzed the translator, a local Tibetan, who was our guide.

'Be patient,' he smiled. Everything will happen as it should.'

I felt a helplessness and frustration tinged with dis-appointment. 'All this effort. The young medics excited and ready to teach, and a very long way from home. And no one. What a bloody waste,' I thought.

I lay back on the cool grass and closed my eyes, trying to quell my increasing anxiety. Then it all started happening at last. The ground started to shudder as if the Gods were drumming the earth to wake it up. I leapt to my feet to see a monk galloping straight towards us at breakneck speed. What a glorious sight! His saffron robes flowed out dramatically behind him and he came to a halt with a flourish.

The monk jumped down, dragging a big saddlebag behind him. Swiftly he took items one by one from his bag: a thick Tibetan rug on top of which he placed a bright yellow piece of silk, carefully smoothing it flat with his hands; then a conch shell; an ornately carved bell; and a long book of scriptures. Then, seated in a lotus position, his head tilted downwards, eyes closed, he started to rock back and forth, chanting quietly under his breath, lips moving rapidly. John and Steve watched him, rapt.

Meanwhile, a young boy who had accompanied the monk

appeared, laden with twigs and leaves. He positioned himself next to the monk and lit a small fire, reaching into the saddlebag for juniper and incense to throw on top of it. He looked up, glanced in our direction and smiled, occasionally ringing the carved bell.

An hour went past. We gazed at the incense spiralling upwards, twisting and turning. Then, as if drawn by the magic of the ceremony, a crowd started to appear. They came by horse, by mule, on motorbikes with red and yellow ribbons streaming from the handlebars, by truck and even on foot. Appearing in silhouette on the top of the mountain ridges surrounding us, they paused for a moment. Each of the nomads was dressed in their traditional clothes that hung to the floor. Many were wearing horsehair-woven visors to protect their eyes from the glare of the sun.

A woman appeared on horseback next to me with her young infant daughter strapped to her back, then a man astride a huge black yak with his young daughter in tandem. The girl looked about eight years old and was wearing bright red, green and pink silks and a fancy hat. Another Tibetan was twirling a prayer wheel as he trotted up to us. Then came a procession of old and disabled men and women, many carried on the backs of young, strong men. And all around, darting back and forth, weaving in and out of the line of people, were rosy-cheeked, runny-nosed Tibetan children, giggling as they played chase.

I looked around as the group gathered and settled down as if on a festival picnic. A pot appeared and was soon bubbling with tea, suspended over a fire. Bottles of *chang*, a locally-brewed alcoholic drink, were piled up in one corner. Everyone brought something to contribute. Small circles of men were soon sitting on the grass, chatting and weaving. Each one had produced a hand-held spindle attached to wool that was peeping out of their pockets.

Steve turned to me. 'What do we do now?' he said.

We were sitting apart from the nomads. No one was approaching the area where we had set up our teaching equipment and my students could sense that we had reached a point where we needed to start or we might well lose our audience.

There was no way I was going to let that happen. 'Don't worry. I've a few tricks up my sleeve.' Little did Steve realise that I meant it literally.

I rummaged in my bag, hoping that I had remembered to pack my secret weapon. My little bag of magic, always my great ally in times like this: icebreaker, crowd-puller and, at times, a tool to resolve conflict and calm tense situations. Magic tricks never fail to break down language barriers – they need no translator. And they always seem to dissolve fear with fun and laughter.

I brought out some large and colourful silk scarves – red, gold and blue – and waved them in big circles above my head. This immediately caught the attention of the children who stopped and stared in surprise. I lay the scarves on the floor and took out my favourite magic trick. Cups and balls is one of the oldest and most amazing magic tricks in history, first performed by Roman conjurors as far back as two thousand years ago.

One by one, I took out my three wide-mouthed cups – one yellow, one red and one blue – and three small red balls and placed them on the mat next to me. I beckoned to the children to come closer but they did not move. I decided to start, hoping that curiosity would overcome their apprehension. With showman taps of my magic wand on each cup and a low bow, I started the performance. The balls passed through the solid bottoms of the cups; they jumped from cup to cup; they disappeared from one cup only to appear in another place altogether; and sometimes I made them vanish completely.

Out of the corner of my eye I saw Steve and John looking dumbfounded and a little embarrassed, as though their mad aunt had just done something a bit over the top at a family party. But the Tibetans were mesmerised. Not just children, but also women who peeped out shyly from behind their men, giggling, and the elders who grinned their toothless grins. I carried on for more than twenty minutes until finally I had to give up, having run out of material.

Afterwards, Steve strode up to me and put his arm around my shoulders. 'You're a bit of a dark horse, Linda,' he said. 'We will have to watch you. Who knows what else you're going to pull out of that bag of yours.'

Next to him, John was punching the air with his fist. 'You rock, Linda! They loved you.'

'Well guys, now the ice is broken, let's get the job done, shall we?'

I put the cups and balls away and picked up our teaching aides – a plastic baby doll and a portable picture-based flip-chart on healthy pregnancy. The translator announced our programme and the crowd listened intently.

There seemed to be many more men than women present.

'Shouldn't we should encourage the women to come forward,' John whispered. 'Surely they are our target audience…not these old men.'

I remembered hearing about the ancient Tibetan custom of polyandry, still commonly practiced, where a woman can marry several brothers at the same time. The logic behind this is that fertile land is scarce and, if each brother marries a wife, the family land will be divided, further impoverishing the group. By sharing a wife, the family is kept strong. No one knows who the true father of the children is but this doesn't bother them: they are all one family.

I looked at the motley assortment of granddads, uncles and brothers gathered at the front, waiting eagerly. We had little choice but to start. The women were still hiding behind the menfolk but we'd winkle them out in due course.

'Tsering, please ask the group to form a circle and sit down on the grass'.

Steve and John circled the outside of the group like sheepdogs guiding their flock into the pen. I could see by the determined look on their faces they were not about to lose any of them. In the middle of the circle, I placed a large towel and Sally, our plastic doll. Steve and John knew their cue: it was their time to take centre stage. Heads held down they walked nervously forward, the crowd glued to their every move.

John, by far the more outgoing of the two, became ringmaster, doing a quick spin around the group, breaking into a skip. 'Tashi Delek!' – 'Hello' – he shouted. Meanwhile, Steve deftly set up the flipchart and got the props ready. The circle started to get smaller, closing in on them with curiosity. They were brilliant. For hours they patiently acted out their message with diagrams on the flipchart and role-play, using various members of the group. It was exciting to see how keen the Tibetans were to learn. They asked so many questions and took turns to role play in the middle of the circle: holding the baby doll; practising clearing out its mouth and nose; and carefully placing it inside their *chuba*, snug and warm. Frequently the group, embarrassed at some activity, burst into laughter. We taught basic hygiene – hand washing, bathing the baby, even some breast-feeding techniques. The crowd were hungry to learn and it was a magical sight. They never got bored, even when we kept coming back to the three key messages. Soon they were chanting it like a mantra: 'Always use a clean knife; clear the baby's airways; keep the baby warm!'

Now that Steve and John were successfully in the swing of things, I could relax and enjoy the show. At one point, I noticed that a pretty young Tibetan girl had become totally smitten by Steve. She would not leave his side and was gazing at him devotedly, touching his hair lovingly while he was trying to demonstrate the baby-care. He was getting more and more flustered and clearly had no idea how he should handle it.

Red in the face, he turned to his friend. 'Over to you, mate. I'm off to teach tooth-brushing' – and in a flash he had scarpered to the children's group, deftly avoiding the clutches of his admirer.

'Steve's got a girlfriend!' I heard John sing out to his hastily departing back.

Of course, the two students were elevated straight to gurus. Our translator had been very clear as to the reason of us being there that day – to teach mother and baby care – but when the nomads had realised skilled medical practitioners would be present they were like bees circling a honey pot. I had warned Steve and John that this would happen everywhere we went but they looked very nervous nonetheless. Every ailment arrived, from rickets to blindness. It was overwhelming. Club feet, huge goitres, TB, skin infections and broken limbs, hanging in a crumpled mess that had not been properly fixed.

'This is crazy,' said Steve, panicking. 'We've only read about most of these cases in a textbook. I'm really not sure I can do this.'

John put his hand on Steve's shoulder. 'Yes, you can. Look, we are the probably the best they've ever had. We'll take it slowly, see them together, pool our knowledge.'

It was amazing to see the resourcefulness of this pair. One by one they examined each patient, offering what advice they could. It was a trial by fire and one they would never forget. Then it was done, and the day was nearly over.

'I need an ice-cold beer' said John, as he slumped down on the grass exhausted. They both looked utterly drained, emotionally as much as physically.

'Well done, lads, you walked on water today. You should be really proud of yourselves.'

Steve looked upset. 'We were rubbish. We had no way of doing it properly. No way of checking the signs and symptoms. If only we could have done more!'

I couldn't bear to see Steve disheartened after all his great work. 'Look, just look at them, Steve.'

Even though it had been a long day, the Tibetans were still buzzing, discussing the day's work animatedly. 'They will put what we've taught them into practice. It's what we came for. You did great.'

The crowd still lingered, reluctant to leave, but the sun was setting and the wind was picking up. Most of them had a very long journey home. As we said our farewells, an elderly man pushed his way through the crowd to me. He draped a *kata*, the traditional Tibetan silk scarf, around my neck in farewell, saying as he did so:

'We welcome visitors from the outside world, but not too many. Did you know that we Tibetans don't bury our dead. We carry the corpses to a mountaintop and carve them up to make a sky burial. We call the vultures, one by one, who descend from the heavens and carry our loved ones away.'

I didn't know quite where this conversation was leading but was listening to the old man, rapt. He continued, 'We would like to invite you as our honoured guest to witness this. Will you come?'

Before I could nod, he added quickly, 'We would need to conceal you for your own safety.'

I was aware that the Chinese had recently banned foreigners from seeing these ancient Tibetan rituals but how could I refuse such an honour? It seemed like tomorrow was going to be yet another venture into the unknown.

CHAPTER EIGHT

FRIENDS IN HIGH PLACES

Morocco

On Tuesday 10 December 1997, Richard Branson, Per Lindstrand and Steve Fossett were at an air force base outside Marrakesh, Morocco. Their team had just started to inflate the canvas of their hot air balloon when disaster struck. A huge gust of wind caught the balloon and it broke free from its moorings. Untethered and unmanned, it sailed off over the Atlas Mountains, two Moroccan police helicopters and Branson's Lear jet in pursuit. At one point it reached an altitude of 55,000 feet before it finally came back to earth. It wasn't the first time these persistent adventurers had tried to achieve the record for a round-the-world balloon flight. The previous January they had taken off from the same base but were forced to land in the Algerian desert.

You may wonder what a runaway hot-air balloon has to do with me...

Many a failure has spawned a great success, and not necessarily one that has been planned for. Richard Branson may not have achieved his record-breaking goal but his time in Morocco gave him a growing love of the country which had played host to his team. It was time to put back. In 1998, he bought a crumbling fortified citadel, Kasbah Tamadot, in the foothills of the Atlas mountains. In 2005 it opened its doors to tourists, rebuilt as a luxury boutique hotel. A responsible tourism project on a grand scale, the business and its employees had a real commitment to make things better for the local Berbers. In 2010 Branson asked me to get involved with two community initiatives.

I didn't hesitate. Over the years it has become easy to sniff out when the commitment is real or when it is manicured for a photoshoot opportunity. However good the plan, if the heart isn't in it, it is bound to fizzle out halfway through. It wasn't the first time I had worked with Virgin Unite, the non-profit foundation of the Virgin Group – I had seen them in action in Soweto when I witnessed the infectious passion Richard and his team have for community uplift – but helping the Berbers was to become a mission very close to my heart.

There are many hotels that spring up along the glorious coastlines and beauty spots of the world which play no active role in the community. Some of them sit on a few acres of turf in the poorest of countries. Using precious supplies of water for golf courses and swimming pools, they ship in almost all their food supplies, building materials and staff from abroad. The hotel makes money for its owners, barely a sou of which is invested in the local community. If asked why food is being imported for the guests, the answer is, invariably, that their customers have certain expectations, which the owners have a duty to meet. Kasbah Tamadot is a living illustration of how this does not have to be the case. It never fails to deliver quality service and products to its guests but always alongside an ethos that is branded strongly on its literature and website. Guests know that the hotel has a 'commitment to the community'. That is, in itself, a strong part of its pull. Many travellers feel uncomfortable shut within the walls of their luxury hotel compound, with absolutely no interaction with the indigenous people. They seek to get stuck in with the local culture, to experience things that will widen their horizons.

I had read in my guidebook to Morocco of the Moorish proverb that said, 'The Earth is a peacock. Morocco is its tail', and there is something majestic in the red cities, proud kasbahs, and soaring mountains. We took the mountain road to the village of Asni, climbing further into the foothills, past thousand-year-old Berber villages and crumbling forts. I felt like I had stepped back a millennium. A place frozen in time – if you could only Tipp-ex out the telegraph poles. For the last part of our journey the road deteriorated to little more than a single track, sometimes tarmac, sometimes mud, which clung precariously to the mountainside. There was no guard rail between our jeep and the eye-watering drop of 80 metres to the valley floor. I took confidence from my driver, who looked like an FBI agent in his designer shades and who coolly assured me he had driven these bends hundreds of times before. After an hour, we had our first glimpse of Kasbah Tamadot, perched at the edge of a valley against a backdrop of snow-capped peaks, like an enchanted citadel from *The Arabian Nights*.

By now it was dark which only added to the mystery of the place. We entered via huge, carved doors, which seemed to be begging you to say 'Open Sesame', and I was led along a candlelit pathway to my room. The next morning, I had the chance to explore the hotel. It was beautifully decorated with statues and mosaics; pink rose petals scattered in a reflecting pool; a Rapunzel tower adding to the romance. I allowed myself a little time to revel in its opulence and tranquillity before immersing myself in the community outside its fortified walls and getting down to business.

Before opening the doors of the hotel, Virgin had invested two years in training the local Berbers to be waiters, cooks, housekeepers and receptionists. This wasn't a mean feat – with formal education ceasing for local girls at 12 years and for boys at 14, it had been a challenge to teach the adults English to a standard that they could converse fluently with the hotel guests. Adding a fourth language to their repertoire – which already contained Berber, Arabic and French – was enough to confuse the most educated of brains. None of them had experience of the hospitality industry: previously they had been farmers, apple pickers, housewives or taxi drivers. The investment had been considerable, and now that the hotel was a smooth-running, flawless operation, Branson was looking for other ways to uplift the community that surrounded it. My first task was to ensure the long-planned community centre was complete by the start of the school term, the following September. The building had been lying unfinished for a while, weeds growing on the foundations, and it needed someone to inject energy into the project. My second was to look at how to improve the local healthcare. (Little did I realise that I would be brushing up my rusty nursing skills before long!)

The next morning I moved to the ex-pat staff house in Asni village, a mile down the hill from the Kasbah. I had three housemates: the head chef and his assistant, brothers from New Zealand; and a flamboyant restaurant manager, a Frenchman from New York. I unpacked my suitcase, which had been my mobile home for the past ten years – a decade in which I'd visited sixteen countries in three continents. I had grown adept at creating my 'space' and in no time my room was a little shrine to my travels: I draped my Tibetan prayer flags over the wardrobe, and on my bedside table I put my carved Buddha from Thailand

and a little thumb-sized silver Ganesh from India. My favourite photo, of Nelson Mandela and His Holiness the Dalai Lama standing side by side grinning, was where I could see it the moment I opened my eyes in the morning. I sat on the bed, looking out at the reddish-brown mountains, dotted with green walnut groves and boxy mud-brick dwellings, and reflected on the richness of my journey. As I did so, the *muezzin* started up, a cacophony of voices calling out from loudspeakers in every village – the Islamic call to prayer. The voices didn't sing in unison but were staggered, like the rounds I used to sing at school. 'Allahu Akbar' ...God is the greatest.

A car beeped outside my window. Zoubair, the long-time manager of the Eve Branson Foundation, had arrived to show me around the local area.

'Bonjour. Ca va?' I called out cheerily as I approached.

Zoubair jumped out of his car to greet me, his English perfect. 'Lovely to meet you!'

I was soon to learn that, before working at the Kasbah, he had been an English teacher at one of the top schools in Marrakesh, a well-educated man with a passion for literature. Zoubair was dressed as if he were going out to dinner, in light-coloured fitted trousers and a striped long-sleeved shirt. I was particularly impressed with his shoes which were made of soft pale-brown leather with a very long chisel toe, similar to 1950s winkle pickers.

'Where are we going?' I asked him.

'Let's go straight to the community centre. You need to see it before talking to anyone else. It's going to be a major job to get it finished.'

As we drove he told me about the Berbers, a tribe who fled to the mountains when the Arabs invaded in the 7th Century. As he spoke, we saw an old Berber tribesman up ahead, walking slowly, his long, dark-brown hooded robe, the *djellaba*, trailing on the ground. He looked as if he had walked off a set of *Lord of the Rings*. As we drew closer I could see that his long hood was being used as an informal pocket: a stick of bread was poking out of it, bouncing as he walked. As we drew near the centre, in the village opposite the Kasbah, we saw a group of school girls, identical in black trousers, white tunics and navy-blue *hijabs*. They waved to us. It felt good to be in a place where Muslim women weren't hidden away or cowed by oppression, who met your eyes with curiosity and confidence.

On the way to the centre, Zoubair tooted his horn at a woman on a motorbike. She swung the bike round and drove it alongside his car.

'Linda, I want you to meet Amina!'

I sensed at once Amina's energy and strong life-force. Everything about her exuded confidence. She had a helmet and goggles over her *hijab* and, instead of biker boots, she was wearing a pair of stiletto *babouche*, the traditional Aladdin shoes but with an extra, sexy twist.

'*Salum alikum*, Linda!'

Zoubair told me we would need to talk in French as Amina had little English. I had been flicking desperately through my French dictionary the previous day, knowing that my worse-than-schoolgirl French would need a dust-off. I caught some of what Amina was saying and Zoubair filled in the rest.

'We are so happy you have come. That community centre in Asni is so badly needed.'

She said that every place would be snatched up as soon as the centre was open, as with the girls leaving school at twelve and so many boys unemployed it would be a safe place for them to continue their education. That was good to hear. I had seen plenty of cosmetic endeavours: projects launched in the right spirit but without the necessary groundwork. Hospitals that no one used, as the community had no access to new parts; school-buildings left to decay. Here, it was clear; the villagers were desperate to have a place that could serve their youngsters, something between a community college and youth club.

I asked Amina what she did.

'I teach at three craft centres in Asni,' she said. 'That's why I need my bike. If you need any help do let me know. I have Sunday afternoons free.'

As we drove away, Zoubair and Amina exchanged cheery waves. He told me that having Amina on his team was a true blessing.

'She's not at all typical of the mountain women,' he said. 'Although Berber social etiquette states that a married Berber woman cannot communicate directly with a man, other than her husband or a male relative, Amina refuses to play by the rules.'

I told him that I was used to similar restrictions in Pakistan.

'We cannot even discuss things on the phone with the Berber ladies,' he said. 'It gets a bit frustrating. I'm used to how it is in Marrakesh, which is much more liberal.'

He said that things were, at least, slowly changing for the better. 'The villagers used to throw stones at strangers,' he said.

'What, foreigners? Tourists?'

'No, a stranger could be someone from the next village!' He laughed.

Zoubair pulled up outside a wild, overgrown garden. 'Here it is,' he said, picking up a stick and starting to flatten the tall weeds and brambles. I was at a loss for words for a moment. Then, bit by bit, the shell of a concrete building appeared. There was rubbish everywhere; as well as a pile of rotting wood which would probably be quite useless now and a heap of bricks under sheets of plastic. Zoubair was huffing – it took a lot of effort to beat a path to the doorway.

'Be careful where you step. There are some ditches under all these weeds.'

I gingerly followed him, putting my feet wherever he had placed his. We stamped the mud and twigs off our shoes at the entrance and stepped through. Inside, the building had the same abandoned feeling, like a deserted ship. Everywhere bore traces of activity, but it was obvious no one had worked on the building for many months. Used cups and plates, empty coke bottles, half-empty cement bags, an old jacket were all covered in thick dust, dirt and cobwebs.

A moment later the Chairman of the Association arrived to give us the tour. Zoubair had explained that all permissions and decisions would have to go through him.

'I am so sorry,' he said Arabic, which Zoubair translated. 'I speak no English. Only a little French.'

I brought out my one word of Arabic: 'La-bass', a word Moroccans use endlessly, meaning 'don't worry'. Then, to cover all bases, I followed it with 'Pas de problème' and 'No problem'.

He looked at me, bushy eyebrows meeting in the middle in a frown of concentration – or consternation, I didn't know which.

I turned to Zoubair. 'Please let him know we will get along famously,' I said, putting my hand on my heart.

That seemed to do the trick, and the Chairman shot off into the first room. The tour of the building had started. He spoke fast, pointing at the unfinished wiring, the shell of a bathroom, toilet bowls standing in a heap in the middle, and a long line of unused paint pots. In every one of the five large rooms and two bathrooms the story was the same: everything was half-finished. It looked like the money had simply run out and that the workmen had downed their tools and walked away. There was much to be done.

'We'd better get going Linda,' Zoubair said, the tour finished.

'It's nearly prayer time.'

We said our goodbyes and headed back to the Kasbah, where there was a mosque onsite for the staff to use. As they had to pray five times a day, building the mosque had been a key element in the hotel's excellent model of efficiency.

I had booked an appointment with Hussein, the administration manager, and was relieved to find that he spoke good English. I needed to get to the bottom of why the centre was unfinished, and picking anyone's brain in French would have been a Herculean task for me. We sat on the beautiful terrace, overlooking the infinity pool, and looked across at farmers tending sheep on the distant hills. Beyond them, Mount Toubkal reared up, a smudge of grey-blue, white-capped and majestic. A waiter brought us some mint tea and Hussein, a calm, measured sort of man, waited while he filled the pot, swished and decanted, in a slow ceremony, before embarking on any conversation. Tea, unlike cooking, was a man's affair in this country and I waited respectfully while it was poured from a great height, and then tasted. He recited a poem about tea, with all the eloquence of a Shakespearian actor, then raised his glass.

'We call it Whisky Berbere!'

I grinned and raised my own. 'Cheers!'

The ceremony concluded, we got down to business. I learned that there were no childcare facilities for the women to use within a 50-mile radius. Berber women had a hard life, shouldering a large share of the agricultural work as well as being responsible for the domestic chores, the collection of firewood and the care of children. I realised that life would get a lot less hard for them if there was a community centre. The schoolroom currently being used was tiny – barely able to hold 40 children – and the teacher, who rarely received any pay, had few materials or toys with which to engage them.

'We really need the centre,' Hussein said earnestly. 'We plan to use the downstairs room as a boys' dormitory.'

He pointed at the craggy mountains and explained that there was no way, in this terrain, that the boys could walk home every night after school, especially once the snows arrived and the villages were cut off. I asked him why the building had stood unfinished for over a year.

'Misunderstanding. Poor communication...Arguments,' he said.

The usual, then, I thought. I told him that I needed to talk to the key person, who would be responsible for builders and deadlines, so that we could agree some goals. I was told Rasheed was my man.

By the time I met with Rasheed the following day, I had come up with a plan for the centre. It was more elaborate than the one that had been discussed but if it was to do The Kasbah justice then I wanted it to be a cutting-edge learning centre, the first of its kind for 100 miles. It would contain a crèche, as well as the boys' dormitory, and would offer evening as well as day school for skills development. Not one part of the building would stand idle, any time – day or night.

We met for lunch in Asni, a town built around a road junction and river valley. I realised, as we drove through it, that it was not so much a town as a collection of villages. The day was Saturday – market day – and the *souk* was bustling. Hundreds of men had come down from their mountain villages to stock up on provisions. There was hardly a woman in sight. Rasheed and I greeted each other. A middle-aged man, well dressed in stylish Western clothes, he looked every bit the successful businessman, I thought.

'Hussein said that you want to experience the hustle and bustle of the *souk*,' he said. 'But first you need to taste the tagine.'

We made our way slowly through the crowd towards an outdoor restaurant with tables on the street. Rasheed went over to one of the waiters to ask what was the special of the day. A few moments later the waiter came to our table, carrying a rust-coloured clay dish with a conical lid. With a flourish he removed it and revealed a fragrant, bubbling mutton stew, cooked with pumpkin, raisins, nuts, quinces and loquats.

'It's been simmering all day in its own juices,' said Rasheed. We were both salivating with expectation.

'Eat! Eat!'

We broke our bread into wedge-shaped pieces – there was no cutlery – and scooped up the stew. We ate ravenously before pausing to discuss the community centre. Rasheed told me he was a builder by trade, an entrepreneur who had built up a successful business sub-contracting. As he spoke, I could see that he had an enthusiasm for the project that went way beyond what it might mean in terms of financial return.

'My children will soon be old enough for the creche at the community centre,' he said.

He asked me when we wanted the centre finished. I had met the other stakeholders and untangled the myriad political and diplomatic reasons the project had stalled. Now that they were all in agreement it only left agreeing a deadline with Rasheed.

'In ten weeks. I know it sounds unfeasible but it's the start of the new school term.'

'*Inshallah*,' Rasheed said with a twinkle. 'You get me the permissions and the cash, I'll make sure it is done.'

He looked at the plans then remarked, 'I do think we need a playground, Linda. There's nowhere safe for the children to play. Not for 40 miles.'

'I'll look at the budget and see what we can do,' I promised him.

We continued to talk about the centre while the waiters

poured our mint tea, increasing the height of the pot until the liquid splashed us both, much to the hilarity of the men sitting at tables nearby. Rasheed then took me on a tour of the *souk*, past towers of brightly coloured spices, stalls selling olives, fresh herbs, or cubes of Berber perfume made from musk and amber. We watched as coppersmiths banged copper sheets to make huge cauldrons, which prompted Rasheed to say:

'If we can have adult skills training at the centre it would be a godsend. There is so much unemployment at present.'

'What do you think about a course in mobile-phone repairing?' I asked. 'It's the one thing everyone seems to have. Even in the mountains.'

'Good idea,' he smiled. 'I can be their first customer. I've got a few lying in a drawer at home which need repairing.'

We stopped to buy some mint. A whiff of roasted sheep's head made me screw up my nose. Rasheed laughed and thrust a few sprigs at me.

'Berber gas mask!' he laughed.

Over the next ten weeks, Rasheed became my most generous-hearted ally. Nothing was ever too much trouble. To save time, he employed teams of men to work simultaneously: painting; constructing a kitchen for the boarders; clearing the overgrown garden; landscaping a playground; digging ditches; and building flood walls. Even during Ramadan, when the workers couldn't eat in daylight hours and tended to get dispirited or grumpy, he worked alongside his men, keeping up their morale. As the centre quickly took shape, crowds of villagers gathered each day to watch and comment, excited to talk about what they wanted to do with it. All of us, builders and managers, were infected by the general buzz of anticipation.

It was touch and go whether we would make the deadline. Rather ambitiously, I had asked various VIPs – including

Richard Branson's mother, Eve, and the district governor of the initiative – to a party on D-day. For the 48 hours before it, Rasheed and his team worked through the night to make everything perfect. They even managed to plant flowers.

It was a wonderful celebration. Everyone turned out for it: men, women and children. Twelve male drummers, dressed head to toe in white, and ten flamboyantly dressed female singers played and sang for hours, everyone joining in. The men and women sang call-and-response choruses, their voices competing with the frenzied noise from the drums. At times, the group broke into a Moroccan form of line-dancing, tassled fezzes spinning. There were speeches and, when it came to my turn, I called out for Rasheed to stand beside me on the platform. He was with his workers, in a group at the back, and when he came up there was cheering from the crowd. His eyes glittered in the flash of the camera bulbs, and I saw that they were full of tears.

At the same time that I had been supervising the building of the community centre, I was also working on another assignment for Virgin. The company wanted me to assess the medical situation in this mountainous area and see how they could assist and upgrade it. I knew I would enjoy this part of the project. Although it had been fifteen years since I had worked as a nurse, I was still fascinated by the medical profession and how healthcare differed in each country. Little did I realise that, before long, I would be mucking in as a nurse whenever there was a need for one at the Kasbah. Some projects in my career as an aid worker, such as that with the Burmese refugees, simply needed me to act as facilitator, getting the best out of a group. Others like this involved rolling up my sleeves and getting truly stuck in.

The nearest well-equipped hospital was over an hour's drive

from the Kasbah, along a tortuous road. There was a countrywide shortage of trained medical staff, and any attempts to lure them into living and working in remote rural areas with poor facilities had been useless. It did not help that the promised 'friendship' pay never seemed to materialise. As a result, what medics there were in these remote places were overstretched to a ludicrous degree.

I began by conducting a public survey, asking a wide cross-section of the community which surrounded Kasbah Tamadot their opinion of the current medical services. There were many complaints, unsurprisingly. However, two names came up repeatedly – men who seemed to be respected to the point of adoration: Hajj Maurice and Abderahim. It was to these 'living legends' that I went first.

Hajj Maurice, I discovered, was the Berber manager of another hotel in the Atlas Mountains, Kasbah Du Toubkal. I had already heard of it: the hotel was managed and staffed entirely by the local Berbers, rather than professional ex-pat hoteliers, and it was a 'responsible tourism' treasure. I was looking forward to seeing it and to meeting the man who was, in a large part, responsible for its success. The farsighted and generous-spirited British owners of the hotel, Mike and Chris McHugo, showed a real dedication to helping the community, energetically raising money for local projects. They gave Hajj Maurice the responsibility to ensure it was well spent. I was keen to meet the man in whom they, and the local villagers, put so much faith.

The road from Asni to Imlil meandered along a dried-up river bed. It was a startling, lunar-like, landscape. My driver snaked his way through the canyon, under rocky ledges, the air getting distinctly cooler as we climbed. Rounding the last hillside, I caught my first glimpse of Kasbah du Toubkal, perched on an outcrop of rock. It took my breath away. Hajj Maurice had asked me to lunch and had warned me that the hotel could only be accessed on foot or by mule. He told me to wear sensible shoes and ask for directions from Imlil, the village tucked away in the valley below.

Imlil, it turned out, was hardly a village: just a small row of shops and restaurants that served the backpackers who wanted to conquer Mount Toubkal, the highest peak in Morocco. A shopkeeper told me where to go and I climbed for fifteen minutes, through fragrant apple orchards and walnut groves. When I reached the top, I was panting. The hotel receptionist told me to sit down (presumably before I collapsed!) and hold my hands over a metal bowl. He proceeded to pour rosewater over them in a traditional Berber greeting. I was then given a date to eat, and a bowl of milk to dip it into.

'Hajj is expecting you. He said to take you to the terrace,' the man said.

I followed him outside and waited for my host, flicking through a picture book, *The Making of Kundun*. Martin Scorsese had used the hotel as a film set in his movie about the Dalai Lama. I looked down at the valley below and wondered how the hell he had got crew and camera equipment up all the way up here.

'Linda! *Bienvenue!*' Hajj said, giving me a warm handshake. The receptionist stayed with us as translator.

I was amazed to see that Hajj, the man with the enormous reputation, was not even five feet tall. His heavy grey *dhalleba* seemed to swallow him up. Despite his slight frame, however, there was an aura about him – something that felt powerfully wise. I told him that Virgin had asked me to assess the healthcare in the local region and asked him what he thought were the key needs.

'There is no phone signal up there.' He pointed to the mountains. I looked at the paths, criss-crossing them like tiny veins, and thought they looked treacherous. 'In an emergency the villagers cannot get hold of anyone quickly. Their only option is to get the sick down to a road and call for help from there. Many don't make it.'

'What medical staff are there?' I asked.

'We have no doctor. Just one nurse. Hameed. Works in Imlil.'

Hajj told me that Hameed was responsible for the total medical care of over 20,000 people.

'Mother and baby care. Vaccinations. Accidents. He does it all.'

Hajj said that there was a high incidence of diabetes in the area. My mind went instantly to all the sweet mint tea I had seen drunk in copious amounts. Heart attacks and strokes were equally common.

'And your nearest doctor?'

'We have a small clinic in Asni. There's a doctor there holds day-time clinics a few times a week. Otherwise it's Tahanoute, which has a small Accident and Emergency. After that, Marrakesh.'

He told me that the conditions at the clinic in Asni were very basic.

'In winter, there's no heating. The mothers have to give birth in the freezing cold.'

It seemed they were desperately in need of midwives as women in this conservative community refused to be tended to by men.

'In Asni clinic alone, there are 620 births a year,' Hajj said.

I was shocked. 'But how on earth do they cope?'

'It's a bit crazy. With the lack of qualified staff here, most women end up giving birth at the hospital in Marrakesh.'

'But that's ridiculous!' I exclaimed. 'It's a ninety minute drive!'

'A long way if you're in pain,' Hajj agreed.

He told me he wanted me to meet Abderahim, their ambulance driver. I told him that his was the other name I had heard most frequently on people's lips.

Hajj smiled tenderly. 'He's a father of three young boys. Loves his family. Loves his job,' he said. 'Do you know, he's never had a day's medical training in his life? All he knows he has learned on the job.'

The more Hajj told me about Abderahim, the more I understood why he was held in such reverence. A man on call 24 hours a day, 365 days a year. And all for less than £25 a week.

'Entirely his choice – the government doesn't pay for him to work those hours,' Hajj said. 'Everyone loves him. He's saved a lot of lives.'

Hearing about Abderahim made my heart swell with gratitude. That there are people like him out there – inspirational role models every one of them – reminds you how powerful and selfless the human spirit can be.

Mohammed, the singing muleteer, was waiting to take me down the hill. I bounced along as my mule navigated the rocky ravines, marvelling at what extraordinary agility the ungainly looking animal possessed. When we got to Asni, Hameed, the nurse, was in his clinic, a long line of customers waiting to see him. I poked my head in.

Hello, I'm Linda. Hajj sent me.'

'Oh, hi. I hear you're a nurse,' he said. 'Why don't you sit next to me and that will give you a feel of what we're doing here. In 30 minutes we can stop for lunch.'

I sat down. We were in an icy, cave-like room. It didn't look anything like a clinic.

'Please excuse the room,' Hameed said, seeing me look round the room, aghast. 'It's the garage for the ambulance. The clinic room is being repaired. I couldn't close up, as the government recommended, so I've parked the ambulance outside.'

He had made good use of the cramped space. Behind a green

hospital screen was a bed for examination purposes. He had rigged up an IV device on the unplastered garage wall. On a desk was a set of baby scales and on the back wall there was a fridge to store the vaccinations.

It was obvious that everyone loved Hameed. He listened carefully and tenderly to people's problems. If a child was in tears they soon dried up when he spoke to them.

Just before lunch, a man rushed in, having fallen off his bike. There was a large, bloody slash on his knee.

'Looks like we will need to sew this one up,' Hameed said.

I asked him how on earth he managed to keep the place sterile. There was no source of water in the room.

'As best we can,' he said with a grimace. 'We use plenty of this.'

He was brandishing a big bottle of bright orange iodine. 'It kills all known germs!'

Over lunch, Hameed described his work. I could see how overstretched and frustrated he was. He wanted to go on training courses but he explained that if he left, there would be no one to stand in for him. He needed more equipment, especially diagnostic items. The government gave them a meagre supply of basic dressings and medicine each month but once that was gone he had nothing until there was a new delivery. It was all so unpredictable and unreliable. What was heartening, though, was that Hameed loved his job in spite of the problems.

'Can I meet Abdrahim today?' I asked, crossing my fingers.

'He was delivering a baby at 3am this morning,' he said, pulling out his phone. 'I'll give his wife a call and see if he's up yet. He sleeps whenever he can.'

He spoke briefly on his mobile, then said, 'You're in luck. He'll meet us at the ambulance.'

When we arrived, Abderahim was cleaning the headlights of the ambulance. Hameed called out to him. He looked up and beamed at his friend. Hameed told him about my project, speaking in Berber. Abderahim turned to me, and I saw how tired he looked, older than his years. He told me that he spoke a little French, but no English. I was used to that by now and my French was becoming a little more fluent every day.

'How long have you been working the ambulance?' I asked.

'Ten years. I delivered a beautiful baby boy in the back last night. We tried to get the mother to the clinic on time but the baby came so quickly.'

Abderahim opened the ambulance door. 'We don't have much equipment.'

There was only a stretcher bed and a stretcher chair, one blanket and a pillow. A small first aid cabinet was on the wall but it was virtually empty. There only seemed to be one bandage inside.

Hameed patted his friend's back. 'Never a day's formal training and he saves lives every week. Whenever he can, he sits in the clinic, listening and learning,' he said. 'He must just be a natural physician.'

Natural physician or no, I reckoned that he would welcome some more training and I knew someone who could give him just that, without his having to take a leave of absence. A Virgin healthcare volunteer, Roger, had been wanting to come out to Morocco for a few months. He had worked over 20 years in the ambulance service and was now a paramedic trainer. It was perfect. I could see exactly how his skills could be put to good use. I called him that evening and asked him to come out as soon as he could.

I met Roger at the airport. He was a large man, from the North of England, with an easy-going vibe. I could tell he would be happy to fit in anywhere. A perfect volunteer.

'That was a close one!' he laughed, after we had introduced ourselves. 'I got stopped by customs.'

'Why?' I asked.

'I'd forgotten to warn them that I was carrying adult and baby resuscitation mannequins. Oops!'

I laughed, imagining the scene. They must have thought they had found a serial killer.

'I've also got a portable defibrillator. I'm surprised they didn't lock me up. All those wires!'

'Poor guys,' I said. 'You must have given them a heart attack!'

'Well at least I had the right equipment on me.'

I hoped Roger wouldn't be fazed by the hectic schedule I had planned for him. It was his first time as a volunteer in a developing country, I learned, but I had visited all of the hotch-potch medical facilities between Imlil and Marrakesh and everyone wanted a piece of him.

He managed three training sessions a day in different locations to groups of midwives, nurses and doctors, covering CPR for adults and children, wounds and bleeding, the recovery position, dealing with choking and how to immobilise broken bones. In response to their eager questions, he updated them on everything from how to manage angina and heart attacks to epilepsy, shock and burns. For many of his students, it was the only medical training they had ever had.

Roger worked hard and loved it. He was shocked by the lack of resources but took it all in his stride. Hameed and Abderahim moved heaven and earth to spend time with Roger, the former shadowing him in most of his training groups, asking detailed questions about each exercise and taking copious notes. For both men, it was like the cool drink of water they had longed for, such was their thirst for knowledge, and they wanted to suck up every word. Abderahim spent every spare minute practising on the resuscitation mannequins, taking great pains to ensure that his technique was correct. For ten days Roger's feet did not touch the ground. He spent many hours in the ambulance with

Abderahim, joking and laughing like old buddies. He was bowled over by their response to him. Infected by their enthusiasm, he was filled with the desire to do more. Nothing seemed to wear him out. He told me that he had never seen such a hunger to learn in all his days as a paramedic trainer.

Roger was like a big, smiley teddy bear and everyone, even the girls, came out of their shells, warmed by his big personality. He was asked by the housemother at a local girl's boarding hostel, Education For All, funded by Mike and Chris McHugo, if he could run a session with them. It was a lovely sight, watching the girls take turns practising the recovery position on each other, a little embarrassed and giggling, but happy to be around Roger. One evening, I asked him if he could squeeze in a basic first aid training session with the local taxi drivers. They were invariably first on the scene of a road accident and I knew that with a little more knowledge they could save lives.

The only time I ever saw Roger knocked out of his comfort zone was when he had to hike up one of the hills. When we set off one day to meet Hajj at Kasbah du Toubkal, he wheezed up the hillside, nearly keeling over at the top.

'I'm not fit enough for this, Linda,' he gasped.

'Don't worry, Roger,' I said, trying not to laugh as he had rosewater poured over his big hands. 'You can ride the mule on the way down.'

The two weeks nearly over, I went to Roger with a list of supplies I thought we should order, making the best use of our budget. I had been over it several times, having consulted countless locals. He checked it over carefully.

'That should do it. There's enough basic first aid stuff there and you'll be able to equip the ambulance too. Abderahim will be dead chuffed.'

It is always to be hoped that volunteers gain as much from

their experience as they give. It is certainly the case for me, and it was for Roger too. There was a spring in his step when he walked across to the departure gate at the airport to catch his flight home. No one had wanted him to leave, but he swore that he would be back as soon as he could.

Over the following weeks all sorts of innovative ideas came bursting through, as Hameed, Abderahim and I put our heads together, brainstorming the best ways to teach the locals more about preventive medicine. Preventive medicine was a new concept for Hameed and 'a stitch in time saves nine' became his new mantra. Hameed was concerned that as Berber was solely an oral language, it was pointless producing pamphlets and literature for his patients. Instead, he became Asni's first video star. We recorded him giving advice, and the films were played on a DVD player at the clinic, where he had a captive audience in the long queue of people that was always waiting to see him.

I sought Hajj Maurice's advice on any sensitive issues as I started to draft a plan of how we might improve the emergency response to the remote mountain areas, literally off the beaten track. I was reflecting on a project I had managed in Thailand, after the tsunami, and the idea came to me that we might be able to use the same model in Morocco. It would be a case of training two people from each village to become 'barefoot doctors', competent in basic first aid. This would save time and lives. We would also provide stretchers to enable the locals to bring the patient to the ambulance. Hajj was delighted with the idea, as the current situation had been a worry to him for a long time, and he immediately got started on making the selection.

The extraordinary community feeling that built up in and around the Kasbah even extended itself to the hotel guests who were always fascinated to hear about the project. Such was the buzz that had been created around the medical uplift programme

that somehow I became the 'honorary medical advisor' to staff
and guests. All very well when it was bruises and scratches but
more demanding when someone's life was at risk. It was over 20
years since I was first at the scene of a medical emergency but my
nursing skills flooded back the night we were called help a young
woman, on the brink of slipping into a diabetic coma.

Joan, a young travel agent from the UK, had been doing a
recce of hotels in the area for her company. She had made friends
with the staff at the Kasbah and, although she had moved on to
stay in another hotel, in a cottage in the grounds, it was to the
Kasbah that she put in a call when she started to feel really
unwell. I was woken at one in the morning. It was the night
porter on the phone who explained that Joan had called him and
that she was feeling unwell.

'Where is she?'

'She is staying at La Bergerie.'

'Give me five minutes. Send a car and I'll be ready.'

I called Abderahim. After three rings he picked up.

'*Salam alikum*'

'*Bonsoir*, Abderahim. Sorry to disturb you. We have an
emergency. Can you come?'

I explained where Joan was staying and he said that he would
pick up Hameed on the way.

His voice was husky, still half-asleep, when he replied in his
broken French, 'On my way, Linda. I will meet you on the road
to La Bergerie.'

Hameed and I were shown to Joan's cottage by the night
porter. The building was tucked away in an isolated part of the
grounds. There was a light on inside but when I knocked on the
door there was no sound. I peered in at the window.

'Quick. You'll need to open the door. She's collapsed.'

The night porter went to get a key and I spoke to Joan through the door, reassuring her that we were there, that she would be okay. A few minutes later we were in her room. The smell of vomit was overpowering. A trail of it led from the bathroom to her bed, where she lay slumped. Hameed checked her blood pressure. It was dangerously low. She was slipping in and out of consciousness and her skin was ice cold and clammy. Her eyes had sunk into their sockets from dehydration. She whispered something and I put my head close to hers.

Her voice was so weak it was almost unintelligible: 'I'm a diabetic. Need insulin,' she whispered. 'Can't keep a sip down. My electrolytes are messed up.'

'Don't worry. We're getting you to the ambulance.' I said. 'Just hang on in there. Everything will be fine.'

Hameed set up an intravenous drip and took her sugar levels. He looked worried.

'Normally we'd take her to the private hospital in Marrakesh but I don't think that would be wise,' he said.

'I agree. It's over an hour away and I don't think she'll make it that far,' I said quietly so Joan wouldn't hear.

By now Abderahim had arrived. He was coolly in control and it relaxed us both.

Look, I will call ahead to every one of the facilities between here and Marrakesh,' he said. 'We'll see who responds first.'

I knew that Abderahim was universally loved by healthcare workers in the region. That is was what counted in an emergency like this. I was sure that someone would pull out the stops for him. I remembered all those occasions when, sitting up front with him in the ambulance, whomever we passed, whether they were on a mule, in a car, or on foot, would wave or beep their horn. My prediction turned out to be true: the main element that ended up saving the girl's life was pure, old-fashioned goodwill. Within seconds, Abderahim had found a doctor willing to help.

'Got one!' he said. 'He will meet us at Tahanoute hospital. Let's get her to the ambulance.'

Abheradim drove fast, taking the bends like a seasoned rally driver, keeping it as smooth as possible. I kept one hand on Joan's pulse. Her eyes were closed.

We're two minutes away,' he said into his phone, warning the doctor of our imminent arrival.

The doctor was standing in the freezing cold, waiting, the gates of the hospital already open. Once inside, he got to work swiftly, setting up multiple IV lines.

'It will take a few hours, but she will be fine,' he said.

I was shocked at the condition of the Accident and Emergency room. The bed sheet was streaked with blood and dirt, there were used needles scattered on the floor, and soiled blankets were piled up by the door.

'Why is it in such a mess?' I asked Hameed quietly.

'No regular cleaners. They come in maybe once a week,' he said. 'The doctors don't have time to clean as well as care for patients.'

By 5am the colour was coming back to Joan's cheeks and she opened her eyes. Hameed called the doctor, who was catching up on his sleep in the room next door.

He checked his patient over. 'You can take her home now.'

I was surprised that he would let her leave. 'Surely she should stay a bit longer?'

Hameed explained the situation. 'They have to free up the bed. There's no other option. The doctor has done his bit. It's up to us now.'

'How do you feel?' I asked Joan.

'Weak...but OK,' she said, putting on a brave smile. She looked around the group standing beside her bed. 'Thank you. You saved my life.'

Then we were back on the road, climbing through the

foothills, the moon illuminating our path so brightly that there was almost no need for headlamps. When we got back to the Kasbah, the staff prepared a bed for Joan, and I took my leave of Abderahim and Hameed. I hugged them wordlessly. Grateful for their tireless labour, the nobility of the 'unsung hero'. 'It is in men like these,' I thought to myself, 'hungry for knowledge, driven to help, that success lies'. All the medical equipment in the world couldn't replace that.

Throughout Joan's ordeal I had kept her family informed of her progress on the phone and via email. After she was better, and safely back home, her mother wrote me an email:

'What you all did was beyond the call of duty and we thank you from the bottom of our hearts. We hear on the news of bad things that happen in the world and sometimes think that there are not many good people around, but you and everyone that helped Joan – the doctors, nurses, and ambulance driver – have certainly restored our faith in human nature.'

The power of kindness, in a people who had so little in the way of worldly wealth, had made its mark on Joan. Over the following months I had several messages from her. Increasingly she felt a desire to 'give back' and was keen to become a volunteer in a developing country.

I had seen Virgin initiating the vision, developing a whole new brand of tourism whose time has come. For the traveller, it is an experience which is not purely physical or sensory, but one which stimulates and broadens the mind. The vision is one that germinates and grows organically, inspiring the minds of all those who come into contact with it.

CHAPTER NINE

THE RIPPLE EFFECT

In Morocco, I had seen 'the ripple effect' work its magic. The image of a seed always comes to mind, falling from a tree into the pond below, disturbing the surface, the ripples broadcasting the seed's message across the still water. Roger, the paramedic trainer who had come out to Morocco to train local health workers, returned to the UK so lit up by the success of his visit that he helped engender a whole new charitable vision in his company – more volunteers are lined up to come out and build on Roger's foundation. Joan, the diabetic whose life we had saved, had felt her life so jolted out of its ordinary groove that she too became fired up with a determination to help, keen to volunteer anywhere in the developing world that needed her skills.

When you are so immersed in the stuff of everyday life, it is hard to put your head above the surface and take a look around. When I was working in Morocco, I met a man who was a walking example of just this predicament, Lee, the chef at Kasbah Tamadot.

Most evenings I didn't manage to make it to the staff canteen in time for supper. I would wander up the back stairs and into the kitchen in the hope that someone would slip me a snack. I'd stand in the corner, waiting until there was a pause, watching the kitchen staff moving seamlessly from one gleaming stainless steel counter to the next, carrying trays of cakes, platters of meat, and glistening puddings. Lee moved around the kitchen with graceful athleticism, tasting sauces and scrutinising each plate before it went out to the dining room. When he saw me he would come over and stand stern-faced, hands on hips.

'Hi Lee. Sorry I've missed dinner again. Is there anything I can eat?'

'No way, mate,' he said in his laconic New Zealand drawl. 'Look, Linda, if you can't make it on time, then forget it.'

He couldn't play it straight for long: his eyes always gave him away. 'What do you want? A cheese sandwich?'

I grinned. 'Perfect! Thank you.'

Lee was a naturally reserved man but over the first couple of months at the Kasbah our conversations grew slightly longer, although never expansive. A dedicated professional and a perfectionist, he seemed driven to exceed his own expectations. He hardly ever took a day off, preferring to catch up on paperwork and hang around the kitchen, to be there in case his team of Berber workers needed him. I could tell that he was curious about my work and I enjoyed talking to him about his. I was intrigued by the man, sensing that he was a bit of a puzzle. I felt that there was something in him, warm but guarded, that longed to express itself.

My mind naturally flicks about making connections between people, wanting them to meet each other, to share their talents and resources. It is a useful skill to have when you need to get projects off the ground. I can be as annoying as a persistent gnat when driven by a new idea, but even the most introverted and taciturn individuals invariably end up being drawn into my plan, if only so they can get rid of the buzzing in their ears! With Lee, it took several weeks of pestering but when he did succumb, he developed a whole new side to his work and discovered things in his own character that he had never given himself the chance to explore.

It all started the day I went to visit a craft centre.

Eve Branson – a veritable philanthropic whirlwind – had asked me to help her find new premises for a group of female craft workers who were currently using a damp garage. I had spotted somewhere I thought might suit their needs, a building high up on a hill near the Kasbah. I arranged to meet Hassan, head of the Community Association, to enquire about availability. To get there I had to climb a path that seemed almost vertical and, as I puffed and panted my way to the top, I wondered how Eve's group would ever be able to get their equipment and sewing machines up there. Hassan was waiting outside, a tall, elegant man with a handlebar moustache and beautiful manners. He took one look at my red face and dashed off to fetch a glass of water. Arriving for meetings in a muck sweat and panting like a dog was by now a familiar experience. The hill climbs never seemed to get any easier. But for now, I was happy to sit and take in the view while my breathing slowly steadied to normal. An emaciated grey kitten jumped onto the table and rubbed against me. I scratched it behind the ears.

'Shoo!' Hassan said, when he saw it. 'These cats know that my ladies will give them the mutton bones so they never let us alone.'

I told him of Eve's craft workers and their predicament. He said that he would happily make space for them.

'That's fantastic,' I said. 'They will be thrilled.'

'Come and see the building,' he suggested. 'I think you will be interested in what my ladies are doing.'

I was happy to oblige, not being in any hurry to tackle the hill again – the path was so thick with mud that I couldn't see any other way of getting down it other than sliding on my bottom. I followed Hassan into the first room where we found a group of women sitting legs apart on mats, earthenware dishes lodged between their knees. Each was rolling small pieces of dough in their fingers.

'What are they making?' I asked Hassan.

'Couscous,' he replied. 'Made from semolina. It's a tradition for us to have it on Fridays, after midday prayers.'

He explained that the semolina, once sprinkled with water and rolled into tiny balls, is dusted with dry flour and then sieved. Any pellets that fall through the sieve are rolled again with a little dry semolina.

'It's a big part of our feast days. At weddings the bride separates the couscous between her husband's family and her own,' he said. 'It symbolises the sharing of happiness.'

Hassan went on to tell me how Berbers make it with *smen*, a preserved butter.

'It gives a wonderful flavour,' he said.

'It seems very labour-intensive,' I said, watching the women massaging the little pellets.

'If you have the time, would you like to taste some?' he asked. I said I would be happy to. The climb had given me quite an appetite.

We continued through to the next room, where shelves on the wall were stacked with honey pots.

'We have hives across the valley,' he said. 'It is wonderful honey. Organic.'

He gave me a spoon and I licked it. Sweetness and fragrance exploded in my mouth, pure and heady.

The next room was where they dried the herbs. Hassan told me that Berbers have a herbal remedy for absolutely everything.

'Thyme,' he said, handing me a sprig. 'A powerful antiseptic and expectorant. They have been using it for thousands of years. Good for bronchitis and asthma.'

'I've heard it's great for stomach problems,' I said.

'For sure. That too. We drink it as a tea.'

He led me to the dining room and we sat down while the women of the house carried in the couscous. It tasted heavenly – not like anything one might find at home.

That made me think of Lee, the Kiwi chef. 'He has got to try this,' I said to myself.

Before I could ask Hassan the question that was on the tip of my tongue, he was there before me, telling me that the ladies could make couscous in any quantity. With his bird-like sharpness he had already read what was in my mind, and was darting ahead.

'What about saffron?' he asked. 'Where does the Kasbah get theirs?'

'I don't know, but I've heard the chef complaining that he spends thousands of Euros a month on it.'

'The most expensive food in the world, gram for gram,' Hassan said. 'The pickers have to collect each stigma from the purple crocuses, one by one. There are only three tiny threads to each flower head.

'Just imagine,' he said. 'It takes 200,000 flowers to make just one pound of saffron.'

He told me that they had started to cultivate saffron on the hillside terraces around the Association building.

'Would it be all right if our head chef paid you a visit?' I asked him.

'That would be our pleasure,' said Hassan, bowing his head.

As luck would have it, the following day Lee came back to the staff house for his afternoon break. We chatted while he made himself a cup of coffee and I asked him where he bought his saffron.

'We buy bucketloads from Marrakesh,' he said. 'Bloody expensive.'

'You know, they're growing it a mile down the road,' I said. 'You ought to pay them a visit. Lovely stuff. Couscous... honey...herbs.'

'I really don't think I can,' he said. 'You know how busy I am.'

'It's only five minutes down the road.'

'Still...' He sighed. If I had been a gnat he would have swotted me. 'Look, I don't promise anything. Maybe next week. If I get a light morning. Tuesday.' He looked at my eager face, knowing he was beaten. '*Maybe.*'

There wasn't a 'light morning', either the next week or for several weeks after that. But my pestering continued... buzz...buzz...buzz...until Lee had had enough. He called to say that he had a free afternoon the following day. I was in Casablanca, but I wasn't going to let the opportunity slip away from me. I asked Zoubair to take Lee to the craft centre.

The following evening, I waited up for Lee, longing to know how the visit had gone.

He bounced into the house. 'Linda! I had such fun,' he said. His usual laconic manner had vanished. 'I haven't felt this good since I got here!'

He told me how much he had loved the produce. 'You know me. I never eat in the mornings. But those ladies wouldn't give up until I had tried the couscous. It's fantastic!'

Lee was thrilled by the food but I sensed that there was more to it than that: he had been charmed by the Berber's kindness and old-fashioned courtesy. Their warm-hearted approach to life and work had inspired him.

His eyes were sparkling with joy when he told me about the crocuses. 'I'll never forget it. The first time in my life I've ever seen them growing. Beautiful, deep-lilac flowers. Purple veins on the petals and tiny little stamens,' he said. 'I've been cooking with saffron since I was a kid and I can't believe I knew so little about it.'

A powerful alchemy had been wrought in Lee that day. The delicate beauty of the flowers, the exquisite taste of the food and the kindness of his hosts had had a transformative effect on this usually taciturn New Zealander.

He was buzzing with ideas, speaking three times as fast as usual: 'We'll buy as much as we can from them, once I'm sure the quality's there,' he said. 'And here's an idea. Once a month I thought I'd cook with the ladies in the Association centre. We can add it to the guest programme.'

I gave Lee a hug.

It was the start of a beautiful trend. Guests jumped at the chance of visiting community projects. Many wrote comments on the website before their visit, asking what activities might bring them together with the locals, or how much locally sourced food was on offer. The ripple effect was beginning to happen in other ways too. Various ex-pat employees at the Kasbah wanted to get involved. When the financial controller asked how he could help it didn't take long to think up some ideas.

'We need to simplify the accounting system for the girls' craft centre so they can get actively involved,' I told him. 'A basic financial literacy course would be great. You could even teach one day a week at the centre if you like.'

Heads wagged; new initiatives unrolled. The idea of 'giving back' was kicking in, sometimes in the most unexpected of places.

I always know when it is time for me to leave. Part of me longs to stay with the friends I have grown to love but the other part knows that my work is done and I should be on my way. Time to move on to the next place, the next project.

A couple of weeks before my flight back to the UK, I had told Lee that I would very much like to throw a leaving party.

'How many would you like us to cater for?' he asked.

'I can't believe that many will turn up. It may be a bit far for some of the medics to travel and the Berbers don't tend to go out in the evenings.'

'Yeah. Eight o'clock and it's lights out.'

'We probably wouldn't get the women,' I said. 'I can't think they'll feel comfortable, knowing there are guys there. What do you think? Maybe twenty?'

At seven o'clock, guests started to arrive: friends who had become dear to me in the months we had been working together. By 8pm, sixty Berbers and a handful of ex-pats had poured through the door of the Kasbah. And they kept on coming. We spilled out onto the terrace in the ice-cold, starlit night. Hussain and Rasheed, Abderahim and Hameed, Hassan, Mike McHugo and the legendary Hajj Maurice.

One of the nurses, Kadeeja, came up to me and placed a large, soft package into my arms. 'It's a dressing gown the same as mine,' she said, grinning.

I remembered all those nights we screeched to the doors of her clinic on one emergency mission or another. She would be waiting for us at the door, blurry-eyed, and there was always something comforting in the sight of her, wrapped in a blue fluffy dressing gown appliquéd with large pink hearts and teddy bears.

I held it up to my cheek and felt its softness. 'Thank you!'

'We won't forget you, Linda,' she said, her eyes sweeping over the crowd of partygoers. 'Not one of us.'

Atticus Finch, in *To Kill a Mockingbird*, said you never really understand a person 'until you climb into his skin and walk around in it.' My son Graham was seven years old when I first had the inkling that he was getting the idea. I had tried to raise my children to think of a broader world than the one that was just outside our front door, to experience things that might at first seem foreign to them. I can still hear my father saying, '*Vive la difference!*' and I always knew that I wanted my kids to travel the world and feed their curiosity. I didn't want them growing up wrapped in cotton wool or unable to embrace a wider understanding of the world or a bigger vision for it.

We went to Egypt the summer Graham was seven. In Luxor we stayed in a hotel on the edge of the Nile. At the back of the building was a patch of waste ground, a sizeable area of dirt and rocks, where a group of children hung about, playing games or kicking around a football. Every day, on returning to the hotel after an excursion, thirsty and footsore, we would head down to the garden area to relax and have a drink. Graham would run off immediately to join the kids on the waste ground. He looked like a shiny penny in his bright new trainers and T-shirt. The others were barefoot and shirtless, wearing only knee-length shorts. My daughter and I would watch his blond head bobbing about, as the boys wheeled like seagulls, and I marvelled that children of any tribe can join in with each other's games seamlessly, without any need for language. For them it is the most natural thing in the world.

Graham had been so proud of the new kit I had bought him for the holiday. But, as the days passed, I detected a change in him, a new awareness. On our last day in Luxor, when he went out to play with the boys, he gave away his Nike trainers and T-shirt. He didn't say much about it, but from that day I sensed that his attitude had changed.

Now, twenty years on, Graham is a lance corporal in the Rifles. His battalion is stationed in Helmand Province. He is still as committed and thoughtful as ever. His rules of engagement are different from mine, soldier versus aid worker, but they do have a common thread. He is proud of me and I of him.

At one point, during the cyclone in Pakistan, we were working within 50 miles of each other. Graham was guarding the Afghan border with thirty other soldiers in a PB, one of the 'pillboxes' dotted along it. His mates would tease him – a running joke:

'Look, it's Graham's mum. Over there. The one in the burkha!'

He said he always half-expected to see me coming over the hill.

'Volunteering' is not for everyone. There are times when it doesn't fit, such as when you are busy raising a family or in the thick of progressing your career, but there are windows in many people's lives when it is the perfect answer, even though the idea may not have taken shape in their minds. I spent years in a job that had no meaning other than its ability to put food on the table. That is how it is for many people. And, for us, the 'mid-life crisis' strikes a particularly hard blow. I think of it as an expression of the soul's cry for meaning: 'What is it all for?' 'What do I really want to do?' If you don't articulate that cry, anatomise it, and respond to it then you could be heading down a one-way street to depression. A whole generation of young-at-heart baby boomers have come to this moment in their lives. Some may be straight off down the road to the Harley-Davidson dealer, others might be reading *Eat, Pray, Love* for all they're worth. But there are those who decide to embrace change in an active way, with both hands. Better off than their parents had been at their age, and with a wealth of leisure time at their disposal, they cast around for a meaningful way to spend their time.

You can decide to be a volunteer or mentor without whizzing off to far-flung places. Certainly, what I chose to do wouldn't suit everybody. There is a real need for mentorship at home, in every community. And the more people put their hands up, the more that ripple effect spreads.

EPILOGUE

'Be the change you want to see in the world'

Mahatma Gandhi

In 2012 Linda Cruse launches the Be The Change Academy.

Be The Change Academy

Business Leaders – we need you!

To be stretched and challenged personally and professionally is not easy when you have reached the top. Be The Change Academy will enable you to use your entrepreneurial skills and business acumen, to assist in solving some of the worlds intractable problems. Join with other global business leaders to assist charitable organisations to solve challenging real-life problems in some of the world's poorest communities by using a hand-up business led approach. At the same time, learn something about yourself.

Sue Stockdale, Women Presidents' Organisation Chapter Chair, Author and Polar Adventurer:

'When Linda Cruse spoke at the Women Presidents' Organisation's London Chapter's annual retreat she related four stories from her twelve years of aid work on the frontline. The stories were so inspiring that our members asked how they could get involved. The 'Be The Change Academy' is a perfect vehicle for us to do just that.'

To find out more and to register for one of the Be The Change trips email: linda@lindacruse.com or go to www.lindacruse.com

The Women Presidents' Organisation (www.womenpres identsorg.com) and the Young Presidents' Organisation (www.ypo.org) are already on board. It chimes with their 'genius of the group' approach and they will be the first of many such organisations and individuals to whom Linda will throw down the challenge.

'Go the extra mile, it's never crowded'

Anon

The Academy and Emergency Zen

Limited places will be available for the Academy Ambassadors to experience Emergency Zen, Linda's personal development course – so that they can combine a personal journey with a professional one.

www.lindacruse.com

linda@lindacruse.com

www.facebook.com/lindacruseauthor

www.facebook.com/lindacruse.bethechange

www.linkedin.com/in/lindacruse

www.twitter.com/linda_cruse

www.emergencyzenonline.com

What they say...

Sir Richard Branson
'Linda makes the impossible, possible. What a great adventure.'

Peter Hopkirk, Author of *The Great Game*:
'Linda understates her extraordinary selfless achievements often in very, very dangerous circumstances and surroundings. Altogether she is an amazing woman with unique abilities. She has been described as a firewalker, a good luck charm, a talisman. She is in fact a magician. Readers will love it.'

Robert Davies, CEO of The Prince of Wales International
Business Leaders Forum:
'Linda Cruse's passion and commitment to people is evident in her wonderful work. She is a lady whose actions speak louder than words and whose dedication to her goals inspire others to partner with her. She has won the respect and admiration of the business community as well as the NGO and charity sector, which in turn has enabled her to broker valuable partnerships to aid recovery in these devastated tsunami areas. Linda's enthusiasm knows no borders; she takes every challenge with a vigour that is a lesson to us all.'

Geoffrey Bush, Director of Corporate Citizenship, Diageo:
'Extraordinary dedication and inexhaustible energy in the relief of suffering and poverty. She gives so much to other people, her energy, her time, and always her love. A delight to meet up with

277

and be inspired again about what can be achieved in the world. She is totally selfless and she constantly demonstrates her commitment to helping others. She has devoted so much of herself, to help make a better life for other people.'

Tweedie Brown CBE:
'Linda Cruse will surely take her place amongst those heroines of history who have changed society in a major way. Her story of adventure, adversity, audacity and achievement, along with her genuine pioneering spirit and engaging warmth of character, inspires others to achieve their true potential. She is up there with the Florence Nightingales and Amelia Earharts of this world, who have blazed the trail to greater enlightenment and improved the lot of their fellow human beings.'

Nelofar Currimbhoy, President, Shahnaz Herbals, India:
'She has a broad smile, bags of enthusiasm, a great sense of humour and never ceasing optimism, which is infectious. I can only be left quite breathless at the speed and energy she plunges into dreadful situations. It's the sheer positive energy she exudes that propels her and others alongside her. Linda is absolutely my inspiration, as I am sure she must be for so many who have had the opportunity to meet this tireless soldier of a kinder sort. When everyone else is rushing out, Linda is rushing in.'

How You Can Get Involved

Getting Involved – Making a Difference

If you feel inspired to roll up your sleeves and get involved below are some of the great organisations I have encountered over the years.

1. Chance For Change

Chance For Change is a new international NGO which is committed to inspiring and enabling young people who have experienced challenging life circumstances to take responsibility for their own future direction. With initial projects in the UK, Nepal and Malawi, Chance for Change creates opportunities that enable participants to begin a journey of personal growth. Travelling and journeying in wilderness environments, enables participants to broaden their horizons, realise their talents and acquire new skills which will give them the potential to take their place as the community leaders of the future.

Chance For Change puts the focus on strengths not weaknesses; on assets not deficits and invests in young talent, inspiring and motivating them to become entrepreneurial global citizens. www.chanceforchange.org.uk

2. People and Places

People and Places offers a service of integrity to thinking people – people who want to use their skills and experience to make a real difference, and know how and where their money is spent.

People and Places is an international, award-winning volunteer recruitment organisation – a social enterprise, where any profits are covenanted to charity. Established in 2005 to match international volunteers to community projects, we are guided by their mutual need to gain real benefits – a 'win-win' experience for communities and volunteers alike. This approach is fundamental to delivering responsible, accountable, ethical, sustainable travel.

Core values are mutual respect, service, partnership, transparency and sustainability. In Africa, Asia, the Caribbean, Europe and South America, projects are initiated, developed and managed by local people for the benefit of their communities. The organisation's role, through the volunteer programme, is to enhance their own abilities – enabling them to build the lives they would wish for themselves.

People and Places believe that volunteers who are willing and able to contribute their expertise, skills and time for the benefit of others, should be provided with quality volunteering opportunities and be well supported through their entire volunteer experience – before, during and after their placements. www.travel-peopleandplaces.co.uk

3. Education For All

World change starts with educated children. An educated girl educates the next generation.

At present few girls from rural communities in Morocco continue their education after primary school. Individually, we may not be able to change the world but together we can help make a difference to a few lives – and indirectly to many more.

For more information and to know how to get involved please visit: www.educationforallmorocco.org

4. Project Trust

Project Trust lets you experience life in Asia, Africa, Latin America or the Caribbean, not as a tourist but as a valued member of a local community. Long-term projects of eight or twelve months will give you plenty of time to explore your new surroundings, whilst working in your community will provide you with an incomparable intimate experience of the inner workings of your chosen country.

Taking a year out will change the way you look at the world. You'll have to rise to new challenges on a daily basis and learn skills that will stay with you for life, not just your time overseas. In fact, the skills you pick up will enhance your CV and future career prospects. You may be one of hundreds graduating with a degree from your university, but you will be one of the few who can say they've lived and worked overseas before having even entered further education! And if you have decided that university is not for you, a year out with Project Trust before entering the world of work could still give you an invaluable foundation of life experience for the future.

Project Trust has been refining and redefining its programme since 1967. Compared with many gap year organisations they send only a handful of volunteers overseas each year, all of whom are 17–19-year-old school leavers, handpicked and carefully matched to their project. www.projecttrust.org.uk

5. Real Volunteers

Real Volunteers Ltd aren't just passionate about travel – they live it, eat it, walk it, breathe it and dream about it! They are a dedicated team of experienced wanderers who have clocked up hundreds of thousands of miles and collected enough crazy stories to dine out on for a life-time! They know that exploring this fascinating planet is addictive – however, they believe that it's not just about the number of places you visit; it's what you do when you get there that tells you who you are. That's why they have spent weeks, months and years scouring the planet to find places, people and projects that could benefit from your help. They know that time is a precious commodity but if you can spend some helping those who need it, the benefits will be immense and the memories and friendships forged unforgettable.

Over the last five years, they have visited dozens of projects throughout Asia, Africa and Latin America in order to be able to match you to the perfect one, where your skills and passion will make a real difference. For anything from teaching in Ghana to helping sea turtles in Costa Rica, they offer a tailor made, personal service that won't cost you the earth. Whether you choose to volunteer for a week or a decade, they can assist you from start to finish and ensure you get as much support or as little interference as you want.

The team at Real Volunteers Ltd also actively fundraises for its partnerships overseas and has done all sorts from running marathons to getting naked in order to support them! They even give 10% of each registration fee to a carefully chosen UK charity and never pass any costs on to the projects you visit. Every Real Volunteer counts and you really can Be The Change! www.realvolunteers.co.uk

6. Responsible Tourism

Responsible Tourism is, in the words of the Cape Town Declaration, about using tourism to make 'better places for people to live in and better places for people to visit'. It is about enabling people to use tourism rather than to be used by it. We all make choices when we travel. Tourism is what we make it – as Jost Krippendorf pointed out in his seminal work, *The*

Holiday Makers, 'Every individual tourist builds up or destroys human values while travelling'.

Tourism can contribute to sustainable economic development, to the maintenance of cultural and natural heritage; it can create employment and bring development to remote rural areas. But tourism is not a pollution free industry; it creates greenhouse gas emissions, consumes water and creates waste. It can displace farmers and exclude fishermen from beaches and cause changes in land values with profound consequences for local communities. The interactions between people of different cultures can bring understanding and a feeling of solidarity encouraging philanthropic behaviour. But it can also accelerate social change contributing to the homogenisation of our world. And some forms of tourism facilitate prostitution, paedophilia and crime.

Responsible Tourism is a movement of people, travellers and businesses committed to using tourism to make our world a better place and to pass on its rich cultural and natural diversity to our children. It is our, and their, heritage. Will you take responsibility and travel to make a better world?

Email Harold@haroldgoodwin.info or visit
www.haroldgoodwin.info/links

Responsible Tourism Awards
www.responsibletourismawards.com

How to contact Linda

Web: www.lindacruse.com
Email: linda@lindacruse.com
Facebook: www.facebook.com/lindacruseauthor
or www.facebook.com/lindacruse.bethechange
LinkedIn: www.linkedin.com/in/lindacruse
Twitter: www.twitter.com/linda_cruse

www.emergencyzenonline.com

'We cannot all do great things, but we can do small things with great love'

Mother Teresa of Calcutta

'Give a man a fish, you feed him for a day. Teach him how to fish, you feed him for life'

Lao Tzu